The Essential Guide to Intellectual Property

The Essential Guide to Intellectual Property

Aram Sinnreich

Yale UNIVERSITY PRESS

New Haven & London

Published with assistance from the
Ralph S. Brown Memorial Publication Fund.
Published with assistance from the foundation established in memory of
James Wesley Cooper of the Class of 1865, Yale College.

Yale University Press books may be purchased in quantity for educational,
business, or promotional use. For information, please e-mail
sales.press@yale.edu (U.S. office) or sales@yaleup.co.uk (U.K. office).

Set in Janson type by Integrated Publishing Solutions.
Printed in the United States of America.

Library of Congress Control Number: 2018956596

ISBN 978-0-300-21442-0 (paperback : alk. paper)

A catalogue record for this book is available from the British Library.

This paper meets the requirements of ANSI/NISO Z39.48–1992
(Permanence of Paper).

10 9 8 7 6 5 4 3 2 1

These are really the thoughts of all men in all ages and lands, they
    are not original with me,
If they are not yours as much as mine they are nothing, or next
    to nothing,
If they are not the riddle and the untying of the riddle they are
    nothing,
If they are not just as close as they are distant they are nothing.

—WALT WHITMAN, *Song of Myself*

Contents

Contents

Preface

When my editor at Yale University Press, Sarah Miller, first reached out to me about writing this book, I was both flattered and trepidatious. Flattered because despite the volumes of research I have produced on the subject, I still feel like a neophyte when it comes to intellectual property—a wanderer in the antechamber to the labyrinth, at best. I count myself lucky to know personally some of the world's leading scholars and practitioners of the subject, and the depth of their expertise is a continual reminder to me of how much I have yet to learn.

My trepidation had several dimensions. Beyond the garden variety insecurities that plague every author embarking on a new project, I wasn't sure I wanted to write a course book. My previous publications have been narrative and argumentative in nature. Could I write clinically and without bias on a subject about which I have been such a passionate advocate for so long? Furthermore, after the publication of my previous book, *The Piracy Crusade*, I had promised myself I would take a break from writing about intellectual property altogether for a while, and focus on some of my other, equally absorbing interests.

Despite these reservations, it would have been unwise to reject Yale's offer to submit a proposal. Invitations such as these do not come every day, and I was grateful to receive one. So I chose the only solution that made sense in the face of these conflicting impulses: I proposed a book that would almost certainly be rejected. Instead of a standard course book outlining the rudiments of the law and walking readers through the well-worn perspectives surrounding its origins and execution, I proposed a book that I'd actually want to write and that (I hoped) people would actually want to read: a *people's* guide to intellectual property. A book that would interrogate critically the role that copyright, patent, and trademark play in our cultural, economic, and political lives, and that would illuminate the hidden strings connecting these laws to our experience of everyday life. Of course, it would still offer all of the information required to understand the mechanics of the law, but always with an eye toward emplacing these mechanics within the larger social structures and forces that shaped them and that are, in turn, shaped by them.

To my enormous surprise and gratification, Yale accepted my proposal, and the result is the book you are now reading. Whether you've been assigned this book in a class, picked it up out of curiosity, or are using it to enhance your grasp of the subject for professional purposes, I hope it serves you well. If I have succeeded, the book will not only provide you with enough high-level perspective and nitty-gritty details to dispel some of the confusion and wonky aura that typically clouds people's understanding of intellectual property, it will also communicate to you some of my passion for the subject. I believe, deeply, in the importance of creative expression and scientific discovery, and the better we understand the laws and regulations that enable and inhibit these forms of human ingenuity, the more empowered and ingenious we can become. Thank you for reading. I look forward to your contributions as well.

Acknowledgments

First and foremost, I would like to thank Sarah Miller and Ash Lago at Yale University Press for inviting me to write this book and for serving as my partners throughout the process of proposing, writing, and publishing it. Their professional dedication and expertise show in every page of the result.

I would also like to thank the numerous scholars, advocates, and legal practitioners who have provided information, analysis, feedback, comfort, and perspective as I've worked on the book. These include, in no particular order, Patricia Aufderheide, Laura DeNardis, Eberhard Ortland, Reinold Schmücker, Masha Zager, Jonathan Sinnreich, Michael Francisco, Antonia Putzger, David Karpf, Nicholas John, Jessa Lingel, Nancy Baym, Mark Kaufman, Louisa Imperiale, Matt Rechs, Donte Newman, and Dori Ann Hanswirth. Many thanks to my beleaguered and brilliant friend and doctoral student Fernanda Rosa for helping with the manuscript preparation. And thank you to friends, colleagues, staff, and administrators at American University's School of Communication and Das Zentrum für interdisziplinäre Forschung for providing me with the resources and community that sustained me throughout the project.

Finally, as always, thank you to my close friends and family, especially my wife and partner in all things, Dunia Best Sinnreich, for inspiring me, believing in me, and supporting me as I tilt at the windmills of the world.

The Essential Guide to Intellectual Property

Introduction

What Is Intellectual Property?

What is intellectual property? Sometimes it seems like *everything* is, from the trademarked logos on the packages of our favorite snacks to the televised warnings at the beginning of major league ball games to the copyright notice at the beginning of this very book. It's hard to turn on a television or computer, read a book or watch a movie, or buy a piece of hardware or software without encountering some reminder that the contents of the box, file, or program in question are owned by someone else and that you'll be in trouble if you copy, distribute, or misuse those contents. It's almost as though some mischievous gnome (Santa's Bizarro World twin, perhaps) has traveled around the world putting a sticker saying "*Mine*" on anything beautiful, useful, or interesting.

On the other hand, many consider the concept of intellectual property (often referred to as IP for short) essential for the health and growth of businesses, cultures, and nations. Film and game studios, record labels, publishing, pharmaceuticals, food distribution, consumer electronics, and apparel are just a few of the industries whose business models rely directly on their ability to stop competitors from copying their content, mimicking their brands, or stealing their secrets. Without the protections afforded by IP laws, these companies might not innovate or produce as much, might not employ as many people, and might not make enough money to be profitable. In fact, by one bullish estimate, the economic value of intellectual property in the U.S. is so great, it's equivalent to more than half of the nation's gross domestic product (GDP).[1]

So which is it? Is IP a legal straitjacket allowing private individuals and corporations to stake ownership claims on the world's shared cultural heritage and scientific discoveries? Or is it a set of wings that allow modern society to soar, giving artists and inventors the confidence to bring their ideas to the world, and giving companies and investors the financial security to bankroll those ideas? The answer, of course, is both and neither. IP in America is a complex and contradictory jumble of laws, treaties, policies, contracts, and court decisions whose contours echo both the altruism of the U.S. Constitution and the self-interest of Washington lobbyists. IP has unquestionably played a role in spurring centuries of cultural and scientific innovation, but it's also helped to widen the gulf between "haves" and "have-nots" and, as legal scholar John Tehranian observes, has turned us into an "infringement nation" in which we are all unwitting criminals, technically liable for billions of dollars apiece in damages for running afoul of laws we don't even understand.[2]

This lack of understanding is a crucial problem in IP today and is contributing to the increasingly public and volatile debates over the roles that legal features like copyrights and patents play in our society. The sad reality is that virtually nobody—whether lawmaker, judge, attorney, professor, or even course book author—fully understands the scope and effects of IP, yet we continue to pass new laws and ratify new treaties that only broaden its reach and increase its complexity.

These debates have also spurred an unprecedented public interest in making sense of IP and making sure that it works to the benefit of society at large. Some of this interest has taken the form of political action, such as the widespread demonstrations against the Stop Online Piracy Act (SOPA) and Protect IP Act (PIPA) in the U.S. and against treaties like the Anti-Counterfeiting Trade Agreement (ACTA) and Trans-Pacific Partnership (TPP) around the world (more on this in chapter 8). But there has also been a rise in academic interest in copyright and IP, led by both students and faculty in a variety of disciplines, from the arts to the humanities to the social sciences to the hard sciences. Students preparing for their roles as professionals and citizens are enrolling in IP-themed courses, starting campus groups and societies, and immersing themselves in the debate.

If you are a scholar seeking a deeper, more critical understanding of copyright and IP but wish to avoid the partisanship of advocacy books and the clinical aridity of legal textbooks, this may be the book for you. In the chapters that follow, we will examine critically the history and purpose of intellectual property, the roles it plays in industry, culture, and politics, and the possible futures we face as technology continues to evolve and IP law struggles to keep current. Our focus will be primarily on American and western European approaches to IP, for reasons that will become clear, although we will also spend some time on its role in international relations. By the time you finish the book, you won't know everything about IP, but you'll know enough to participate in the debate and to interpret and apply the laws according to your own point of view, and you'll know where to look next to continue your education.

But before we do any of that, we need to answer the question we started with: What is intellectual property? At the most basic level, IP is a set of legal rights, rooted in legislation, interpreted by the courts, and used for better and for worse by a range of different stakeholders, from individual authors to international conglomerates. In the remainder of this introduction we will explore specific varieties of IP, from copyrights to trade secrets, and consider briefly "how the sausage is made"—that is, where these laws come from and how they're used in practice.

Copyright

Copyright is perhaps the most contentious and visible form of IP, and it plays the greatest role in enabling, constraining, and regulating our media and cultural spheres. It gives the author or creator of a work a temporary monopoly over certain uses of that work. Specifically, only the owner of a copyright can reproduce a work, prepare derivative works (such as translations and dramatizations) based on it, distribute or sell copies of it, and perform or display the work publicly. The owner can also grant third parties the right to do those things as well, in exchange for money or other considerations, or for reasons of generosity, altruism, or self-promotion.

When copyright was first developed in the U.S., the law covered only books, maps, and charts. Today, a much broader variety of media and cultural forms are protected by copyright, including musical compositions and recordings, movies, software, sculpture, poetry, choreography, photography, plays, paintings, and architectural designs (more on the history and gradual expansion of copyright in chapter 1).

In fact, virtually anything can be copyrighted now, as long as it meets a few basic requirements. First of all, *you can't copyright an idea.* We all know someone who walked out of a movie like *Inception* or *The Matrix* saying, "Oh, my gosh, that was totally my idea! I should have copyrighted that—I'd be a millionaire now!" Fortunately, your friend was mistaken. Thousands of people may have considered writing or filming a thriller about a crack team of dream extractors, but only Chris Nolan actually wrote and directed *Inception*. And although you can't make your own adaptation of this particular film without the express consent of the copyright holder, you can certainly write and direct your own film about dream extraction, regardless of whether you came up with the premise or not. By virtue of making the film, Nolan and his studio control the rights to this particular *expression of the idea*, not the rights to the idea itself. In IP scholarship, this distinction is called the "idea/expression dichotomy," and it's considered one of the most important aspects of copyright because it ensures that everyone is free to think what he or she wants and to develop and express new ideas based in part on the ideas that others have shared.

Another requirement for copyright is that ideas be *fixed in a tangible medium*. If you stand on a street corner whistling a tune or describe a plot for a novel to your friends over dinner, you don't get to enjoy copyright protection for those ideas. You have to write them down, record them, or otherwise make sure they're "sufficiently permanent or stable to . . . be perceived, reproduced, or otherwise communicated for a period of more than transitory duration," as U.S. copyright law puts it. Though it's an open philosophical question how "tangible" radio transmissions, online software, and choreography are in reality, the law is fairly straightforward on these matters, and there are innumerable guides available for creators who want to make sure their work is covered, or who want to create a new work secure in the knowledge that they're not infringing on someone else's rights.

It is important to note, however, that just because copyright requires an idea to be expressed in a medium doesn't mean that ownership of a copyright is necessarily the same thing as ownership over its physical expression. For instance, a painter might sell a still life to an art collector but retain the IP in the composition featured on the canvas. In that scenario, if a publisher wanted to release a book featuring the artist's work, the company would need to seek permission from the painter rather than from the collector. By the same token, if the collector wanted to sell the physical painting itself, she wouldn't need to seek permission or share the profits with the painter.

Another important requirement for copyright is that the idea being expressed is an *original work of authorship*. Again, this may sound like a fairly fuzzy concept. Philosophers and critics have squandered vats of ink over the centuries debating the definition of originality, and by the time the author of Ecclesiastes wrote, "There is nothing new under the sun" over twenty-two hundred years ago, it was probably already a well-worn cliché.

Yet, as with the concept of tangibility, U.S. copyright law sets a pretty low threshold for originality, ensuring that as many works as possible fit the bill for protection. The current working definition comes from a well-known 1991 copyright case called *Feist Publications v. Rural Telephone Serv. Co.*, in which one company had copied and republished telephone numbers from another company's directory book. U.S. Supreme Court justice Sandra Day O'Connor, writing the majority opinion that phone numbers don't rise to a protectable level of originality, explained: "Original, as the term is used in copyright, means only that the work was independently created by the author (as opposed to copied from other works), and that it possesses at least some minimal degree of creativity. To be sure, the requisite level of creativity is extremely low; even a slight amount will suffice . . . a work may be original even though it closely resembles other works so long as the similarity is fortuitous, not the result of copying."[3]

Thus, with a bar this low, nearly all works of creative expression merit copyright protection: doodles on diner placemats, snatches of melody hummed into a cell phone's recording software, and even emails are technically covered. The only forms of expression that don't qualify are facts (such as phone numbers), functional or utilitarian objects (such as can openers and clothing), principles (such as the laws of gravity or the structure of DNA), words, phrases, and familiar symbols (though these can be trademarked, as we'll discuss below), and information belonging to everyone, what's known as being in the *public domain*. This is an important concept that will be covered in greater detail in chapter 2, but for present purposes, we can summarize the public domain as consisting of work that predates copyright (such as Shakespeare's plays), work whose copyright has expired (such as Mark Twain's novels), work created by nonhumans like robots or animals (such as monkey selfies, according to a recent court ruling), work that is specifically excluded from copyright (such as documents produced by the U.S. government), and work that has been intentionally granted to the public domain by its author.[4]

Getting and using a copyright is fairly simple. Until 1978, if a creator wanted a copyright for her work, she'd either have to register it with the U.S. Copyright Office (an arm of the federal government) or publish it with a "notice of copyright," making sure that it fit a range of legally defined requirements. Today, however, copyright is secured automatically at the moment of creation—that is to say, as soon as an idea is written down, recorded, or otherwise fixed in its medium. Of course, it still helps creators to publish and/or register their works, especially if there's a chance they might have to defend or assert their copyright claims in court one day.

When America passed its first copyright law in 1790, this limited monopoly lasted for 14 years. If an author was still alive and interested in exploiting his work commercially at the end of this term, he could renew it for an additional 14 years. Today, the terms are much, much longer. Copyrights last throughout an author's life and for another 70 years after her death. If the author is technically a corporation rather than a person, the copyright will last either 95 years from publication or 120 years from creation—whichever expires first. If history is any guide, there is also a good chance that copyright will be extended further before these terms end; for instance, in 1998 terms were expanded by 20 years, bringing many works that had lapsed into the public domain back into private hands. For this reason, many critics of copyright consider today's terms, though technically limited, to last for a "functional eternity."

Another important aspect of copyright in the U.S. is its *transferability*. Only the creator of a work is entitled to copyright at the moment of creation, but the creator can sell, trade, or give the copyright in whole or in part to another party at any point after that. This ability distinguishes America from many other countries, including European Union members, in which an author's "moral rights" over a work can never be broken or traded away. Even in the U.S., it is possible under certain circumstances for a creator who has transferred away her copyright to regain ownership over her work, typically thirty-five years following the initial transfer. This is sometimes called "rights reversion," and at the time of writing, there are several court cases testing the limits of this relatively new legal provision (the law affects only transfers made in 1978 or later, so 2013 was the first year in which it was a viable option).

In summary, copyright is a widely used and highly influential legal instrument allowing individuals and organizations to monopolize creative expression. Any "original" work is automatically copyrighted once it's fixed in a medium, and that copyright will last for a virtual eternity. Most of the movies, books, paintings, computer programs, photographs, and songs you consume are copyrighted, and our cultural environment would probably look very different if they weren't. Yet copyright has its limits, and there are entire industries—and fields of human endeavor—that exist and thrive without it. For instance, you can't copyright a mousetrap or a cold remedy. For inventions like these, we have developed another form of IP altogether: patents.

Patents

Imagine you're struggling with a sheaf of loose papers and desperately need a paper clip, but you can't locate one anywhere. You jury-rig one together, MacGyver style, out of whatever you can find in your kitchen drawer: a bit of string, a length of wire. To your amazement, it works great—better than a regular paper clip would have. "Wow," you think to yourself, "I could make a fortune selling these things." The problem is, you know that as soon as you begin to sell your invention, it'll take about a week for a bigger, more powerful company to copy your design and flood the market with cheaper, mass-produced versions. "Never mind," you think. "Maybe I'll just keep the idea to myself."

This is exactly the kind of problem patents were created to solve. While copyrights give creators a limited monopoly over the expression of their ideas and the distribution of their works, patents offer inventors an even more limited monopoly over the use of their creations. In both cases, the monopoly is supposed to serve as an *incentive* for someone to share his or her idea. Once you've written a song, anyone can learn to play it, and once you've invented a device, anyone can learn to build it. But with your temporary monopoly, only you and the people who get your permission are allowed to exploit your ideas in the marketplace.

There are three basic varieties of patent:

- *Utility patents* cover mousetraps, paper clips, and any other "new and useful process, machine, manufacture, or composition of matter, or any new and useful improvement thereof," as the letter of the law puts it.

9

- *Design patents* cover any "new, original, and ornamental design for an article of manufacture," which could mean a surface decoration like the filigree on a guitar neck, the overall shape of an item, like a steering wheel or a vase, or a combination of the two, like a printed lampshade.
- *Plant patents* cover new varieties of plants that have been discovered or bred by explorers and horticulturalists. For example, I currently own the illustration and now-expired patent paperwork for *hedera helix*, a new variety of ivy discovered by Walter S. Hahn of Pittsburgh, Pennsylvania, and granted on January 15, 1952.[5]

Between these three categories, a surprisingly broad range of inventions, designs, and organisms may be—and are—protected legally as monopolies. These include everything from predictable categories like pharmaceuticals and electronics to more bizarre examples like a patent for the "comb-over" baldness-concealing hairdo (U.S. patent #4022227) and a patent for a method of exercising a cat (#5443036). There's even a patent application for a method of patent litigation (#20080270152).

In fact, the U.S. Supreme Court has ruled that patents may cover "anything under the sun that is made by man" other than "laws of nature, physical phenomena, and abstract ideas."[6] The only limitations are that inventions must be "useful," in the sense of achieving a specific stated goal; "novel," both in comparison to other inventions and in terms of general public awareness; and "nonobvious," a vague, oft-debated, and relatively new requirement that essentially means that people skilled in the subject matter addressed by the patent wouldn't smack their heads and say "Duh" if they heard about it.

This last point is notoriously difficult to pin down. For instance, in 1997, online retailer Amazon.com received a patent for "1-click" checkout, a business method allowing consumers to buy an item

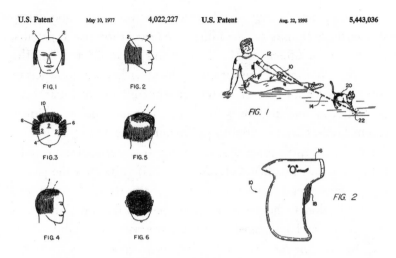

Figure 1: Patent illustrations for comb-overs and cat exercises.

with only a single click of the mouse. Despite facing widespread criticism and even derision for claiming ownership of this head-smackingly obvious concept, the company has held the patent in the U.S. ever since (although Europe's patent office has continually rejected Amazon's claims), and has even licensed it for considerable amounts of money to competitors such as Apple.

Unlike copyrights, patents are not created instantaneously when new inventions are developed; they still require a registration process. To obtain a patent, an inventor must apply to the U.S. Patent and Trademark Office (USPTO) after first making sure that the invention doesn't already belong to another patent holder or to the public domain. In the old days, this used to entail a grueling search through reams of paper records. These days, the USPTO keeps its entire database online, so it's much easier for an individual, organization, or patent attorney to make sure there is no "prior art" (the legal term for preexisting IP) conflicting with the patent's central idea.

Once a patent is granted, it lasts for one twenty-year nonrenew-
able term, beginning on the filing date (except for design patents,
which last for fifteen years). Though this is far shorter than the
"functionally infinite" author's life plus seventy years accorded to
copyrights, it's still long enough to generate billions of dollars each
year in economic incentives for American patent holders. Utility
patent holders are required to pay maintenance fees to keep their
patents active three times over the twenty-year term, at three and a
half, seven and a half, and eleven and a half years after the patent
was granted; failure to do so means that the IP might lapse into
the public domain and cease to be property. Like copyrights, patents can be sold and transferred from one party to another; however, because the term is shorter, there is no opportunity for rights
reversion: once transferred, a patent stays transferred, at least until
it gets transferred again.

Roughly half of all patent applications are eventually granted by
the USPTO. For instance, in 2013, there were 571,612 utility patent
applications and 277,835 grants. These numbers have grown steeply
in recent years: in 2000, 157,494 utility patents were granted, and
the number was only 61,819 in 1980. Although I began this section
with a hypothetical anecdote about a lone inventor creating a new
kind of paper clip, the reality is that the vast majority of patents
granted in 2013—almost 93 percent—were held by corporate entities, and only forty companies, led by IBM, Samsung, and Canon,
accounted for roughly one-fourth of all patent grants for the year.

Because the requirements are so vague, the subject areas are so
arcane, and the IP is so potentially lucrative, there is a great deal of
litigation over the ownership and validity of patents, and a great
deal of criticism over the current patent system (more on this later
in the book). In recent years, patent reform has emerged from the
wonky policy world to become a mainstream political issue. In 2014,
for instance, President Obama promoted it as an agenda item in his

annual State of the Union Address. Yet, with accelerating techno-logical advancement, the number of things "under the sun" that are "made by man" (or woman) continues to balloon with each passing year, and this probably means that the number of patents will con-tinue to grow as well, along with the degree of controversy surround-ing them.

Trademarks

Imagine you're a clothing designer, and your mission in life is to make an indestructible pair of jeans. Graced with your unique stitch-ing style, high-quality materials, and attention to detail, your jeans last three times as long as a standard pair and cost only twice as much. Consumers flock to your website and retail partners, buying your jeans faster than you can produce them.

Then a problem arises. Your friends start sending you the link to another website that sells jeans that look just like yours—but at a far lower price. Not only are these competitors underselling you, they're also giving you a bad rep; while their clothes might look identical to yours, they fall apart much more easily, and you're con-cerned that your lovingly crafted designs might come to represent shoddy workmanship in the eyes of your customers. If you can't somehow differentiate yourself from these charlatans, the future of your business is in peril.

The challenge is, clothing design isn't copyrightable (it's a func-tional object), nor is it patentable (you didn't invent a *new* method for making jeans, you just did a better job at following the old method). Fortunately for you, there's a third IP option that fits the bill perfectly: trademark. You can protect your reputation and dif-ferentiate yourself from the competition by adding a logo to your jeans, or even possibly by claiming that your unique stitching style is itself a mark that distinguishes you as the creator of the jeans in question. Once you receive your trademark, your customers can shop confidently, knowing that you and only you were responsible for producing those wonderful jeans. If any other manufacturers try to use your logo or trademarked stitching style in their work, they're potentially liable for infringement, and you can take them to court to recover your losses.

The scenario I have just outlined is the classic use case for trademarks and their legal sibling, service marks. They function as a guarantee to consumers that a given product or service was created by a specific party, who can thus be held accountable for the quality of the work. They also protect the providers of goods and services by distinguishing their work from competing (and potentially inferior) work. Brand names can be trademarks, but so can logos, tag lines, design elements, and even more abstract symbols like colors, sounds, and smells.

Trademarks don't need to be claimed or filed in order to have legal merit, but it certainly helps when it comes to protecting or asserting them in court. In order to claim their trademarks, many manufacturers place a ™ symbol on or near the mark in question. As with copyrights, a greater degree of legal protectability comes with federal registration, which requires an application process that can take a year or more. Once the USPTO issues a certificate of registration, the rights holder may use the ® symbol (for "registered trademark") instead of ™. Unlike copyrights and patents, trademarks don't automatically expire after a fixed term; they are granted for ten-year periods and may be renewed at the end of each period as long as the mark is still in use.

In America, the oldest trademark still in use is for Underwood Deviled Ham, which has used a playful depiction of Lucifer on its packaging since 1870. Other nearly as old examples include John Deere's jumping buck (1876), Coca-Cola's swooping cursive lettering (1886), and Johnson & Johnson's signature with the red cross (1886). Elsewhere in the world, far older manufacturers, such as

Figure 2: Underwood Deviled Ham logos, 1870–present.

brewers Stella Artois and Löwenbräu, have employed their trademarks since at least the fourteenth century.

Once a trademark is granted, it is protected not only against identical marks but also against any that might entail a "likelihood of confusion" among the consumer base. For instance, if you open a fast food restaurant chain and call it "McDonnald's," the extra "n" isn't going to protect you against a claim of trademark infringement; it's reasonable to assume that the average hungry commuter wouldn't notice the difference—at least until mid-burger, when the damage is already done. On the other hand, there's a McDonald's hardware store in Fort Lauderdale, Florida, allowable because (despite your opinion regarding the edibility of a Big Mac) it's unlikely you'd confuse its inventory for anything you'd see on the Dollar Menu.

Yet the "likelihood of confusion" standard entails a lot of gray area (what if the hardware store offered coffee to its customers, or what if toy wrenches and screwdrivers were included in Happy Meals?), and trademark holders often engage in litigation to clarify and claim uses at the boundaries of their control. McDonald's, for instance, has attracted both critical and laudatory attention for suing a range of businesses around the world for employing the "Mc" prefix in their names. Some suits, such as a trademark action against Bay Area café McCoffee (owned by a woman named Elizabeth Mc-Caughey—say it out loud), have been successful; others, such as a suit against a Malaysian restaurant called McCurry, have not.

Some IP critics also argue that the range of symbols and expressions that can be trademarked has surpassed the law's intended function, and that instead of protecting consumers from fraud, trademark has become a mechanism for the privatization of public culture and the stifling of free and critical speech. In his 2005 book *Brand Name Bullies*, IP reform advocate David Bollier documented hundreds of cases of corporate "overreach" in what he calls the "pursuit of perfect control."[7]

These include many hilarious but chilling examples, such as Toho, owner of the "Godzilla" trademark, trying to shut down a website called Davezilla.com, and Fox News's attempts to litigate against a parody book by comedian turned politician Al Franken for using its trademarked phrase "fair and balanced." They also include the successful trademarking of seemingly universal sensory and cultural experiences, such as the color pink, the letter O, a "smell reminiscent of roses," and the sound of a lion roaring. As in the case of copyrights and patents, the challenge when it comes to trademark law is providing just enough protection to shield and incentivize legitimate creators (like our jeans designer) without generating undue burdens or limitations on the public speech and commercial freedoms enjoyed by the rest of us (like Elizabeth McCaughey).

Other Forms of IP

Because of their central roles in regulating public speech, technological innovation, and market competition respectively, copyrights, patents, and trademarks are the most widely discussed forms of intellectual property, and thus will be the central subjects of this book. Yet there are other varieties of IP as well, both in the United States and elsewhere in the world.

Trade secrets, such as Google's search algorithm and Coca-Cola's soda pop recipe, can be worth billions of dollars and are often central to corporations' business strategies. No organization like the USPTO exists to keep track of these secrets (they're secret, after all), and there's no limit on their term, yet they instantly become part of the public domain once they're exposed, regardless of the legal circumstances of that exposure. Trade secrets are also very limited forms of protection in that they don't prevent independent creation by third parties. Thus, if you stumble upon the exact recipe for Coca-Cola in your kitchen one day, the company's IP will not prevent you either from creating and selling your own competing taste-alike product or from sharing your discovery with the world at large.

The *right of publicity* is a valuable form of IP that gives individuals the ability to prevent others from using their name or likeness in a commercial context. In the U.S., this right is granted by individual states rather than the federal government. In one notable case in California, television game show hostess Vanna White successfully sued consumer electronics manufacturer Samsung for using a robotic likeness of her without her consent in a television commercial for its videocassette recorders.[8]

Other nations sometimes develop forms of IP that do not exist in the United States, typically because the legal category may be in conflict with American constitutional rights or because it has failed to muster sufficient political support for enactment at either the federal or state level. One such example is *database rights*. As I discussed above, the *Feist* decision made it very clear that in the U.S. a "minimal degree of creativity" is required to warrant copyright protection, and phone books do not rise to this low bar. Yet in several other legal systems, including those of the European Union and Russia, even a database consisting entirely of factual, noncreative information is eligible for protection as a form of intellectual property.

The Architecture of IP Law

As this cursory overview has demonstrated, not only are there several varieties of IP but each has different legal contours, such as term of ownership, scope of protection, registration requirements, enforcement procedures, and so forth. Yet this is just the tip of the proverbial iceberg. In practice, IP is far more complex, confusing, and just plain messy than it is in theory. While it's beyond the scope of this book to explore every corner of this legal labyrinth, any scholar of intellectual property needs to have a basic understanding of the institutional and procedural dynamics that surround this body of law. The next chapter will delve into the history of this field, but for the remainder of the present introduction, I will outline in broad brushstrokes the key elements of today's IP system.

American intellectual property law, like all American law, is rooted in the U.S. Constitution. Specifically, article 1, section 8, which enumerates the "Powers of Congress," gives our legislators the ability "to promote the Progress of Science and useful Arts, by securing for limited Times to Authors and Inventors the exclusive Right to their respective Writings and Discoveries." If we think of intellectual property as a building, this short sentence fragment is its foundation. All copyright and patent laws, policies and procedures are ultimately weighed in light of whether they fulfill this mandate, and in fact a quick search of U.S. Supreme Court documents shows that the language of this clause has been quoted verbatim dozens of times by the justices.[9]

Despite (or maybe due to) the brevity and vagueness of this constitutional mandate, the letter of IP law itself is much more verbose. At the time of writing, the most complete and up-to-date version of U.S. copyright law, embodied in title 17 of the United States Code, takes up over 350 single-spaced pages on a PDF provided by the U.S. Copyright Office website.[10] Patent law occupies over 100 pages, and trademark law 260.[11] To continue the architectural metaphor, this statutory level makes up the ground floor of our IP building.

Where did all these laws come from? How could fewer than thirty words in the Constitution spawn such a massive edifice? The short answer is that they were all written by senators and congresspeople, mostly at the behest of interested parties such as individual creators, IP-driven industries, and the lobbyists they hire to further their agendas in Washington (more on this in chapter 5). According to publicly available data, over four hundred companies have lobbied the government on copyright, patent, and trademark issues each year for the past three years, employing over fourteen hundred individual lobbyists and spending over $690 million on this issue at the federal level in 2014 alone.

Of course, wealthy industries aren't the only ones to have a say in our laws. Individual creators have contributed to the debate as well, and have done for centuries. Mark Twain, chafing at the proliferation of unauthorized editions of his work, famously advocated for longer copyright terms and international copyright "harmonization" (mutual recognition and alignment of the laws' contours), even testifying at a 1906 congressional committee meeting on copyright. More recently, musicians like Sheryl Crow, Metallica, and Rosanne Cash, filmmakers like George Lucas and Steven Soderbergh, and popular authors like Scott Turow have all testified before Congress to share their views about intellectual property law.

Those of us who aren't lobbyists or celebrities play a role in shaping IP law as well. Most intellectual property bills are well under the public radar, succeeding or failing based largely on a combination of their merits and their political viability. But every so often, and increasingly frequently in recent years, the American public (as well as the global public) speaks up in large enough numbers to help tilt a bill toward or against passage. One relatively recent example of this is the aforementioned case of SOPA and PIPA, corresponding bills introduced into the House and Senate in 2011. These bills, initially supported by a majority of lawmakers, were widely criticized for their potentially devastating impact on free speech and privacy as well as the undue burdens they would place on a variety of internet-focused businesses and communities.

With help and encouragement from web publishers like Reddit, Wikipedia, and Google, a day of protest against SOPA and PIPA was held on January 18, 2012. Over a hundred thousand websites shut down completely or limited their functionality for the day, and over 10 million American voters spoke up via emails, petitions, phone calls, and other channels to ask their legislators to reject the bills. Within two days after the protest, House Judiciary Committee chairman Lamar Smith, who introduced SOPA into the House of Representatives, announced that the committee would "postpone consideration of the legislation until there is wider agreement on a solution."[12] The bills effectively died that day, although this hasn't prevented Congress from reintroducing key elements of SOPA and PIPA under different names. Three years after the internet blackout, a similar bill called the Cybersecurity Information Sharing Act (CISA) was signed into law by President Obama with little fanfare or protest.

Sometimes, even those outside our nation can play an important role in shaping our IP laws. This generally happens through international trade agreements and treaties. As we will explore further in chapter 6, IP treaties can be a powerful diplomatic tool and have implications that extend far beyond the realms that we usually associate with intellectual property. Although the United States initially resisted entering into such accords, it became a signatory to the Paris Convention for the Protection of Industrial Property in 1887 and never looked back. According to a tally compiled by the World Intellectual Property Organization (WIPO), America has signed well over a hundred treaties in the past century and a half, the majority of them since 1990.[13] All of these agreements require the U.S. to adapt its laws to their contours, generally by ratcheting up the scope of IP coverage, infringement policing, and/or liability in some way.

Many of these treaties are developed and negotiated via the United States Trade Representative (USTR), which is staffed by appointees, and sometimes elected representatives have little or nothing to do with the process until the accords are ratified and have become binding with respect to U.S. law. This fact has led some legal scholars to complain, as University of Ottawa law professor Michael Geist put it, that such tactics amount to "a blatant attempt to sidestep Congressional approval" in the creation of new IP legislation.[14]

As a result of these processes, the U.S. currently has, by WIPO's count, over 160 standing federal laws, rules, and regulations related to intellectual property. But for those creators and industries that rely on IP for their work and livelihood, the laws are still maddeningly vague. How much of a song can a hip-hop DJ sample in a mix without permission? When is it permissible for a television news organization to use a photo by a third party in a story? Does putting a document on an internet server count as "public accessibility" for the purposes of establishing the validity of a patent? How distinctive does an ice cream truck's name need to be in order to keep video game developers from using it without permission in their virtual worlds? How racially insensitive must a football team's name be before its trademark becomes invalid?

The letter of IP law doesn't provide answers to these questions; instead, they are decided in the courts (all of the examples above are from actual litigations). Not all IP lawsuits lead to a decision by a jury or judge; in fact, most of them are settled out of court. Many of those that do end in a decision are appealed to a higher court. And, of course, those cases that are finally decided serve as precedent only for the region in question; a New York district court decision might inform a California judge's decision, but it has no precedential power over it.

To complicate matters further, court decisions that become influential pieces of case law (the technical term for legal interpretation based on judicial decisions rather than legislation) sometimes become adopted as statute (the technical term for law as written). For instance, "fair use," an important concept we'll explore in chapter 2, was first introduced as case law in an 1841 suit about a George Washington biography, but it wasn't codified as statute until over a century later, in the Copyright Act of 1976.

Even more confoundingly, sometimes courts will adopt a legal standard or philosophy that the legislature has explicitly rejected. For instance, in 2004 Senator Orrin Hatch introduced the Inducing Infringement of Copyrights (INDUCE) Act, which would have made it illegal for someone to even *suggest* that someone else should violate copyright. The bill never made it into law, but this didn't prevent the Supreme Court from unanimously adopting "inducement" as an unprecedented standard when holding file-sharing network Grokster liable for infringement the following year.[15] Since then, the inducement standard has been a powerful element of copyright case law, despite the Senate's unwillingness to pass a bill regarding it.

Because this is such a large, complex, and diverse legal field, it's

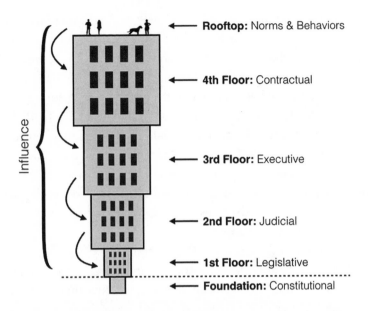

Figure 3: The architecture of IP law.

difficult to quantify the size or scope of IP case law. Yet, with tens of thousands of IP-related lawsuits in U.S. courts each year, it's safe to say that by any measure the case law dwarfs the scope of statute, delving into innumerable corners of the law never even considered by lawmakers. To return to our architectural metaphor, we can think of case law as the second floor of our building (as you may now realize, our building is constructed like an inverted pyramid, with the smallest bits at the base and growing ever larger with each successive level).

If the first floor of our building was built by the legislative branch of our government and the second floor was built by the judicial branch, the third floor is constituted by the executive branch. Once IP laws are written and interpreted, there are several state and federal organizations and institutions tasked with the responsibility of enforcing and facilitating the laws. Chief among these are the U.S. Copyright Office (which is, at the time of writing, technically a department of the Library of Congress) and the U.S. Patent and Trademark Office. These two organizations serve too many functions to enumerate here, but one of the chief among them is maintaining publicly searchable registries of IP. Using the USPTO's website, for instance, I was quickly able to discover that someone named Matt Sinnreich (no relation of mine) co-owns a trademark for "Tickle Room," used in the context of hats, shirts, and nightclub and bar services, registered only weeks before my search took place. Not only are these databases useful tools for IP owners, they're also fascinating cultural archives!

In addition to their roles as IP registrars, the Copyright Office and the USPTO also play a central role in analyzing and promoting IP policy both domestically and abroad, advising lawmakers and leaders about these issues and administering statutory licenses (which are established by Congress rather than agreed upon between parties). The USPTO is by far the larger of the two organizations, currently employing over ten thousand people, compared with fewer than four hundred at the Copyright Office.

In addition to these two agencies, the government employs numerous other parties whose roles involve enforcing or facilitating IP law, in whole or in part. These range from presidential appointees like the Intellectual Property Enforcement Coordinator (IPEC; sometimes referred to as the "IP czar") to auxiliary arms of the federal government like the U.S. Department of State's Office of International Intellectual Property Enforcement (IPE) to more generalist departments and actors such as the Department of Justice, the office of Immigration and Customs Enforcement (ICE), and state attorneys general. The role of the government at both the federal and state levels in policing, enforcing, and promoting intellectual property has grown considerably over the past few decades, as newer legislation has created entire offices dedicated to this purpose (such as IPEC) and increasingly tasked generalist offices such as ICE with IP-specific mandates.

The fourth floor of our IP edifice has nothing to do with the government, at least not directly; we build it ourselves with the licenses, contracts, and other interpersonal and interorganizational agreements that populate daily life and business in our mediated culture. When a recording artist gets his lucky break and signs that major label contract he's been angling for, one of the first things he does is assign the copyrights for his recordings to the label. When a research scientist takes a prestigious faculty job at a university, she's often required to sign away the patent rights to any of her future discoveries as a condition of taking the job. When you signed up for an Instagram account, the terms of service (TOS) agreement you probably didn't read requires you to grant the company a "nonexclusive, fully paid and royalty-free, transferable, sub-licensable, worldwide license to use the Content that you post" (there's nothing particularly onerous about this; most social media services' TOS have some version of this clause).[16] In a world where so many forms of expression are technically intellectual property, it's difficult to develop any mediated relationship between people and/or organizations that doesn't include some kind of contract or license setting out the legal terms of that relationship.

This puts our society somewhere between a rock and a hard place. If we didn't rely on so many contracts and licenses, there might be legal mayhem; in 2015, four hundred hours of video were uploaded to YouTube *every minute*. That's roughly the same amount of video that was produced by the global film industry during *an entire year* a mere century earlier. Without some fundamental ground rules, we'd have no way of coping economically or culturally with the ballooning volume of information we produce as a society.

On the other hand, licenses and contracts typically serve to further limit our control over information above and beyond the strictures already imposed by IP law. This is almost always a unidirectional process in which individual creators and consumers cede their rights to commercial organizations without any corresponding sacrifice on the other side. As many legal scholars have observed, this dynamic creates a widening gap between our laws, our ethics (what we think is right), and our norms and practices (what we actually do), which seems like a recipe for disaster in its own right.

There are no simple solutions to this dilemma other than some form of IP maximalism (granting commercial entities total control over our information sphere) or minimalism (essentially putting all information in the public domain), neither of which is particularly feasible, or even desirable to most people. Ultimately, each of us makes our own way through this dense and confusing jumble of laws, policies, and practices, negotiating our paths based on what we need to do, what we want to do, what we're allowed to do, and what we think is right.

Sometimes we fall afoul of the law, like the millions of people around the world who have been threatened with legal action for distributing copyrighted work online. Often the law serves us well, enabling us to profit from our ideas and creations or simply to make the most of our media culture, consuming, reconfiguring, and sharing the movies, books, songs, and games we love most.

Mostly, though, we just keep our heads down and go about our business, unsure of the legality of our actions and hoping to fly under the radar if we unwittingly commit an infringement. To complete our architectural metaphor, we can think of these individual decisions informing our daily journeys through the ever-evolving mediascape of networked society as the roof of our building. Regardless of what the law says, how it's interpreted by judges, how it's used to mediate our institutional relationships, and how well we understand it, what we actually do is meaningful—and sometimes it even has ripple effects back down the chain, contributing to future changes in the laws themselves. If the Constitution at the base of the building is the epitome of IP in theory, our daily lives and inter-actions constitute IP in practice.

Hopefully, you now understand the architecture of today's IP laws better than most—or at least better than you did before. But how did we get here? Why did the Constitution include the foun-dations for intellectual property in the first place, and how and why has it evolved into the massive edifice we know today? We will ex-plore some of this long and fascinating history in the next chapter.

ONE

The Origins of Intellectual Property

Imagine you're one of the founders of a new republic in a territory recently liberated from colonial subjugation. In addition to setting up the basics—infrastructure, schools, currency—you've got to develop a set of laws to guide the conduct of your citizens. Some of these would be obvious, such as laws against murder, rape, and arson. Others might be aspirational, related to the kind of republic you wish to build, such as laws requiring mandatory military service or publicly funded university education. But here's the question: would it occur to you to create intellectual property laws? If so, why? What purpose would they serve your fledgling nation?

These days, with international treaty organizations like WIPO and major political powers like the United States pushing for global adoption of such laws, the answer might seem obvious: of course you'd want to have IP, even if for no other reason than greasing the wheels of international trade. But a couple of centuries ago, the answer was nowhere near as obvious. In fact, for most nations throughout most of history, IP didn't exist at all. It wasn't part of the Code of

Hammurabi, written in ancient Babylon in 1750 BCE. It wasn't part of the Law of the Twelve Tables, written by the ancient Romans in 450 BCE. It didn't appear in the Code of Justinian, written for the Roman Empire in the sixth century CE. It didn't appear in the Great Qing Legal Code, first established in China in 1644. While most of these legal systems had very clear notions of property (and its analog, theft), none of them entailed any concept that ideas or their expressions could be propertized. So where did this notion originate and, more to the point, *why* did it originate?

The simple answer is that intellectual property as we know it originated with new cultural ideas and modes of production that emerged in Europe in the fourteenth and fifteenth centuries. Two radical new paradigms developed more or less simultaneously during this era, both of which are central to our story. In Italy, and later throughout Europe, the Renaissance gave rise to the modern notions of artistry and authorship. No longer was creative labor such as painting, music, and literature viewed as merely a skill, craft, or trade developed and shared within a guild or profession; instead, it became evidence of the talent, imagination, and even genius of an individual creator. It was during this period, for instance, that painters began signing their names to their works and that patrons began to pay a premium for work by "masters" of their arts (previously, as art historian Michael Baxandall has demonstrated, patrons were more concerned with the type and quality of materials to be used in the artwork than they were with who made it).[1]

Meanwhile, in Germany, a goldsmith named Johannes Gutenberg invented the printing press, which meant that, for the first time, creative expression could be mass produced.[2] This in turn meant that the business of culture could be organized like any other manufacturing industry: large companies with expensive machines creating identical products for large regional, nationwide, or even international markets (in fact, publishing was one of the first sectors to be "industrialized"). It also meant, however, that cultural expression could be produced, distributed, and consumed via market channels, without the participation (or even the permission) of either the church or the royal court.

While these two developments might seem to conflict directly with one another, they are actually flip sides of the same coin. In the older era, when everything was made by hand, the artistry and authenticity of a cultural work was rarely in doubt (except in the case of forgeries). In the newer era of cultural mass production, the signature of a creator became proof of a given work's uniqueness, and an assertion of sole authorship provided a human element that made a work more palatable and relatable in the case of new, machine-made cultural products. In short, one might say that the modern notion of the "artist" became necessary only at the moment that culture entered into mass production.

In the centuries that followed, these developments contributed directly to a fundamental reorganization of European society marked by the rise of new and disruptive belief systems (for example, Protestantism), new and disruptive social philosophies (like the Enlightenment), new and disruptive economic systems (such as industrial capitalism), and new and disruptive political systems (for example, constitutional monarchies and republics). We cannot possibly understand the origins of intellectual property separately from the tectonic shifts that shook Europe to its foundations during this era. It's not simply that IP, like these other new ideas, was inspired by Renaissance notions of authorship and individuality and the transformative potential of the printing press—although this was most certainly the case. Rather, IP emerged at this time because it was a *catalyst* for these other changes.

By crystallizing the notion of authorship in the form of copyright, IP law validated and formalized the concept that each individual has his or her own unique perspective, and that the cultural world is comprised of autonomous actors, collaborating and competing in the "marketplace of ideas." By giving publishers and manufacturers the ability to own and stockpile copyrights, patents, and trademarks in the same way they would raw materials and machines, IP law naturalized the transition to a mercantile economy and demonstrated that few if any dimensions of the human condition are entirely separate from the marketplace. In short, the concept of intellectual property is integral to the entire Enlightenment project and to the emergence of what, in retrospect, we have come to call "modernity."

The United States of America, which was conceived from the same philosophical materials and which emerged just at the apex of this social moment, was the first nation to be created with intellectual property as a fundamental building block of its legal system. It should come as little surprise, therefore, that two and a half centuries later, the nation is the world's chief exponent of IP rights and the chief exporter of IP. In the intervening years, copyrights, patents, and trademarks have evolved and expanded in conjunction with new technologies, cultural movements, and social philosophies, to the point where our nation's founders might barely recognize them (let alone approve of them). The pace of change has only continued to accelerate, and today a book written on the subject of IP might be out of date by the time it's published a year or two later. Yet to understand these changes and the evolving philosophy of intellectual property, we must start at the beginning, with the origins of copyrights, patents, and trademarks, in the days before America was even a gleam in its founders' eyes.

IP Before America

Intellectual property didn't spring into the world fully formed, like Athena jumping from the head of Zeus. Instead, more like a mortal, the law had a gestation period, an infancy, and a slow, sometimes painful path to maturity. Copyright was first conceived in England about a century after Gutenberg's printing press, when the government of Queen Mary I granted a Royal Charter of Incorporation to the Company of Stationers of London in 1557. The company at the time was in the midst of a centuries-long evolution from a medieval-style guild of bookmakers and purveyors of writing materials such as ink and paper into what today we might call a "trade organization," primarily representing the interests of the country's most powerful publishing companies. This charter would prove to be a crucial element in that transition.

Among other things, the charter empowered the company to grant any of its members the exclusive right in perpetuity—sometimes referred to as a "stationer's copyright"—to publish a given work within England. Anyone who violated this right would face disciplinary action, the wrath of fellow publishers, and potentially crippling exclusion from the company. This served a few purposes for company members, chief among which was eliminating competition within the industry (which had been exerting a downward pressure on book prices—a boon to buyers but a threat to sellers). It also gave them a strong sense of entitlement. As historian Adrian Johns argues, the exclusivity conferred on company members by this practice "became the principal element in Stationers' common notions of right and wrong conduct in the trade" and "would survive to be enshrined in legal notions of copyright for hundreds of years after this."[3]

Yet, from the very beginning, the Company of Stationers' charter also had a second, equally vital function. From the perspective of the government, the charter served as a way to keep tabs on powerful publishers, limiting the politically subversive potential of the printing press (which would play a central role in the political upheavals that rocked European monarchies in the centuries to come, including the American Revolution). In the words of legal scholar

Lyman Ray Patterson, "This policy made it convenient for the government to give the stationers large powers . . . in order to have them serve as policemen of the press."[4] This political sleight of hand—binding publishers' self-interest with the government's—remains an integral dimension of copyright law and IP policy to this day, nearly half a millennium later.

Of course, stationers' copyrights weren't truly copyrights in the sense that we use the word today. For one thing, although the power to grant them was bestowed via government charter, the copyrights in this case were binding only among members of the company, not the law of the land. For another, stationers' copyrights were granted directly to publishers, not to authors themselves. At this point in time, the notion that intellectual property existed in order to support or incentivize creators—something many take for granted today—was not even part of the rationale for such policies.

The power of the stationers' company to bestow copyrights, as well as its role both in policing works that infringed copyrights and in censoring "seditious" books on behalf of the government, was further increased over the next century and a half, first via a series of Star Chamber decrees and finally via the Licensing Act of 1662, which definitively required a publisher to obtain a stationer's copyright before it could print a work. When this law expired in 1694, the Company of Stationers was suddenly deprived of the tremendous power it had wielded for the past century and a half, and the English publishing industry was plunged into chaos. The House of Commons, newly empowered following the Glorious Revolution of 1688, had a very different agenda than the monarchical government that had first granted the company its charter, viewing the Company of Stationers as a corrupt tool of the crown, "impowered to hinder the printing [of] all innocent and useful Books."[5] It was at this moment that the major book publishers pivoted, switching their political allegiances to Parliament, repositioning themselves as defenders of "authors' rights," and lobbying for a statutory copyright law.

This new strategy bore fruit a few years later when Parliament enacted the Statute of Anne in 1710. This is often referred to as "the first copyright law," though of course scholars of the subject have debated whether and to what degree that claim is accurate. What we can say for certain is that, unlike the expired acts and charters that it updated, the Statute of Anne specifically enabled authors, rather than just publishers, to own copyrights (although these rights were assignable, which meant that publishers were likely to end up controlling them in most cases), and it extended this right to the entire universe of authors and publishers rather than just to stationers' company members. The statute also introduced the notion of limited copyright terms, setting them to expire after fourteen years, with a renewal option for an additional fourteen years. Over the course of the eighteenth century, this law was continually debated, litigated, and refined, and by 1774 it had evolved into something definitively modern. In Patterson's words, "Copyright had ceased to be a publisher's right and had become an author's right."[6]

England wasn't the only nation to develop a proto-copyright system during these years. As the printing press spread across the European subcontinent, religious and political powers of various kinds sought to control its revolutionary potential by granting monopoly privileges to designated publishers and authors, though details of these commissions varied from time to time and from place to place. However, no other nation empowered the publishing industry to police itself and to grant such privileges on the government's behalf, and no nation developed an actual copyright law prior to the Statute of Anne. For these reasons, and because England's system would soon be adopted to a large degree by the United States, where IP would reach its global apogee, the history of copyright in these other nations is not as central to our story.

The history of patents is intimately tied to the history of copyright. In their earliest years, in fact, the two mechanisms were virtually indistinguishable. In the medieval era, a "patent" was simply a letter from a political power conferring some kind of privilege on the letter holder. In the sixteenth and seventeenth centuries, many publishers throughout Europe operated under the aegis of a "printing patent" from a given monarchy, state government, or office of the church. In England, this practice was common even after the stationers' copyright was developed and, according to Patterson, "printing patents were the more desirable of the two" because they "covered the most profitable works."[7]

The notion of the patent as we now think of it—a monopoly granted to an inventor by the government—was another subcategory of this general practice, and its origins can be traced back to the Italian Renaissance, especially in Venice. In 1447, this powerful independent republic passed the first statutory patent law, which provided inventors a ten-year window of exclusivity for their devices. There was an important caveat, however: in order to receive a patent, an inventor had to share his or her discovery with the state, which was free to use it without further permission or payment. While this bears some structural similarity to the modern American patent system, in which inventors register their work with the government in exchange for a twenty-year monopoly, the intent was very different. In the case of Venice, the state shared in the inventor's secret for its own benefit. In the modern system, the state incentivizes the inventor to reveal his or her secret for the benefit of society at large.

As with copyright, the first patent law that would be recognizable by today's standards was enacted in England. In 1624, Parliament passed the Monopolies Act, which challenged the power of the crown by immediately nullifying all previous patents and by establishing itself as the sole patent-granting authority in the country.

The explicit purpose of this policy was to eliminate the toxic level of royally condoned monopolization, which was seen as an obstacle to growth and innovation across a range of industries. The act also broke new ground by emphasizing the *public interest* inherent in the discovery and widespread adoption of new ideas, granting patents only to the original inventors of a given technology. This legal vision was so transformative, so integral to the political vision of what we would now refer to as a "free market," that the statute continues to serve as a reference for modern patent laws around the globe, and has achieved what legal scholar Chris Dent calls "an almost idealized status within patent law."[8]

The Monopolies Act is also seen by many social historians as a watershed moment in the genesis of the industrial revolution: by making new discoveries public and rewarding their creators for sharing them, the argument goes, the act created the ideal conditions for the rapid technological advancement that we have witnessed over the past four centuries. Of course this, like all broad claims about IP, is a dangerous oversimplification. As historian Christine MacLeod argues in her exhaustive history of the early English patent system, "The connection between inventing and patenting is historically tentative," at least until the laws and the broader patent system matured at the end of the eighteenth century.[9] Even today, although patents are routinely used in research and advocacy as a de facto index of overall innovation, this claim is widely critiqued; as *Washington Post* writer Dominic Basulto recently wrote, "Patents might be a better proxy for how litigious American business has become rather than how innovative a specific company or industry has become."[10]

Intellectual Property in Early America

Intellectual property is in America's DNA. As discussed in the introduction, article 1, section 8 of the U.S. Constitution gives Congress the power "to promote the Progress of Science and useful Arts, by securing for limited Times to Authors and Inventors the exclusive Right to their respective Writings and Discoveries." It didn't take long for our legislature to take advantage of this power. The nation's first IP law, the Patent Act of 1790, was signed into law in April of that year, with the Copyright Act of 1790 following a few weeks later. These were still very early days for American law; only two days before the Copyright Act's passage, the Constitution was ratified by Rhode Island, the last of the thirteen original states to do so. The First Amendment, which established a constitutional basis for free speech and freedom of the press (often seen as intimately related to intellectual property law in both theory and function), wouldn't be ratified for another year and a half.

Given the rapidity with which Congress created intellectual property laws (faster, for instance, than it chartered the first national bank, established a federal postal service, or created a navy), it's clear that, far from mere afterthoughts, copyrights and patents were integral to the founders' conception of what America should be and how it should operate. Yet despite this rapidity and focus, there was significant disagreement among the founders on these matters from the years leading up to the nation's establishment to long after these initial laws were passed.

While the nuances of this debate are far too complex to go into, we can glimpse its rough contours in the differences between James Madison's and Thomas Jefferson's approaches to intellectual property, reflected in their public letters and other writings. The two men agreed on many things: they were wed to the principle of individual liberty, to the value of property as a pathway to liberty, and to the importance of a rich and vibrant public sphere, where the self-ruling citizens of a democratic republic could freely share and debate ideas, allowing the best ones to rise to the top and influence the laws of the land.

The problem is, these aims can contradict one another. To put it simply, the more that ideas and inventions are treated as the exclusive property of a single individual or organization, the less freely they can be adopted, adapted, and exchanged, and the more impoverished the public sphere risks becoming. Therefore, the challenge is to find an optimal set of intellectual property laws (what, in today's parlance, we might call a "sweet spot") that serve maximally to strengthen liberty and self-governance and minimally to impede the sharing of knowledge and ideas. Finding this optimal political balance (while also balancing more mundane but equally important economic interests) was where Madison and Jefferson differed.[11]

Madison believed that England was a good model to follow. In 1788, he authored Federalist Paper No. 43, which proposed the text that eventually became article 1, section 8, clause 8 of the Constitution, granting authors and inventors sole ownership over their writings and discoveries for a limited time. In support of this text, he wrote that the value of intellectual property laws was self-evident: "The utility of this power will scarcely be questioned. The copyright of authors has been solemnly adjudged, in Great Britain, to be a right of common law. The right to useful inventions seems with equal reason to belong to the inventors. The public good fully coincides in both cases with the claims of individuals."

Thus, according to Madison, there is no conflict between propertizing the expression of ideas and the "public good." As copyright scholar William Patry explains, this was "based on a belief that the enlightened self-interest of individuals will, collectively, always work to benefit society."[12] Property, in other words, gives people a personal investment in something, and therefore, if we want citizens to be personally invested in developing and sharing ideas, what better way than to grant them ownership over them?

Jefferson, on the other hand, was skeptical of intellectual property and resistant to the idea of granting a monopoly over ideas (or their expressions). In a widely quoted and brilliantly written 1813 letter to Isaac McPherson, a miller concerned about the extra costs of using patented equipment, Jefferson laid out his principal objections:

> If nature has made any one thing less susceptible than all others of exclusive property, it is the action of the thinking power called an idea, which an individual may exclusively possess as long as he keeps it to himself; but the moment it is divulged, it forces itself into the possession of every one, and the receiver cannot dispossess himself of it. Its peculiar character, too, is that no one possesses the less, because every other possesses the whole of it. He who receives an idea from me, receives instruction himself without lessening mine; as he who lights his taper at mine, receives light without darkening me. . . . Inventions then cannot, in nature, be a subject of property. Society may give an exclusive right to the profits arising from them, as an encouragement to men to pursue ideas which may produce utility, but this may or may not be done, according to the will and convenience of the society.

Furthermore, Jefferson confessed, even though America had adopted the English practice of granting such rights to authors and inventors decades earlier, he still wasn't convinced it had been for the best. In his words, "It is a fact, as far as I am informed, that England was, until we copied her, the only country on earth which ever, by a general law, gave a legal right to the exclusive use of an idea. In some other countries it is sometimes done, in a great case, and by a special and personal act, but, generally speaking, other nations have thought that these monopolies produce more embarrassment than advantage to society; and it may be observed that the nations which refuse monopolies of invention, are as fruitful as England in new and useful devices."

In other words, for Jefferson, the costs of monopolizing ideas threatened to exceed what little benefit there was. If most of the great scientific discoveries and works of art and literature had been developed and shared without the benefit of copyrights or patents, he reasoned, then how useful could they be as an enrichment to the public sphere and as a boon to the public good?

Ultimately, the final text of the Constitution and the resulting laws in 1790 and beyond were something of a compromise between these differing notions. Even at his most enthusiastic, Madison still acknowledged the dangers of monopolization, while Jefferson accepted the political necessity of intellectual property, though he continually sought ways to limit its power.

Though Jefferson lived in France during the mid- to late 1780s while Madison stayed in the U.S. helping to develop the Constitution, he still weighed in from afar; in a 1789 letter to Madison, for instance, he suggested that the Constitution specify that "Monopolies may be allowed to persons . . . for a term not exceeding—— years, but for no longer term, and no other purpose." If this passage had indeed been included in the Constitution, the last two centuries of intellectual property law (and consequently American culture and industry) would have unfolded rather differently; an explicit limit on the scope and term of IP laws would have meant that Congress couldn't expand either without amending the Constitution itself—a far greater political barrier than a simple majority vote.

In the centuries since the Constitution was ratified and the first intellectual property laws were enacted in the U.S., legislators, courts, and regulators have sought to maintain the delicate balance established between Jefferson and Madison, chasing the "sweet spot" as new technologies, new cultural forms, and new economic models have contributed to radical changes in our society and in the ways that we express our ideas. The Constitution's emphasis on IP as an *incentive* for creators to share their work and as a *temporary* monopoly granted by the state, rather than a moral right divinely bestowed upon authors and inventors through the mystical act of creation, has continued to inform copyright, patents, and other forms of intellectual property as they have evolved to accommodate these changes.

Yet, because Jefferson's clause wasn't included in the final text, nearly everything else about IP, especially copyright, has changed in the years since then. As we will explore in the following section, monopoly terms have expanded drastically over the past two centuries, the range of cultural artifacts that may be owned has ballooned, and policing and enforcement of IP infringement has been elevated to a national and international priority on par with counterterrorism and combating organized crime.

The Growth and Expansion of Copyright

Copyright in the twenty-first century bears little resemblance to the visions espoused by Madison and Jefferson. In fact, IP laws have been continually updated, expanded, and strengthened since they were first enacted. According to the U.S. Copyright Office's own tally, the longest period in American history *without* a new piece of copyright legislation was just under seventeen years—from 1802 to 1819. All told, between 1790 and 2008, Congress passed at least ninety new laws related to copyright, an average of one every two and a half years. And this tally leaves out legislation that was proposed but not enacted as well as treaties and judicial decisions, to say nothing of other domestic IP laws covering patents and trademarks, let alone international laws.

To put it simply, intellectual property law has never been fixed, static, or consistent. It is always in flux, due in part to the emergence of new technologies, cultural forms, and economic models, but also in large degree thanks to the tireless lobbying of IP-based industries such as publishing, music, film, software, apparel, and pharmaceuticals. And though the details differ from year to year, bill to bill, and industry to industry, the general trend is toward what some legal scholars, like Lawrence Lessig and David Bollier, call "maximalism."

This term refers to an expansion of legal control over culture and technology that downplays the incentive-oriented mandate of the Constitution and creates exactly the kind of commercial monopolies that Jefferson warned about. According to these critics, IP is no longer calibrated to occupy the sweet spot between too much and too little control, and now threatens to undermine the democratic virtues it once aimed to serve. Of course, proponents of these newer, stronger laws have always argued that just the opposite is true; without constant vigilance, they say, new technologies will abet "piracy" on a massive scale and thus destroy the very industries that have subsidized so many of our cultural and technological achievements over the past few centuries.

Whichever interpretation you prefer, the facts are fairly straightforward. To begin with, copyright's term has been extended considerably by Congress over the years; in 1790, the law offered authors a fourteen-year term, followed by an optional fourteen-year renewal term. Today, copyright lasts for the duration of an author's life plus seventy additional years, or a fixed ninety-five-year term in the case of "works for hire" (in these cases, authorship technically belongs to a corporation, which has an infinite potential lifespan). This expansion didn't happen all at once, but rather in increasingly frequent bits and bursts. As Lessig observes in his book *Free Culture*, for instance, Congress extended existing copyright terms eleven different times in a forty-year period ending at the turn of the twenty-first century.[13]

This expansion is likely to continue for a fairly straightforward reason: Mickey Mouse. The Sonny Bono Copyright Term Extension Act of 1998 (CTEA) was frequently referred to by commentators and critics as the Mickey Mouse Act (or some variation thereof)

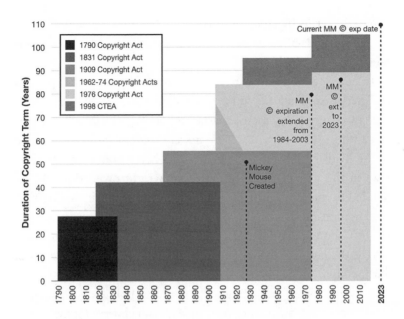

Figure 4: Copyright term expansion timeline, 1790–2017. (Adapted from Zachary Crocket, "How Mickey Mouse Evades the Public Domain," January 7, 2016, *Priceonomics* (blog), https://priceonomics.com /how-mickey-mouse-evades-the-public-domain/.)

because if it had not extended copyright terms by twenty years, the first cartoon featuring the famous character, *Steamboat Willie* (1928), would have passed into the public domain in 2003. This would have made the lovable little rodent fair game for anyone, from Disney's competitors to its fans to its detractors, to use without permission or payment. The prospect of losing monopoly control over its mascot was a terrifying prospect for Disney (then, as now, one of the two largest media companies in the world), which lobbied and advocated aggressively for the CTEA. Today, twenty years later, the twenty-year reprieve granted by the law is due to expire, and at the time of writing, there have already been some efforts to further extend copyright terms by an extra thirty years (for instance, a draft copy of the Trans-Pacific Partnership trade accord leaked in 2013 contained this proposal).

In addition to an ever-expanding term, the scope of copyright has increased drastically in the years since the 1790 act. Originally, the law covered only maps, charts, and books published by American authors (foreign works were not covered, much to the chagrin of the British publishing companies that had lobbied for copyright laws in the first place). Since then, copyright protection has expanded to include a broad range of creative works, including musical compositions in 1831, photographs in 1865, motion pictures in 1912, sound recordings in 1972, and computer programs in 1980. Today, the law says that copyright applies to all "original works of authorship fixed in any tangible medium of expression, now known or later developed," including but not limited to literary works, musical works, dramatic works, pantomimes and choreographic works, pictorial, graphic and sculptural works, motion pictures and other audiovisual works, sound recordings, and architectural works.[14]

The scope of copyright has expanded in other ways as well. Beginning in 1891, for example, America recognized the copyrights of foreign authors. This was partially a response to the first major international copyright treaty (the Berne Convention, signed in 1886, which the U.S. didn't technically join for another century) but also a sign that America's copyright industries were becoming large and powerful enough to benefit from copyright protection abroad more than they did from the ability to distribute foreign works freely at home.

Beginning in 1856, U.S. copyright also expanded to give authors the right to authorize or prevent the creation of derivative works, which current law defines as those "based upon one or more preexisting works, such as a translation, musical arrangement, dramatization, fictionalization, motion picture version, sound recording, art reproduction, abridgment, condensation, or any other form in which a work may be recast, transformed, or adapted."[15] This category itself has expanded over the years, most drastically in the 1909 Copyright Act, which gave copyright owners the exclusive right to "make any other version" of a protected work—a vague enough phrase to cover a very wide range of creative adaptations.

During the nineteenth century, copyright's scope also began to expand beyond the right of publication into other uses of protected works. For instance, in 1897, music publishers, who already enjoyed copyright protection for printed scores, were given a new and extremely valuable right: public performance. From this point on, concert halls, nightclubs, and other public venues were required to pay a royalty to rights holders every time one of their songs was played. As the twentieth century progressed, this right was extended to performances on radio, television, and eventually the internet, and today it generates billions of dollars in annual revenue for composers and their publishers.

While this may seem a very natural and straightforward kind of copyright protection to those of us who have never known a world without it, think for a moment about what a massive abstract leap it was at the time. Copyright, which had served for the past sixty-six years merely to prevent one music publisher from *printing* a score controlled by another without authorization, was suddenly used to prevent musicians from *singing or playing* a song, and music in the air (an intangible, ephemeral abstraction) was subjected to the same kind of monopolization and control as music on paper (a tangible commodity).

Thus, the scope of copyright has expanded significantly over the years—both in terms of the kinds of works that may be copyrighted and in terms of the uses covered by copyright. Before we move on, it is important to note one more major expansion in scope—perhaps the most important, if we're measuring purely on the basis of numbers. For the nation's first two centuries, Americans who wished to hold copyrights in their works had to register those works with the government, essentially asking for permission to exercise a monopoly over the expression of their ideas. Everything else, by default, was a part of the public domain. This meant that only those who had a financial interest in exploiting their work would go through the trouble of protecting it, while the vast majority of creative expression remained free and open for anyone to use.

All of this changed with the Copyright Act of 1976 which, for the first time, ensured that every copyrightable work (as we have discussed, an increasingly extensive category) was protected immediately from the moment of fixation in a tangible medium of expression. The moment the law was enacted in 1978, every snapshot, napkin doodle, and home video instantly became a protected work. Today, roughly 225 million Americans carry around smartphones and wearable computing devices, capturing and sharing trillions of pieces of information each year. Every text, email, photo, video, screenshot, audio clip, blog post, status update, meme, and animated GIF we make instantly enjoys the same level of copyright protection as a Hollywood movie, and each of them, as well as any derivative works based upon them, will stay protected for the duration of our lives plus another seventy years, assuming copyright terms aren't extended again in the next century or so.

The upshot of these changes is this: when copyright began in the U.S., it covered a limited range of uses, for a limited variety of works, for a limited span of time—reflecting the spirit, if not the letter, of Jefferson's cautious language. Today, nearly every piece of cultural expression is private property—and will remain so for generations. Whether you consider this development a boon for creators and creative industries or a dangerous obstacle to free expression, there can be little question that it represents a significant change in the

cultural and economic landscape, with far-reaching political and social repercussions.

The Growth of Patents and Trademarks

Since the passage of the first U.S. patent law in 1790, this form of
intellectual property has evolved as well—though not in ways that
are as obviously radical as copyright law. For one thing, the term of
a patent has grown very slightly. Like copyright, it was initially set
at fourteen years, but this term has grown by only six years rather
than by an order of magnitude. For another, the scope of coverage
hasn't expanded much because it was pretty broad to begin with.
According to the 1790 act, a patent could be granted to anyone who
"invented or discovered any useful art, manufacture, engine, machine, or device, or any improvement therein not before known or
used." Today, the law covers anyone who "invents or discovers any
new and useful process, machine, manufacture, or composition of
matter, or any new and useful improvement thereof."[16] Again, these
changes are meaningful but not nearly as sweeping as copyright's
expansion from a handful of printed products to a universe of mediated expression. Finally, unlike copyright, patents still require registration with the federal government, which means that a great
many useful but noncommercialized discoveries and inventions are,
by default, in the public domain.

Yet, despite the fact that patents' term, scope, and registration
process have remained relatively unchanged over the past two centuries, there have been some significant alterations in the letter of
the law, in its judicial interpretation, and in its application to industry and technology. Some examples include the extension of patent
protection to foreign nationals and the establishment of a federal
Patent Office in the early nineteenth century, the gradual expansion
of patent coverage to new realms of technology and industry (rang-

ing from fabrics to plants), and the development of a specialized design patent (as opposed to the more traditional "utility patent"). As with copyright, changes to patent law began to accelerate in the middle of the twentieth century, spurred in part by the creation of the Court of Appeals for the Federal Circuit in 1982, which is the only federal appellate-level court with the jurisdiction to hear patent case appeals.

As both an effect and a cause of these relatively recent legal developments, the number of patents and patent-centered lawsuits has climbed steeply in recent years. According to the USPTO's most recent tally, there were more patents granted in the U.S. in the past thirty years (1986–2015) than in the two centuries before that (1790–1985).[17] And as the number of patents has grown, the number of patent lawsuits has increased commensurately. According to analyses based on federal data by IP attorney Gene Quinn and accounting firm PwC, the number of patent litigations in America rose roughly eightfold in a three-decade span, from about eight hundred per year in the early 1980s to nearly sixty-five hundred in 2013.[18]

What accounts for this abrupt uptick in patent applications, grants, and lawsuits? Part of the answer has to do with the accelerating pace of technological change in the wake of the "digital revolution": there are many legitimately new devices and processes enabled by these platforms and catalyzed by the massive investment that's gone into the tech sector and into other sectors transformed by it. Yet the novelty of these new technologies and concepts has also created an incentive for mischief in the form of opportunistic patent filings and litigations initiated by unscrupulous parties seeking to take advantage of the lack of technical expertise in the USPTO and the courts, and there is little question that a substantial portion of recent patent applications and lawsuits can be attributed to these mischief makers.

Finally, as we will explore further in the conclusion, there has been a drastic increase in "patent trolls," entities that seek to use their IP not for commercial purposes but rather to make money through litigation or the threat of it. According to analyses by White House legal adviser Colleen Chien, troll-initiated lawsuits accounted for 62 percent of all patent litigation in 2012, leading the federal government itself to call for legal reforms raising the bar for "novelty" and "nonobviousness" and establishing lower-cost alternatives to pricey IP litigation.[19]

Although copyright and patent laws were priorities for America's founders, there was no statutory trademark law in the United States during the nation's first century. While common law concepts such as "passing off" (in which one manufacturer attempts deceptively to trade on the good name of another manufacturer) did exist, there wasn't a single federal trademark case until 1844, and no trademark legislation until 1870.[20] Even in the early twentieth century, the exclusive rights of trademark holders in the U.S. were fairly limited; under the acts of 1876 and 1905, trademark was violated only when the infringing party sold a piece of merchandise with "substantially the same descriptive properties" as the infringed party.

Modern trademark wasn't born until 1946 with the passage of the Lanham Act, a far more comprehensive law that expanded the scope of trademark infringement to cover anything that "is likely to cause confusion" on the part of consumers, while eliminating the requirement that someone be "willfully" deceiving in order to be found liable. In other words, a company could now be sued successfully and its business halted if its logo looked or sounded a bit too much like another company's, even if its products and services didn't compete directly, and even if the similarity was completely coincidental.

Needless to say, this broader notion of trademark protection opened the door to a whole new universe of legal disputes, which in turn helped to further propel the legal powers of trademark holders.

As in the cases of copyright and patent, the mid-twentieth century marked the beginning of a rapid expansion in the scope and power of this form of intellectual property. In the U.S., according to WIPO, total trademark registrations per year have risen steadily over the past few decades, with more than an elevenfold increase from 1980 (under 19,000) to 2015 (almost 220,000).

This is not merely an American trend; globally, annual trademark registrations have risen more than sixfold in three decades, from under 700,000 in 1985 to over 4.4 million in 2015. As with copyrights and patents, the rate of litigation has grown steeply as well. According to data compiled by law professor Matthew Sag, for instance, the number of trademark cases in the ten most IP-litigious U.S. district courts doubled between 1994 and 2014.[21]

Summary

As this brief review demonstrates, intellectual property laws have changed considerably since their origins at the dawn of the modern era. Copyright, which began as an instrument of cartelization for British book publishers (and a means of censorship for the British crown), evolved into an author's right, and though its American origins were modest in their term and scope, the law has come to cover a very wide range of cultural expression and activity for a very long period of time. Patents, initially a dispensation granted to select elites as a political favor, evolved into a widely used instrument to encourage the public sharing of specialized expertise, yet also emerged as a chief bulwark against competition for technologists and researchers across a range of sectors. Trademarks, once a simple legal recourse to prevent a specific variety of fraud, have expanded their mandate to ensure that market newcomers aren't "confused" with existing products and services in the minds of consumers.

Over the centuries, and especially in the decades since World War II, the number of cultural works, discoveries, inventions, products, and services covered by these legal instruments has grown by orders of magnitude, and the courts have been increasingly burdened with the task of splitting IP's ever-finer hairs, attempting to distinguish original from derivative, novel from known, and genuine from counterfeit while staying mindful of potential precedents and chasing the Constitution's implicit sweet spot between too much and too little protection and control. In the meantime, as we will explore more throughout this book, the stakes continue to rise, as IP infringement is policed to an ever-greater degree by state and private entities and as legal penalties climb ever steeper for those found liable. As the economic and legal stakes have grown, so have the social ones; IP critics decry increasing "maximalism" and warn of dangers to free speech, free markets, and cultural and technological innovation, while industry groups and others continue to lobby for ever-stricter laws, citing threats of "piracy" and raising the specter of diminishing profits and disappearing jobs.

For better or for worse, the continuing growth of intellectual property has made it one of the chief instruments of international trade, one of the most valuable commodities in the market, and one of the most hotly contested arenas in the world of policy. Yet, despite its sustained expansion over the centuries and its recent postwar boom, IP does have its limits, both legally and functionally. Though it may seem contradictory, many of these limits have grown stronger and more clearly defined even as IP itself has expanded its footprint throughout the cultural realm and the marketplace. We will explore these limits, and the limits to these limits, in the following chapter.

TWO

The Limits of Intellectual Property

In the introduction and first chapter, we explored the many varieties of intellectual property law, the wide range of cultural artifacts and social practices that may fall under their purview, and the historical emergence and expansion of these legal instruments. Today, IP plays a more central role in our business and culture, is worth more economically, and is more assiduously policed and prosecuted than at any other point in history.

We live in a society so thoroughly permeated with IP that its ubiquitous signs and symbols are virtually invisible to us (ever notice the ® marks next to the logos on your favorite box of cereal while you're enjoying a nutritious breakfast?), while arcane copyright and patent disputes in fields as disparate as music, technology, and pharmaceuticals have become standard fodder for workplace water cooler moralizing and late night television humor.

Yet, despite the dominance of intellectual property in our daily lives and global cultural environment, it still has some important limits in terms of both its scope and its power. Thanks to legal concepts like the public domain, term expiry, fair use and safe harbors, there are some places IP just can't go and some things it just can't do. As we will explore in this chapter, these limits are clearly necessary for free speech and free markets, and are ultimately beneficial even to rights holders themselves.

Understanding the Commons: Tragedy or Treasure?

Sometimes the limits of intellectual property are described by IP maximalists, industry representatives, and others as impositions on the rights of patent, trademark, and copyright holders themselves, a state-sanctioned land grab of rightful private property. If I can pass on my precious silver and china to my descendants without it eventually falling into the hands of the public, one version of this argument goes, then why can't I pass on the copyrights to my work in similar perpetuity?

At other times, the limits of IP are even decried as a form of *legal trickery*, a technical loophole in the law exploited by pirates and counterfeiters to abet their crimes against the rightful owners of cultural expression and scientific discovery. Creators who assert their right to exploit the limits of IP for artistic or commercial purposes may be accused of "hiding behind fair use" or "hiding behind the DMCA" (Digital Millennium Copyright Act, a 1998 copyright law discussed further below), as though this right were merely a façade or an obstacle thrown in the path of justice.[1]

Yet, to many legal scholars, these perspectives get the story backward: IP isn't a natural right, unfairly fettered by a thousand legal shackles. To the contrary, IP laws themselves are the shackles, impinging on the freely shared knowledge and culture of humankind at large—often referred to as *the commons* (or, more specifically, the "cultural commons"). While this imposition may be beneficial for some, or even necessary at times, it should never be forgotten that every piece of work protected by intellectual property is, de facto, a diminishment of the commons, an appropriation of a public good, and an incursion on the rights of free speech and commerce.

What, exactly, is the commons? And where does this idea come from? The term itself is centuries old, and it encompasses far more than merely the world of knowledge and expression—in fact, it applies to everything within the human sphere of experience that isn't explicitly owned by a single individual or entity, such as the air we breathe, the planet Jupiter, the D major scale, or the Pythagorean theorem.

In Middle English, the term *commons* (sometimes singularized) also applied specifically to land that was communally owned by residents of a town or village, collectively maintained and used for agriculture and livestock. Beginning in the thirteenth century and continuing in waves throughout the next five hundred years, these common lands were "enclosed" with hedges and fences, converted from public to private property.[2] This process was anything but peaceful; it fueled riots, rebellions, and ridicule, including an anonymously penned eighteenth-century poem that summed up centuries of anti-enclosure sentiment perfectly in its first stanza:

> You prosecute the man or woman
> Who steals the goose from off the common
> But leave the larger felon loose
> Who steals the common from the goose.[3]

Of course, the enclosure of the commons was not universally reviled. For one thing, the landowners whose wealth was increased by the process benefited immensely from the policy. But there are also those who hold that enclosure benefited everyone throughout society, especially the poor, because it allowed the land to be used more efficiently, producing a higher volume of food and other necessities for a European population that soon began to boom with the onset of industrialization.

Figure 5: Engraving depicting Kett's Rebellion, a violent protest against enclosure of the commons in England in 1549.

This perspective was epitomized in a 1968 article by biologist Garret Hardin, in which he coined the term *the tragedy of the commons* to describe what happens when a resource is owned by everyone and no one at the same time. If there is a limited amount of common grass for grazing, for instance, each shepherd has an incentive to maximize the size of his or her own flock to get the most grass. While this strategy might benefit the individual shepherd relative to his or her competitors, it ultimately causes the grass itself to be overgrazed, which denudes the land and thus hurts everyone. In Hardin's poetic words, "Ruin is the destination toward which all men rush, each pursuing his own best interest in a society that believes in the freedom of the commons. Freedom in a commons brings ruin to all."[4]

As attractive as the idea of a "tragedy of the commons" might be (especially to those who benefit from enclosure and its modern equivalent, privatization), there are many scholars who question its validity, both theoretically and practically. For one thing, to assume that the market is the only viable method of managing resources successfully simply flies in the face of historical evidence—even when it comes to the enclosure movement itself. In the words of political scientist Susan Jane Buck Cox, "Perhaps what existed in fact was not a 'tragedy of the commons' but rather a triumph: that for hundreds of years . . . land was managed successfully by communities."[5] Hardin himself eventually modified his idea somewhat in response to such critiques, acknowledging that he should have called it "the tragedy of the *unmanaged* commons."[6]

Even if the tragedy of the commons does apply in the case of a finite and tangible good like a parcel of land (which can be overgrazed) or a pond (which can be overfished or polluted), there's no clear reason to believe it applies in the case of an infinite, and perpetually shifting, *cultural* commons. As Thomas Jefferson pointed out back in chapter 1, "He who receives an idea from me, receives instruction himself without lessening mine." In more contemporary economic terms, Jefferson's point is that cultural artifacts typically differ from material ones in that they are neither "rivalrous" (one person's use doesn't limit another's), nor "excludable" (one person can't prevent another from using it). Without rivalry and excludability, how can there be tragic overuse or wasteful underutilization?

Yet, despite the absence of such tragedy, many legal scholars have voiced concern that the cultural commons is indeed being enclosed—especially in the wake of major copyright revisions enacted in 1976 and 1998, and the resulting lengthening and strengthening of the law described in the previous chapter. Law professor James Boyle has gone so far as to call this a "second enclosure movement," arguing that "once again things that were formerly thought of as either common property or uncommodifiable are being covered with new, or newly extended, property rights."[7]

In 2001, law professor Lawrence Lessig, sharing a similar assessment, cofounded a new organization called Creative Commons, dedicated to encouraging artists, authors, and other rights holders to make their work available for reuse and redistribution. As we will discuss further in chapter 8, the "open" licenses created by Creative Commons have been used on over a billion photos, songs, videos, books, games, and other works to date, but perhaps the organization's more significant accomplishment has been to bring far greater public awareness to the *existence* of a cultural commons, and to the social value of resisting its further enclosure.

The Tragedy of the Anticommons

Another critical perspective on the "tragedy of the commons" comes from law professor Michael Heller, who argues that, while Hardin's ideas may have some validity, they tell only half the story at best. If too little ownership may lead to a tragedy of overuse, he reasons, then too much ownership may result, conversely, in tragic underuse. Heller calls this the "tragedy of the anticommons" and warns that such scenarios are not only theoretically possible but are demonstrably causing "gridlock economies" in markets ranging from pharmaceuticals (where too many patent holders have prevented a major drug maker from releasing a potential cure for Alzheimer's disease) to documentary films (where too many copyright holders prevented *Eyes on the Prize*, the definitive film about the American civil rights movement, from airing for two decades).[8]

Thus, Heller argues, it doesn't make sense to keep ratcheting up intellectual property law, using the specter of an anarchic and polluted commons to justify ever-stronger protections for a growing mountain of copyrights, patents, and trademarks. A well-balanced IP policy must also guard against the opposite threat—a world so thoroughly privatized that no idea can be effectively deployed or communicated, resulting in terminal cultural and scientific gridlock.

The Public Domain

The term *public domain* is often used, even by some legal scholars, interchangeably with *the commons*. Broadly speaking, they connote the same basic principle and apply to the same set of cultural and material artifacts—the universe of ideas, expressions, inventions, discoveries, and objects that aren't owned by anyone in particular and therefore are free for anyone to use, modify, or distribute without explicit permission.

Yet, unlike the commons (a term that does not appear once in the text of American copyright statute), the public domain is a legally recognized concept. Although U.S. copyright law never defines the term outright, it is used repeatedly to refer to works that aren't protected, either because they're ineligible, their term has expired, or they originate in a country that lacks a treaty agreement with America.[9]

Yet, as James Boyle has observed, legal scholars working at the forefront of IP studies tend to embrace a more "granular," "complex" view of the public domain than the one suggested by the letter of the law. For them, the term isn't a negative category (works *not* covered by copyright) but rather an affirmative one that also includes "reserved spaces of freedom inside intellectual property," such as the right to quote from someone else's work or to make a backup copy of a CD for your car.[10] To these scholars, all of the limits to IP's power that I will be reviewing throughout this chapter contribute directly to growing the public domain, and this "space of freedom" must not only be maintained but actively nurtured and celebrated by creators, regulators, and citizens at large in order to preserve individual liberty and a vibrant cultural sphere.

To achieve this, Boyle argues, we must agree upon an affirmative definition of the public domain—one that explicitly defines our shared intellectual commons as clearly as copyright law defines individual intellectual property. In his words, "We have to 'invent' the public domain before we can save it."[11]

Copyright and Patent Expiry

One of the most important limits on the power of intellectual property is the fact that copyrights and patents are available only for a limited duration. As you may recall from the previous chapter, the U.S. Constitution gives Congress the power to grant IP rights only "for limited times," and though these terms have expanded over the years since the Constitution was first ratified, they are still technically finite (despite the fact that they seem to be lengthened another few decades every time Mickey Mouse's copyright comes close to lapsing).

Once a work's term has definitively expired (currently, twenty years for most patents and an author's life plus seventy years for most copyrights), it "lapses" into the public domain and becomes accessible for unlimited, unpermissioned use by everyone and anyone. In the case of patents, putting inventions and discoveries in the public domain means that they can be manufactured far more cheaply and distributed far more broadly; for instance, a recent analysis by healthcare researchers found that Americans saved $1.2 trillion over the course of a decade by taking generic (public domain) drugs instead of their patented equivalents.[12] It also means that inventors and researchers can develop innovative new technologies and business processes by improving upon the existing ones without asking for permission from, or paying a hefty fee to, their potential competitors.

The public domain is a valuable asset when it comes to cultural expression as well. Although copyright takes far longer to expire than patents do, many works that have lapsed are still both culturally and

Figure 6: Poster for *10 Things I Hate About You*, 1999.

economically viable, even a century or more after they were first authored. To choose one example, William Shakespeare, who died four hundred years ago, currently has a writing credit on 1,357 commercial films, according to the Internet Movie Database.[13] These films range from familiar titles like *Hamlet* and *Richard III* to obvious adaptations like *Rosencrantz and Guildenstern Are Dead* to less obvious ones like *10 Things I Hate About You.*

Collectively, films based on Shakespeare's work have generated billions of dollars in revenue, on a scale comparable to the *Star Wars* and *Harry Potter* film franchises. Even creators less famous than the Bard account for a significant amount of value in their public domain contributions. One recent analysis in the *Harvard Journal of Law and Technology* estimated that public domain photographs on Wikipedia—a fairly narrow slice of the commons—have a total value in the range of a quarter of a billion dollars per year.[14] For comparison's sake, that's roughly the same amount of money paid at auction annually for the top five pieces of fine art combined.

Other forms of intellectual property, such as trade secrets and trademarks, don't expire unless they cease to be secret (in the former case) or cease to be used commercially (in the latter case). The constitutional mandate to grant IP for "limited times" doesn't apply to these forms of property because they are based on the commerce clause (article 1, section 8, clause 3), which includes no such constraints. Yet it is an interesting question whether such limits *would* generate the same kind of cultural and economic value that is gained by allowing patents and copyrights to enter the public domain once their terms are complete.

Fair Use, Creative Freedom, and Consumers' Rights

Another crucial check on the power of intellectual property is the principle of "fair use." There is perhaps no legal concept in the world of IP that has been more fiercely contested, more thoroughly examined, more vilified, more celebrated, and more misunderstood than the 176 words of American copyright law that lay out the purpose and function of this right. At the most basic level, fair use says that in certain cases, people can access, modify, reuse, and/or distribute a copyrighted work without permission and still be innocent of infringement. The reasoning, according to federal appeals court judge Pierre N. Leval, one of the leading legal interpreters of fair use, is this: "The copyright is not an inevitable, divine, or natural right that confers on authors the absolute ownership of their creations. It is designed rather to stimulate activity and progress in the arts for the intellectual enrichment of the public."[15]

In other words, if we take literally the Constitution's mandate that IP laws "promote the Progress of Science and useful Arts," then we must draw a line limiting the power of intellectual property rights when they cease to fulfill that function, and especially when they risk *impeding* progress in these fields. This is all well and good in principle, but the question remains: how can we establish whether a given unpermissioned use is helping or impeding the progress of art and science? Without knowing that, we can't establish what's fair and what isn't. And unless we know which uses are fair, we can't possibly know whether the user in question is liable for copyright infringement.

The letter of the law is maddeningly vague on these points. It acknowledges that some uses might be more fair than others, "such as criticism, comment, news reporting, teaching . . ., scholarship, or research," but doesn't either rule out other uses explicitly or protect these uses definitively. Instead, it offers four "factors" for judges and juries to weigh when deciding whether a given use is fair: the *purpose and character* of the use, such as whether it takes place in a commercial or nonprofit context, and whether the use is "transformative"; the *nature* of the copyrighted work, such as whether it is a work of fact or fiction; the *amount and substantiality* of the portion used, such as a one-second sample compared to a three-minute song; and the *effect of the use upon the potential market* for the work. These factors are based directly on an opinion written by Supreme Court justice Joseph Story back in 1841, and although fair use was a staple of copyright case law in the subsequent century and a half, the principle did not become statute until the Copyright Act of 1976.[16]

Interpreting fair use, especially in the decades since the law was written into statute, has become a complex and high-stakes game of brinkmanship for media, communications, and information companies. On the one hand, news organizations, record labels, movie studios, and others recognize that reusing the work of others is integral to their businesses, and they rely heavily on their fair use rights on a daily basis. On the other hand, these same organizations are extremely cautious about protecting their economic interests in the work they themselves produce, and would like to control and profit from that work whenever possible.

This has led some very prominent media organizations to weigh in publicly on both sides of the issue—not duplicitously but merely because the line between fair and unfair can be very contingent and case-specific, and because the same law can benefit one part of a large company while it limits another. For instance, News Corporation chairman Rupert Murdoch, chafing at Google News's practice of aggregating stories from his journalism properties, notoriously proclaimed in 2009 that "there's a doctrine called fair use, which we believe to be challenged in the courts and would bar it altogether."[17] Yet Fox News Network, a company founded and overseen by Murdoch, has gone out of its way in recent years to defend its fair use rights in several prominent cases, including some in which works of journalism by third parties were allegedly used without permission on social and digital media by Fox-related properties.[18]

Ultimately, despite the innumerable fair use cases that have passed through our courts over the past two centuries, there is still a significant amount of legal uncertainty stemming from the vague language of the statute, the often conflicting or contradictory opinions handed down by judges, and the rapidly evolving nexus of culture, technology, and commerce. How much do the "purpose and character" of a use need to "transform" the original work in order to make a use fair? What do "commercial" and "noncommercial" mean in the context of online communities and social media platforms? Do new digital uses of copyrighted work, such as mash-ups and re-mixes, pose any potential harm to existing or future markets? These seemingly fundamental questions are still in dispute, often between large corporations, and often over the course of many years of litigation and at great cost.

This uncertainty and economic risk make fair use difficult in practice for individual artists (who might want to use other work fairly in their own creations) and consumers (who might want to use the movies, songs, and games they love fairly in the context of their own digitally mediated social lives). Because there are no legal "bright lines," fair use claims can't be tested until you've been sued for infringement. Given that even minor infringement cases typically cost about a quarter of a million dollars to litigate, asserting such rights has historically been a daunting prospect for many individual artists and consumers, who have often opted instead to "fly under the radar" and hope they don't get sued.[19]

Recognizing this fundamental flaw in the system, legal scholars Patricia Aufderheide and Peter Jaszi have worked with many existing creative communities, such as poets, documentarians, dancers, journalists, online video producers, visual artists, librarians, and academic researchers, to create "codes of best practices" instructing each community about its fair use rights and how to assert them with confidence.[20] If the letter of the law doesn't provide "bright lines," they reason, there's no reason such communities can't self-educate and develop their own guidelines based on case law and common practice. Although these codes are fairly new, they've already borne fruit; recent survey research published by Aufderheide and myself has shown that, when these best practices are observed, more creators exercise greater liberty at lower legal risk and financial cost.[21]

There is also another glimmer of hope on the horizon for fair use rights: growing support for a small-claims court dedicated to adjudicating cases of alleged copyright infringement in which the financial stakes are relatively low and in which the statutory damages would be capped at a more reasonable level. Such a court would embolden a broader range of creators and consumers to exercise their fair use rights, secure in the knowledge that a loss in court wouldn't bankrupt them. Although this court doesn't exist yet at the time of writing, it was recently endorsed in a white paper published by the U.S. Department of Commerce's Internet Policy Task Force—a promising step in the right direction.[22]

Although fair use is almost always discussed, and typically exercised, in the context of copyright, there are analogous checks on the power of some other forms of IP. U.S. trademark law has an explicit fair use provision that allows advertisers to use the marks of their competitors in advertisements comparing goods or services, and allows anyone to parody, criticize, or comment upon trademark owners through the use of their mark. The law also protects the third-party use of trademarks for news reporting and commentary, and for any "noncommercial" purpose, though the way the law is written, these scenarios are not categorically "fair use."

Rights of publicity (covered by laws that vary state by state) are also typically limited to specific commercial contexts: hence the booming trade in unauthorized biographies and the legion of paparazzi who follow celebrities around, snapping and selling candid shots—the less flattering, the more valuable. Patents and trade secrets, however, don't have any analogous protections—perhaps because the IP they cover is more functional than expressive in nature, and therefore not understood to require First Amendment exceptions. Yet many legal scholars have argued that there should be "patent fair use," in part because of the anticommons problems identified by Michael Heller. Law professor Katherine J. Strandburg has gone so far as to develop a four-factor test analogous to the one used in copyright law, although she acknowledges that it "seems unlikely" that either courts or Congress will adopt such a doctrine anytime soon.[23]

It is important to distinguish fair use from two other limits on IP that are often confused with it. First, there is the *"de minimis" doctrine*, which gets its name from the Latin phrase "De minimis non curat lex," or "The law does not take notice of trifling matters." Basically, this principle says that certain things are too small to warrant copyright protection in the first place—for instance, a three-note musical phrase or a one-sentence synopsis of a larger work.

By the same token, there are some uses of copyrighted works that are so minor they don't constitute infringement because the portion taken wouldn't be sufficient to deserve protection on its own. One recent example is the 2009 Jay-Z song "Run This Town," which used a short, unlicensed sample of Eddie Bo's "Hook and Sling—Part I" in the mix. TufAmerica, the company that owns the copyright to the Bo recording, sued the rapper for infringement. Jay-Z ultimately prevailed because, in the words of Judge Lewis A. Kaplan, the sample had "essentially no quantitative significance" relative to the original recording, and the word "Oh," which made up the entirety of the sample, "is a single and commonplace word. Standing alone, it likely is not deserving of copyright protection."[24]

Though Kaplan's conclusion might seem obvious to most readers, especially those raised on the kind of minimal sampling that is so common in musical genres like hip-hop and electronic dance music, it actually represented a major departure from precedent.

For the decade before Kaplan's ruling, no one had dared claim de minimis for a hip-hop sample because of an infamous Sixth Circuit case *Bridgeport v. Dimension,* in which the judge ruled that the principle didn't ever apply to this musical technique, laying down the strict edict of "get a license or do not sample."[25]

The other doctrine often confused with fair use is called fair dealing. While a few nations, such as Israel and South Korea, have adopted American-style fair use laws in recent years, they are still somewhat uncommon, in part because most other nations don't have a constitutional right to free speech that must be reconciled with IP rights. Instead, many countries (including former British colonies in the Commonwealth of Nations) have a fair dealing provision in their copyright laws, and these provisions are typically weaker and apply in fewer circumstances than American fair use practices. Under most of these laws, while scholars and educators may enjoy some limited freedom to employ copyrighted works without permission, such freedoms are not extended to standard practices among visual artists, documentary filmmakers, and other creative communities.

In addition to fair use, there are several other rights enjoyed by both consumers and creators under American law that limit the scope of intellectual property controls. An excellent example of consumers' rights is the first sale doctrine. Basically, the law says that once you purchase a physical copy of a protected work—such as a book, CD, or Blu-ray disc, it's yours to "sell or otherwise dispose of" in any way you like, without permission or risk of infringement and without any shift in the rights to the creative work embodied on that copy (you may sell a Kendrick Lamar CD, but that doesn't mean you own the composition or the master rights to "The Blacker the Berry").

This doctrine is the reason there are used record stores and the reason a home rental market for movies first emerged. In other words, by placing such a limit on copyright, Congress generated billions of dollars worth of sales and rental fees above and beyond the first sales of the items in question, growing the size of the media economy considerably.

Unfortunately, the first sale doctrine, easy to apply in the case of physical goods, gets a bit murkier in the case of digital formats, which are rapidly becoming the primary distribution platform for movies, music, and games. How can you resell an MP3, let alone a streaming version of a song you accessed through Spotify or Apple Music? The Internet Policy Task Force recently took a stab at addressing these issues (in the same document that recommended a small-claims court for copyright infringement) and ultimately came up empty-handed. While acknowledging that "some of the benefits traditionally provided by the first sale doctrine ... are not replicated" in a digital environment, the task force didn't recommend updating the right for application in a digital context because it "could curtail at least some of the flexibilities of new business models."[26]

In this case, the government is apparently willing to let some consumers' rights fall by the wayside to err on the side of protecting IP holders. On the other hand, the first sale doctrine is still growing stronger when it comes to physical products. The U.S. Supreme Court recently ruled that if a book is legally published overseas and intended for an international market, it can still be imported and sold in the U.S. without permission from the publisher—even if it undercuts the market for a higher-priced domestic edition slated for American consumers.[27]

While the first sale doctrine exemplifies how consumers may benefit from limitations on copyright above and beyond their fair use rights, there are similar spaces of freedom for artists and other creators as well. A good example is "compulsory licensing," a facet of copyright law in which rights holders are *required* to allow third parties to use their work, typically according to specific parameters and at statutory rates. For instance, songwriters control the copyrights to their musical compositions, giving them the choice to allow or prevent a performing artist from making a recording of a new song. However, once the song has been recorded and distributed in the U.S. by one artist, songwriters can no longer prevent additional artists from making their own "cover" versions (as long as they pay the statutory "mechanical" royalties set by Congress). Even though this limits the power of copyright to a certain extent, it contributes to a robust musical culture and a thriving music economy.

To pick one example from a virtually infinite list, both Jimi Hendrix's and Bob Dylan's careers were aided immeasurably when the pioneering rock guitarist covered the celebrated songwriter's composition "All Along the Watchtower" in 1968, generating a much bigger pop hit, and a far more frequently played classic, than Dylan's original version. The cover version may never have been made if Dylan had been able to refuse permission to the relatively unknown Hendrix (his own version had been released only a few weeks earlier, and the new version was direct market competition from a disruptive upstart) or to charge a licensing fee higher than Hendrix's label was willing to pay. This would have been a tragedy for both artists and fans alike; twenty years later, when I saw Dylan perform the song live in concert, he opted to play Hendrix's version rather than his own—a tacit acknowledgment that the cover had become the definitive recording.

Secondary Liability and Safe Harbors

Sometimes the unpermissioned user of a copyrighted work isn't the only one on the hook for infringement; a third party who assisted in or benefited from that infringement may also be found liable. This concept has never been codified in statute, yet it is well enshrined in American case law and is typically referred to as "secondary liability." There are three varieties of secondary liability:

- Contributory infringement, in which a third party is aware of an infringing activity and directly causes or "materially contributes" to it;
- Vicarious liability, in which a third party both supervises or controls the infringing party and benefits financially from the infringement;
- Inducement, a relatively new judicial standard in which a third party distributes tools capable of infringement while promoting their infringing uses.

All of the exceptions to copyright that apply to direct users also apply to these third parties. For instance, if I help a student of mine to produce and distribute a documentary film using materials copyrighted by a third party, I might be sued for contributory infringement. But if my student successfully defends her film as fair use, then I am relieved of any liability as well.

Yet even if supervisors, employers, technology manufacturers, and other third parties were liable only if one of their employees, friends, or customers actually broke the law, it would still represent a significant legal risk; a large company might have thousands of employees, and a tech company might have millions of customers. Any one of them could theoretically infringe on intellectual property, opening the door for secondary liability. Thus, an added layer of protection is sometimes provided to these organizations.

One important case of this added protection against secondary liability comes in the form of the "safe harbors" accorded to "online service providers." Back in the 1990s, when it first became clear that the internet was going to become a major force in business, culture, and society at large, Congress struggled to reconcile the exciting prospects for this new platform with concerns from legacy media industries that it would abet large-scale digital copyright infringement. The compromise solution was the Digital Millennium Copyright Act, a copyright law that says large internet companies such as search engines and internet service providers (ISPs) are *not* responsible for the infringing actions of their users as long as they make it easy for rights holders to identify possible infringements and, when such infringements are identified, take them down promptly (often referred to as a "notice and takedown" policy). Over the past twenty years, this law has been criticized heavily from virtually every side (more on this in chapter 8), but there can be little argument that these safe harbor provisions have been vital to the ongoing success of ISPs, wireless data companies, and interactive sites and services from Google to Facebook to Wikipedia, and in fact to the innovation and durability of digital communication platforms overall.

Unfortunately, the future of this compromise is in peril. Several media industry trade groups have called in recent years to have the notice and takedown provisions in the DMCA and in other countries' copyright laws replaced with new ones requiring ISPs, search engines, social media services, and other digital communications platforms proactively to police their own networks and eliminate suspected infringing materials—essentially censoring the internet on behalf of copyright holders—or risk secondary liability.

Clearly, this proposed "notice and stay down" policy would be difficult to follow without also removing many noninfringing materials, including virtually every example of fair use on the internet. At the time of writing, the U.S. Copyright Office is undertaking a public study to evaluate whether such a policy should supplant or modify the DMCA's safe harbor provisions. Regardless of the immediate outcome of these deliberations, it seems likely that large media companies will continue to push for such policies until they are enacted, or until the DMCA safe harbors are otherwise weakened to the point of obsolescence (more on this in chapter 5).

Unprotected Cultural Forms

Another way in which the power of intellectual property is limited by law can be seen in the cultural forms that *aren't* covered. As we explored earlier in this book, the law excludes copyright ownership for certain categories of objects and information, including facts (such as phone numbers or sports statistics), ideas (such as zombie movies or breakup songs), and purely functional objects (such as can openers or shoelaces). Yet we have also seen the law expand to encompass previously free forms of expression, such as musical performances, photography, and computer programs.

Because copyright is always being renegotiated and reinterpreted through treaties, legislation, case law, and policy, and because culture itself is always changing in unexpected ways, the borders of the law are kind of like the lines of a fractal: the closer you look at them, the less distinct they become. And that means that while phone numbers and movie genres are unlikely to merit copyright protection anytime soon, the cultural forms closest to the border may eventually slip over the line from "unprotected" to "protected."

There are several fields of cultural production, such as fashion, food, and stand-up comedy, that are not currently covered by copyright in the United States—though some creators and businesses in these industries have publicly called for their work to merit protection, and there have even been several bills drafted to bring fashion design within the scope of copyright (most recently, at the time of writing, the Innovative Design Protection Act of 2012, sponsored by New York senator Charles Schumer). At first glance, the benefits of extending copyright to these forms might seem obvious. First of all, one might argue, it's only fair; why should a painter get to own the image on her canvas while the designer of an equally beautiful and creative evening gown can be "knocked off" with impunity? Why should a famous comedian with a book deal get to copyright his published jokes while an up-and-comer on the nightclub circuit who hears one of her one-liners repeated by a late night television talk show host must grin and bear it? Why should a pioneering chef shoulder the economic and reputational risk of developing a new recipe, only to see the dish served by his less innovative competitors down the street once it's been perfected?

Second, this is an era in which billions of people carry around tiny internet-connected microphones and video cameras in the form of smartphones and "wearable" computing devices. Virtually everything noteworthy (and innumerable trivialities) transpiring in public ends up being captured, distributed, and archived for perpetuity on one or more social media platforms. Given this fact, how can we maintain a clear legal distinction between works that are recorded in a "fixed, tangible medium" (such as books published by comedians) and those that aren't (such as jokes told on a nightclub stage)?

These concerns are legitimate. The lines demarcating what's copyrightable and what isn't are neither clear nor perfect, and some creators who may "deserve protection" in many people's eyes are not currently entitled to it. To be fair, however, it cuts both ways: several works that do currently enjoy copyright protection may fall short of the mark in many people's esteem. Until very recently, for instance, the song "Happy Birthday," unquestionably a part of our shared cultural commons, was both protected and assiduously policed by its copyright holder, the music publisher Warner/Chappell. This ended only after it was firmly established through lengthy litigation that the composition was based on an earlier work now in the public domain.

Yet to argue the merits of copyright scope expansion on these terms is to miss the point altogether. Remember that intellectual property in the United States is not a *moral* right. It doesn't exist to reward creators, or to confer creative legitimacy on genuine innovators while punishing derivative wannabes. Nor is it supposed to certify *authorship* by making sure that every piece of cultural expression is duly assigned a singular creator. Its function is to promote the progress of arts and science, plain and simple. And in the case of creative professions like food, comedy, and fashion, in which so many individual creators are constantly trying out slightly new variations on timeworn formulas (chicken soup, mother-in-law jokes, three-piece suits), reacting and revising in response to instantaneous audience feedback while navigating regional and temporal variations in taste and style, it makes sense to err on the side of openness rather than overprotection.

Letting chefs, comics, and fashion designers "riff" on one another's work ultimately does more good than harm—it contributes to a more vibrant, more diverse market for cultural goods in which a larger number of creators can take risks and ultimately reap the rewards for their successes. As law professors Kal Raustiala and Christopher Sprigman argue in their book *The Knockoff Economy: How Imitation Sparks Innovation*, "Creativity can persist even in the face of widespread copying. Indeed, in some instances creativity occurs *because* of copying."[28]

Finally, the absence of copyright in these fields doesn't necessarily mean that derivative creators and knockoff artists who choose to exploit their peers' innovations rather than invest the energy, resources, and risk required to innovate for themselves will "get away with it." Copyright is hardly the only tool that creative communities have in their arsenals to police the fuzzy border between creative influence and theft. While copyright litigation requires a bevy of lawyers, hundreds of thousands of dollars, and years of patience to reach a conclusion, one critical social media post or article can do far more damage in a far shorter time by leveraging reputational pressure and tweaking the fickle tastes of the audience—without recourse to legal remedies.

In 2016, for instance, the rapid upward trajectory of comedian Amy Schumer's career was slowed significantly by accusations of joke stealing from three other female comedians. The flap was widely covered in the press, and Google currently returns roughly one hundred thousand results for the search term "Amy Schumer plagiarism." Though it's still unclear whether or to what degree Schumer is guilty of the transgressions she's been accused of, let alone what effect it will have on her reputation and financial viability over the course of her career, the stakes are far higher than the $450,000 maximum statutory fine associated with three counts of willful copyright infringement. Schumer's 2015 film *Trainwreck* grossed over $140 million at the box office worldwide; that means if only half a percent of her fan base opted not to see her next film because of these allegations, the financial costs would already be higher than a loss in court. In fact, it seems abundantly likely that the plagiarism scandal may have contributed to a much greater pressure on Schumer's earning potential; the following two films in which she starred, *Snatched* (2017) and *I Feel Pretty* (2018), have, at the time of writing, collectively earned only about $109 million at the box office worldwide.

Thus, despite the absence of copyright protection, the creative community in the comedy world apparently does an excellent job of maintaining its standards, rewarding innovation, punishing unethical behavior, and holding the powerful accountable to those on lower rungs of the professional ladder. Extending copyright protection to cover jokes would not be likely to improve upon this system, but it would certainly limit the ability of newer, less powerful comics to add their voices to the mix by burdening them with the risk of crippling litigation costs and fees—even if their jokes fell on the right side of the ethical line but were in a legal gray area. Would this outcome "promote the Progress" of the "useful Art" of comedy? Or do the exceptions and limitations to intellectual property serve a valuable and necessary role in this case and many others like it?

THREE

Intellectual Property and Industry

Thus far, this book has been about intellectual property *in theory:* what it is, why it exists, where it came from, what it can and can't accomplish, and how it must be balanced and adapted to serve the needs of multiple competing interests while being weighed against multiple other competing rights. For those of us who like to geek out in the fuzzy realm of abstract ideas or to plumb the sociopolitical implications of every word in a judicial decision, that stuff can be fun. For the rest of you (what some might call "the sane ones"), this is where the book will start to get more interesting because now we will begin to explore the role of intellectual property *in practice.* Specifically, this chapter will review some of the central roles that copyrights, patents, trademarks, and other forms of IP play across a range of different industries, from the arts and media (music, filmed entertainment, and marketing) to the sciences (technology and pharmaceuticals).

Because we'll be covering a lot of ground in a single chapter, the aim here isn't to give you in-depth expertise in any given field; you won't be able to read the section on film, for instance, and then go take charge of the legal department at Sony Pictures. Nor does the chapter provide you with a comprehensive overview of IP's role in *every* major industry, but these five particular fields are diverse enough to demonstrate a range of approaches to the use of intellectual property and representative enough to indicate how IP may be used in additional business contexts. The point of this chapter is simply to show you some examples of how intellectual property works in the wild, beyond the letter of the law and outside the pages of a textbook. It's important to recognize that despite the mountains of statute and the seas of case law surrounding it as far as the eye can see, IP truly exists not in its abstract form but in the concrete relations it enables among creators, consumers, and the institutions that connect, exploit, and serve them. And despite the elegance and simplicity of the constitutional mandate underpinning IP in America, these concrete relations tend to be anything but elegant and simple. As the old saying goes, "In theory, theory and practice are the same. In practice, they're quite different."

As we skip from industry to industry in this chapter, one theme is important to bear in mind: there is no "god" of intellectual property reconciling one practice or policy with another, making an orderly assessment of it all from on high, counting every proverbial hair on the head of every attorney. IP in practice does not make cohesive sense, and there's no reason it should. Instead, it's better to understand the motley assortment of legal and economic arrangements discussed in these pages as a temporary map of power relations among a diverse group of stakeholders in a range of highly idiosyncratic fields.

Regardless of any highfalutin' rhetoric about the law's ordained purpose, IP in practice is one of many instruments used by organizations and individuals within a complex web of industrial relations in order to make money, reduce risk, and manage competition. In many cases, IP simply represents the ability to sue someone if they deviate from established business practices, and therefore it often serves as the "glue" that binds these industries together, creating a stable enough business environment to ward off market mayhem and inspire confidence among investors and creators. At other times, as we shall see, it has the opposite effect, giving one stakeholder the power to game the system while causing misery and chaos for everyone else. There is nothing contradictory in these divergent outcomes; like a hammer or a screwdriver, IP is merely a tool, and it's often up to the one who wields it to decide whether it will be used for constructive or destructive purposes.

IP in the Recording Industry

Since 1831, when American copyright law was first amended to include musical compositions, the music industry has been fundamentally oriented around this form of IP, and it has been perhaps the staunchest, most visible public advocate for copyright expansion and enforcement in the nearly two centuries since then.

Most of the music industry centers around two specific species of copyright: the "publishing right," which covers an actual musical *composition* as it would appear on a printed score, and the "master right" (created in 1972, also known as the "phonorecord copyright"), which covers the *sound* of a given performance once it's fixed in the form of an audio recording. The publishing copyright is created by default as soon as a composer "fixes" a song in the form of a written score or recorded demo, and the master right is created as soon as a recording artist produces a given recording (in the case of songwriters who compose as they record, these two copyrights might be created in the same instant).

In the commercial music industry, these copyrights don't usually remain the property of the creators for very long; composers typically assign their rights to publishers as part of broader publishing contracts, while performing artists assign their rights to record labels per their recording contracts. The publishers and labels are then required to pay the creators a set royalty rate, usually based on a percentage of the revenues collected via the sale and licensing of the copyrighted works.

In the old days, publishers and record labels earned their shares of the revenues from the copyrighted works through significant industrial investment. Publishers needed printing presses to produce scores, warehouses to keep them, transportation to bring them to retail, and of course extra money for marketing (stoking consumer interest) and promotion (stoking retailer and performer interest). Similarly, record labels needed to pay for access to recording studios, record-manufacturing facilities, warehouses, transportation, marketing, and promotion.

These days, many musicians and composers (including the most commercially successful ones) can accomplish most or all of these tasks on their own using a laptop with an internet connection. Notation software like Sibelius and Finale take the place of printing presses, while digital audio applications like ProTools and Logic take the place of the traditional recording studio. Adding a song to an online retailer like iTunes or Spotify takes minutes and costs practically nothing. And an artist's own social media accounts are often the most important marketing and promotional venues of all; in recent years, performers like Beyoncé and Kendrick Lamar have generated top-selling albums without any advance marketing whatsoever, based largely on direct appeals to their millions of social media followers.

When the internet first emerged as a viable distribution platform, many pundits suggested that record labels and music publishers would rapidly become obsolete because they'd be "disintermediated" (cut out of the equation when creators connected directly with fans) and thus either diminish in power or disappear altogether. Yet not only do both sectors still exist, they have managed to maintain their traditional shares of the recorded music economy, taking control of copyrights and doling out the same royalty percentages to creators that they did in the old days, despite no longer having to pony up for printing presses, record plants, warehouses, and promotion to the same degree they once did.

There are two key reasons for this. First of all, not every recording artist can be a social media maven, and record labels still hold the keys to global promotion and the fame that may come with it. Even though the vast majority of professional recording artists never receive a royalty check (according to record industry accounting, labels rarely recoup their initial investments in producing and promoting a new release, and contracts only require artists to be paid post-recoupment), musical fame can be parlayed into far more remunerative channels, such as endorsement deals and arena concerts.

Second, and more important, record labels and music publishers control not merely the copyrights for new songs but also for most of the older music that is still commercially viable—and this older music is becoming increasingly valuable as it becomes more accessible via digital channels. In 2015, for the first year in history, older albums (which are referred to as "catalog" in industry parlance) outsold newer ones. This would have been unthinkable in the days of LPs and CDs, when brick-and-mortar music retailers like Tower Records and HMV would devote most or all of their shelf space to the hot new releases guaranteed to sell in large quantity. It makes perfect sense, however, in the current era of limitless digital retail shelves, when it costs the same negligible sum to sell a million Justin Bieber albums as it does to sell five albums by Ina Ray Hutton, the "blonde bombshell of rhythm" from the 1930s. Additionally, the licensing opportunities for music have grown dramatically in recent years, as an ever-expanding slate of movies, television shows, commercials, and video games requires a growing supply of fresh (or freshly exhumed) music for their soundtracks.

Between the boost in catalog demand and the boom in licensing, record labels and publishers with deep libraries of copyrighted works can parlay those holdings into decades of reliable income, virtually impervious to short-term market fluctuations and the vagaries of musical fashion, while leveraging their control over must-have catalog to demand multimillion-dollar advances and equity stakes in any new, well-funded music startup that might wish to enter the digital music marketplace. In short, the recorded music sector has largely transformed itself over the past few decades from a manufacturing industry based on the power of physical capital to a licensing industry based on the power of copyright.

IP in the Film Industry

You usually can tell who the author of a painting is because they're holding a brush. Similarly, you usually can tell who the author of a book is because they're typing. These are self-contained forms of creative expression, and while collaboration is not uncommon in either field, each typically conforms to our traditional understanding of sole authorship. But who is the "author" of a motion picture? The list of credits at the end of a film sometimes continues for ten minutes or more and may contain thousands of individual names. While "auteur theory," which came to prominence in the 1950s (half a century after the birth of cinema), holds that a film is the unique creative vision of its director, one could just as easily point to the crucial creative roles of the scriptwriter(s), cinematographer(s), actor(s), or of any number of other skilled contributors, from the lighting director to the wardrobe designer, as evidence that this is an art form without a sole author. To put it plainly, cinema is a form of cultural expression that has large-scale collaboration and industrial production in its very DNA. Yet, without a clear author, how can there be authorship? And without authorship, how can there be a copyright?

Of course, filmed entertainment does rely on copyright protection, just as the music industry does. But while the composer and recording artist are the presumed copyright holders until they assign those rights to music publishers and record labels, there is no such presumptive author in the case of cinema. Technically, according to the letter of the law, films are classic "joint works"—that is to say, they are "prepared by two or more authors with the intention that their contributions be merged into inseparable or interdependent parts of a unitary whole."[1] This means that, in theory, all of the creators who contribute to a film would share in the ownership of the copyright. In practice, however, whichever person or corporate entity is producing and/or financing a film (in most cases, arguably the least creative contribution to the finished product) ends up owning the copyright in its entirety. This is managed by inserting a clause into each contributor's contract stipulating that he or she is merely a "worker for hire" and therefore not entitled to an ownership stake in the results of any creative labor. While some high-power contributors (especially famous actors and directors) may ultimately receive a share of net or gross receipts from the film, this is not a royalty in exchange for copyright assignment (as is the case in the recording industry), but merely an economic concession to star power or another source of leverage.

The copyright for the film itself is hardly the only IP in play when a commercial movie is released. Often the screenplay will have its own discrete copyright that is not automatically transferred to the producer or studio when the film is made. The screenplay itself may be based on a preexisting work of literature or even a non-literary franchise (such as a comic book character or a video game), and those copyrights will typically be retained by their original owners as well, and licensed for use in the film. The music used in the soundtrack—both the original score and any preexisting works—must be licensed for "synchronization," covering both the publishing and the master rights for each recording and composition.

Each of these third-party licenses must be renegotiated for each "distribution window," such as a new region or country, or a new distribution platform. Sometimes filmed entertainment can be considerably altered depending on where and how you see it because the studio is either unable or unwilling to relicense a third-party work from its owner(s) for a new distribution window. This can create opportunities for independent creators to participate in established entertainment franchises; for instance, my own unsigned band has licensed music to television shows for home video distribution, presumably replacing more expensive major-label music used in the original on-air broadcasts.

Finally, copyright isn't the only form of IP at stake when a film or television show is released; in some states, including California, where most big film studios are based, there is a *right of publicity* aspect of the process as well. This comes into play both when a film depicts an actual human being (living or deceased) and when the actors in a film are used for marketing or franchising (for instance, when an actor's face is mapped onto a plastic toy or a video game avatar based on the character he or she portrays).

These laws are somewhat vague—for instance, California statute protects a person's "likeness," a poorly defined term at best. Consequently, the courts sometimes become the arbiters of whether the right of publicity has been violated. In one recent example, a U.S. Army bomb-disposal expert sued the makers of the Oscar-winning film *The Hurt Locker* for portraying him in a bad light, even though the character in the film had a different name. Ultimately, in this case, a federal appeals court decided that the filmmakers' First Amendment rights trumped the soldier's concerns about the use of his "likeness." Yet these kinds of disputes are still common enough that film producers routinely include a budget line item for "errors and omissions insurance" to protect them against claims such as violating rights of publicity.

IP in Marketing

Unlike music and film, which are primarily copyright-driven industries, the business of marketing is typically more focused on generating, maintaining, and exploiting trademarks and service marks, which represent the brands being promoted. A single commercial product will often have multiple trademarks associated with it, such as the manufacturer's name, the manufacturer's logo, the product's name, the product's logo, and other branded elements of the packaging or messaging (such as the trademarked "flowery musk scent" that Verizon Wireless pumps into its brick-and-mortar stores or the trademarked "popping and whooshing" sound that Skype makes when you sign in to the video chat service).

Trademark management is integral throughout the marketing life cycle. Manufacturers, service providers, and the marketing agencies that represent them search trademark databases across multiple countries before launching a new brand or creating a new name, logo, jingle, or design for an existing product or service, making sure that their new marks are sufficiently differentiated to warrant protection, avoid infringement, and make an impression in the minds of consumers.

Once a mark has been registered, a brand owner will often employ a third-party trademark-monitoring service to keep track of government databases as well as media and retail channels to make sure that no one is infringing on one of its existing trademarks, legally challenging the validity of its trademarks, or trying to register a new trademark that's too similar to one of its own. And while trademarks don't expire as long as they're still in use, they do need to be renewed every decade or so (this process can vary based on the nation of ownership and/or registration and the international treaties that may apply).

From the point of view of a commercial brand, trademark management is a high-stakes balancing act. On the one hand, you want your brand to be the first one consumers think of when they are in the market for your product or service. For instance, if you live in the American South, chances are that when you reach for a sweetened carbonated beverage, regardless of its flavor or manufacturer, you call it a "coke" (New Yorkers like me are more likely to call it a "soda").[2] If you're an American or European searching for a vital piece of information on the internet, chances are you're going to "google it." And if you're anywhere in the Western Hemisphere, the odds are that you're more likely to play "ping-pong" than "table tennis."

All three of these popular terms are registered trademarks, and their success is the result of intensive branding over long periods of time (two of the three brands are more than a century old). This often requires continuing investment at a high level. According to its own tally, the Coca-Cola Company currently spends over $4 billion per year on marketing, much of it dedicated to its flagship product, Coke. Google is widely estimated to spend over $1 billion per year on advertising. The marketing budget for Escalade Sports, the current owner of the Ping-Pong brand, is no doubt a far smaller figure, but when Parker Brothers first launched the product in the early twentieth century, it simultaneously invented the brand and the sport, contributing to an enduring association in the minds of consumers.

On the other hand, successful consumer brands must be constantly vigilant lest they become *too* successful. If a trademark becomes synonymous with the category of product or service it belongs to, it risks becoming "genericized." In plain English, that means that, in the eyes of consumers, the trademark has become indistinguishable from the generic name of the product category it belongs to. When this happens, a competing company may initiate a lawsuit or petition the USPTO seeking to establish that the trademark is no longer valid, and that the mark in question has entered the public domain.[3] This has happened to several major brands over the years: "escalator," "thermos," "zipper," and "app store" were all trademarked at one time but have since become legally generic terms (in the U.S., anyway—to make matters more confusing, a trademark can become genericized in one country while remaining valid in another).

There are steps a trademark owner can—and should—take to prevent genericization. For instance, the Xerox corporation actually spent a significant amount of money on a public-awareness campaign to get consumers and media organizations to use the term *photocopy* instead of *xerox* as a verb for copying documents. While it may seem counterintuitive for a company to simultaneously spend money to promote its brand and undermine its brand, in this case it was a successful strategy; Xerox averted a cataclysmic outcome and retains its trademark to this day. Other brands, like Kleenex and Band-Aids, have skirted this same precipice; in their cases, the trademark owners altered their commercial messaging to make it clear that the brand and the generic terms aren't the same thing: for instance, by using the word *brand* in their advertisements, as in "Kleenex brand facial tissues" and "Band-Aid brand adhesive bandages."

IP in the Technology Industry

The tech industry, a vague but frequently used term that covers computer hardware and software as well as the telecommunications platforms that connect these devices and the content and services that are distributed and accessed via these platforms, relies heavily upon intellectual property. Yet this sector is also one of the epicenters of debate and dissent against today's IP regimes and is

Figure 7: Kleenex public awareness campaign, 2015.

continually at the bleeding edge of IP law and policy, exploring tensions and conflicts that have no obvious resolution in either the letter of the law or the annals of case law.

Perhaps it is only natural that an industry based on channeling the flow of data is so deeply engaged in larger abstract questions about the propertization of information (these are themes we will explore more thoroughly in the second half of the book). Yet there is also an instrumental, concrete dimension to the relationship between tech and IP. This is a sector based on accelerated innovation, painstaking interface design, and complex technological interdependencies, and the ability to monopolize components and set standards can be crucial to the success or failure of an enterprise.

Intellectual property is central to all of these processes. This applies throughout the broad spectrum of tech-related businesses and strategies, from Apple's "walled garden" approach to keeping customers locked into long-term relationships with its hardware, software, and services to Google's "platform agnostic" approach to cornering the market on consumer data to Facebook's combination of the two approaches, leveraging its "social graph" to both monitor and shape the relationships among consumers, businesses, and brands.

One of the most interesting aspects of IP in the tech world is that, unlike virtually any other product of human creativity, computer software is both copyrightable (as a work of authorship) and patentable (as a work of invention). Copyright was first extended in the U.S. to cover software code in 1980, and in pushing for international treaties for software protection a few years later, the U.S. argued that beyond any "remaining doubt," software programs were "not considered to be patentable, but could only be protected under the copyright law."[4] Yet a little more than a decade later, the USPTO published legal guidelines for patenting software, and since then, both forms of IP have routinely been applied, sometimes to the same computer program.

Strategically, copyright and patent protection each has its own strengths and weaknesses for software publishers. Copyright lasts far longer than patents but covers only the exact code that comprises a program. Thus, while copyright can be used to police unauthorized copies and prevent the creation of derivative works for a functional eternity, it has no power to prevent competitors from "reverse engineering" a piece of software and creating a program that achieves the same ends via different technical means.

Patents, on the other hand, last for only twenty years, but if the software embodies an "inventive concept" that "solves practical problems," patenting it can prevent rivals from duplicating its functionality, even if they write their own code from scratch. In recent years, especially since a 2014 Supreme Court decision on the subject, the bar for a successful software patent claim has been raised significantly, leading almost four-fifths of the patents challenged in court to be invalidated in the year following the decision, according to one legal analysis.[5] Thus, software companies in this new legal era should think hard about the inventiveness and problem-solving potential of their programs before applying for patent protection in the U.S.

IP always entails a lot of "gray area," but this is even more true in technology than in most other fields. Tech tends to be poorly understood by legislators, judges, and regulators because it changes so quickly, requires such an arcane set of skills to produce and evaluate, and (in part due to the first two factors) because it's surrounded by an air of cultural mystique. This leads to some interesting challenges. A good example is the long-running legal battle between tech hardware titans Apple and Samsung, which originated with a handful of patents related to the iPhone's shape, features, surface finish, colors, and user interface. Their initial litigation, which began in 2011, was seemingly tipped in favor of Samsung by the U.S. Supreme Court in December 2016, though less than two years later, a jury in the U.S. District Court system ended up awarding Apple over half a billion dollars in damages. A second trial, initiated in 2012, was ultimately decided en banc (by all the judges on the federal circuit court), delivering another victory for Apple, especially once the Supreme Court declined to reconsider the decision in 2017. At the time of writing, however, the war between these two tech behemoths continues on several other fronts; each party has filed multiple claims against the other in at least a dozen courts in nine separate nations.

Can one company "own" the design of a flat, rectangular device with rounded edges? Should Apple be able to prevent Samsung from having a "home button" on its phones or force it to pay handsomely to include one? Do these features live up to the requirements that patented designs be novel and nonobvious? Moreover, are the justices on the U.S. Supreme Court, or any court, really equipped to answer these questions? There are no clear answers—at least, not until long after the smoke has dissipated from these multiple litigations. Nor will the answers, once we have them, shed much light on future disputes over design and utility patents involving platforms that haven't been invented yet.

Another large unresolved issue at the intersection of tech and IP is the widespread use of "standard form contracts" such as end user license agreements (EULAs) and terms of service (TOS) statements. Even if you've never heard of these acronyms, you've probably agreed to hundreds or even thousands of them in your lifetime, binding yourself to the terms set forth in these iffy legal documents. This has happened every single time you've downloaded and installed a new piece of software, then hit a button marked "agree" after not reading the preceding forty pages of dense legalese. And who can blame you for not reading it? One scholarly analysis found that if software customers read merely all of the privacy policies they encounter in a given year, they'd have to dedicate about thirty workdays to the task.[6] Given that TOS and EULAs are of comparable lengths, reading all three would mean you'd spend a quarter of your waking life just reading the fine print for these sites and services.[7]

Of course, nobody—not even legal scholars, consumer advocates, or tech CEOs—ever actually does that. Another analysis found that fewer than one in five hundred software shoppers actually accesses any given EULA, and even the tiny fraction of a fraction that *do* "do not, on average, spend enough time on it to have digested more than a fraction of its content."[8] This has been a bit of an open secret in the tech industry for decades; back in 2004, in fact, a software firm called PC Pitstop hid a note in its EULA offering $1,000 to the first person who emailed the company at a given address. It took over four months and three thousand downloads before someone actually took the company up on its offer (which was honored).[9]

The fact that every one of us routinely agrees to contracts we don't read, and that an entire multibillion-dollar industry is built on this dubious legal practice, is bad enough. Even worse, however, are the terms of many of these agreements. In addition to placing sometimes extreme limits on customers' privacy, access to legal recourse, and freedom to use their own property in the ways they choose, TOS and EULAs often contain clauses undermining consumers' intellectual property rights to their own work. For instance, at the time of launch, the TOS for Facebook's virtual reality headset Oculus Rift included the following clause: "By submitting User Content through the Services, you grant Oculus a worldwide, irrevocable, perpetual (i.e. lasting forever), non-exclusive, transferable, royalty-free and fully sublicensable (i.e. we can grant this right to others) right to use, copy, display, store, adapt, publicly perform and distribute such User Content in connection with the Services. You irrevocably consent to any and all acts or omissions by us or persons authorized by us that may infringe any moral right (or analogous right) in your User Content."[10]

In other words, Facebook demanded unilaterally that users permanently abandon any of the control over their own creative work that copyright technically affords them. Following some negative publicity, the company eventually removed the word *perpetual* from the terms. While this clause, with or without "perpetual" in it, may seem burdensome and extravagant, it's actually quite typical; popular social media platforms like Snapchat, Pinterest, and Instagram (which is also owned by Facebook) have added similar clauses to their TOS, as have thousands of other sites and services.

Sadly, although there has been a significant degree of outcry over the implications of these practices among consumer advocates and legal scholars, and occasionally some from the general public, it is unlikely that the law will be reformed to prevent these overreaches, at least anytime soon. Yet some courts have acknowledged the essential unfairness of these agreements, and it is conceivable that TOS and EULAs will continue to diminish in both power and prevalence if there are additional rulings against their enforceability in federal litigations.

IP in the Pharmaceutical Industry

Intellectual property plays a central role in the pharmaceutical industry, a massive sector that garners nearly a trillion dollars each year from the worldwide sale of prescription drugs, enjoying a higher profit margin than any other industry, even banking.[11] Companies like Novartis, Pfizer, and Roche, each of which nets more per year than the collective box office revenues of the entire global film industry, rely upon patents to protect the compounds they develop in their research labs or acquire from third parties, trademarks to establish and maintain their brands, and international trade agreements to maintain the market value of their products. These practices have been both celebrated as an exemplar of IP's role in supporting innovation, productivity, and profitability, and criticized as a case where IP serves to pad corporate coffers while keeping life-saving medicine out of the hands of those who need it most.

Like most patents in the U.S., the European Union, and elsewhere, drug patents typically last twenty years. Yet, unlike most patent-based industries, in which a manufacturer introduces the patented invention, process, or discovery to the marketplace soon or immediately after filing, it can take ten to twelve years for a patented pharmaceutical to go through its full cycle of research, development, and regulatory approval before the drug in question is actually available for purchase, leaving only eight to ten years of protection remaining for the manufacturer before the compound enters the public domain.

Furthermore, because many new drugs follow major breakthroughs in science and medicine, valuable pharmaceutical patents tend to be filed in waves rather than in a consistent volume from year to year. This periodicity can be very profitable when a fresh wave brings a raft of new blockbuster drugs to market, but it can be treacherous when one of those waves crashes. This is exactly what happened in the early 2010s, when the pharmaceutical industry faced one of the largest mass patent expirations in history, leading to what some scholars and analysts called a "patent cliff." In the course of a few years, some of the industry's best-selling drugs, including Lexapro, Lipitor, and OxyContin, entered the public domain, threatening roughly a quarter of a trillion dollars in sales by the original patent holders between 2012 and 2015, according to one analysis.[12]

This shortened span of monopoly protection and high level of market volatility, along with the fact that a new drug costs so much to develop and market (varying research pegs this figure at anywhere from $161 million up to $2.6 billion, according to a recent controversial study), has led pharmaceutical companies to seek various ways of extending their monopoly rights beyond the natural lifespan of the patent.[13]

One of these tactics has been lobbying successfully to update patent law, extending the term of protection under certain circumstances. Another tactic is promoting patented drugs to doctors while giving them money, gifts, free travel and/or meals, a mostly legal (though ethically questionable) practice that has been shown by multiple researchers to increase the likelihood that doctors will prescribe these drugs instead of their cheaper, often equally effective, generic equivalents.[14] Another tactic is paying the manufacturers of generic drugs illegally to delay the release of their cheaper alternatives into the marketplace.[15] It is difficult to assess the frequency of this practice, given its illicit nature, but allegations and investigations related to it are fairly common and widespread.[16]

Another common tactic for extending the market value of patented drugs is called "evergreening." This tactic takes many forms, but generally it revolves around creating a minimally differentiated version of an existing product, updating it just enough to meet the low threshold of novelty and nonobviousness required for a new patent to be granted. It doesn't take much: new patents may be granted for a drug entering the public domain if it's delivered via a new method (for example, an inhaler instead of a pill), provided in a new dosage, combined with another drug, or even if the molecule's structure is simply replaced with its own mirror image (a process called enantiomerization). In some countries, including the United States and India, evergreening has been significantly reduced in recent years through targeted legislation and judicial oversight, though it remains a widely recognized problem in other countries, such as Canada and Australia.

Even once a drug patent has entered the public domain and generic alternatives have been introduced, the brand name that was originally used to market and sell it remains valuable intellectual property. Few readers are likely to recognize the generic chemical name sildenafil, yet the brand name under which it's been marketed for two decades—Viagra—is well known around the world. This name recognition goes a long way; although Pfizer no longer holds a patent on sildenafil for most uses in most countries, worldwide revenues from Viagra have continued to increase in recent years (though the company has acknowledged in its public filings that these revenues are negatively impacted somewhat by competition from generics).

Sometimes a pharmaceutical trademark can be even more valuable than a patent. Above and beyond the value of name recognition, there are some institutional benefits to controlling the branded version of a pharmaceutical, even if the drug is in the public domain. For instance, Medicare, the U.S. government healthcare program that covers tens of millions of aging and disabled people, many of whom would otherwise lack access to medical care, often buys brand-name drugs in bulk quantities from manufacturers yet lacks the power to negotiate prices for those drugs or to use the existence of a generic alternative as a form of leverage. Consequently, drug manufacturers, especially those who control valuable trademarks, can essentially set their own prices, with sometimes tragic consequences.

This is exactly what happened in the fall of 2015, when Turing Pharmaceuticals, a company run by former hedge fund manager Martin Shkreli, acquired the U.S. marketing rights to Daraprim, the brand-name version of a generic drug called pyrimethamine, for $55 million. Turing immediately raised the price of the medicine, which is used to treat life-threatening infectious diseases such as toxoplasmosis, from $13.50 to $750 per tablet—a 5,555 percent increase. While Medicare was required to cover this precipitous price hike (at a considerable cost to taxpayers), Turing's new price effectively made the drug inaccessible to many people with other forms of coverage or with no insurance at all. Although theoretically the generic version of pyrimethamine could still be created and sold at a lower cost, there was little practical incentive for any pharmaceutical manufacturer to do so, given the relatively low incidence of toxoplasmosis and the market dominance of the Daraprim brand.

It is impossible to say how many people died, faced prolonged illness, or incurred significant financial hardship as a result of Turing's price hike, but for many onlookers, any number would be unacceptable. This story sparked a considerable amount of outrage in the press and among the populace at large when it became public, yet because there was evidently nothing illegal about Turing's practice, little could be done to remedy the situation. Today, it simply remains a cautionary tale about the dangers of underregulation and unchecked greed, and an informative case study regarding the relative value of trademarks and patents in the pharmaceutical industry.

Conclusion

As this brief review illustrates, intellectual property plays a central role across a range of different industries, generating revenue, shaping business practices, and mediating relationships among creators, consumers, and the organizations and institutions that comprise the marketplace connecting them. In contrast to the simplicity and focus of IP's constitutional mandate and the clinical precision of copyright, patent, and trademark law, IP in practice is clunky, confusing, and contradictory and, as often as not, its uses inhabit legal and ethical "gray areas" in which the applicability or enforceability of a given arrangement depends on whether it's tested in court and if so, what a judge or jury might say.

Despite—or because of—its many idiosyncrasies and practical imprecision, there can be little question that intellectual property, in all its forms and manifestations across the numerous industries it shapes, generates significant economic value. A recent report published by the USPTO estimated that "IP-intensive industries" (roughly a quarter of all the business sectors that make up the U.S. economy) collectively account for about 28 million jobs and generate about $6.6 trillion in value annually, comprising more than a third of America's gross domestic product. Even if those numbers are exaggerated somewhat (a frequent occurrence with broad studies of this kind), it's clear that the report is accurate in its central claim that "IP-intensive industries continue to be a major, integral and growing part of the U.S. economy."[17]

Yet what of the economic hardship suffered by a recording artist whose label never recoups its initial investment in her album, the creative confinement endured by a visionary director bound by a work-for-hire contract, or the agonizing choice between insolvency and infirmity faced by a toxoplasmosis patient in need of Daraprim? How can we assess the value of all that's *lost*, both economically and in human terms, by the use of IP in these industries? This side of the equation is far harder to tally, and though I won't make any claims about its relative size or merits, any critical assessment of IP must acknowledge that it holds the potential for both profit and loss, both benefit and cost. To say that our industries in the twenty-first century are shaped and even propelled by IP is unquestionably true; to say whether we benefit as a society from these uses, or what an optimal use of IP in industry might be, is a matter of opinion and perspective.

FOUR

Intellectual Property and Cultural Expression

In the last chapter, we explored a few of the myriad roles that intellectual property plays in the world of business and commerce. As we discussed, IP is vital across a range of industries, contributing to trillions of dollars in revenue annually in sectors ranging from cinema to technology to pharmaceuticals. This is certainly good news for employees, investors, and all of the other people who share in the profits from these earnings. Yet, recall that the purpose of IP, according to the Constitution and reiterated in some of the most recent judicial rulings, isn't to buoy industry or create profit. Rather, its sole function is to incentivize creators and inventors to share their work with society at large, creating a richer and more vibrant public sphere and a broader body of public knowledge (if I've repeated this point throughout the book, it's because it bears repeating).

How can we tell whether and when IP is achieving what it's meant to achieve? The problem is it's a lot harder to evaluate creative incentivization, cultural vibrancy, and breadth of knowledge than it is to measure revenue. If we look at creators purely as a labor force, we can see very clearly that in nearly every "IP-intensive industry," the people doing the authoring and inventing end up with a relatively small portion of the economic upside, while institutional middlemen tend to soak up the lion's share.

In the music industry, for instance, as we discussed in the previous chapter, only about one in twenty recording artists signed to a record label ever sees a royalty check beyond the initial advance, due to contractual requirements that give the labels the right to recoup all of their (self-reported) expenses before paying the artists their stipulated royalties. As it turns out, this low ratio of commercial revenue to artist remuneration remains more or less consistent across the entire music sector. According to the U.S. government's Bureau of Labor and Statistics (BLS), all "musicians, singers and related workers" in the U.S. earned about $1.4 billion per year on average from 2007 to 2011 (the five most recent years on record at the time I performed this analysis).[1] In the meantime, Americans spend roughly $40 billion per year on musical recordings and events, according to audience-measurement firm Nielsen.[2] This nets out to about three and a half cents of every dollar earned from music ending up in the pockets of musicians themselves. Journalism offers another good example. According to BLS data, American "reporters and correspondents" working "for newspaper, news magazine, radio, or television" outlets earned about $2 billion in 2017. This nets out to almost exactly 3 percent of the $63 billion to $65 billion in annual revenue currently generated by the news industry in the U.S.[3]

For IP-driven industries in which creative expression takes a back seat to more functional considerations, the percentage earned by creators is far lower. For instance, according to the BLS, fashion designers in the U.S. earn about $1.5 billion per year (a collective income on par with musicians and journalists), yet this figure represents a much smaller portion—less than half of a percent—of a much larger industry, considering that Americans spend about $400 billion per year on apparel.[4] Similarly, architects in the U.S. earn about $9 billion per year—about three-quarters of a percent of the more than $1.2 trillion spent annually on construction.[5] The good news here is that IP-driven industries provide meaningful employment for hundreds of thousands of creative professionals in the U.S. and even more around the globe, bringing their work to billions of consumers and audience members. Yet it's a legitimate question whether industries such as these, which pass on only one-twentieth or less of the economic bounty generated by creative work to the creators themselves, are truly effective at incentivizing creativity (rather than merely exploiting it). Furthermore, even if the answer is yes, to evaluate IP's full impact on culture and society, we must *also* explore its less quantifiable costs and consequences, such as the effects of IP on creative communities and the public sphere. Creative expression is not merely a form of labor, it's also the foundation of our culture(s), and in that sense, its value is incalculable.

While we have no hope of quantifying the role that IP plays in shaping creative expression, we can certainly document and examine the many ways in which these two worlds—legal and cultural—interact. In this chapter, we will explore some of these interactions by looking at the history of two forms of cultural expression: music and visual art. In both cases, as we will see, the evolving concepts of authorship and ownership that are encoded into copyright law directly influenced the ways in which artists expressed themselves, and in turn, those new modes of expression helped to shape the evolution of the law.

The aim here is neither to provide a comprehensive overview of art history nor to catalog the innumerable ways in which IP influences culture and vice versa. Rather, these two brief cultural histories serve merely as examples of copyright's important historical and ongoing role in shaping our cultural environment, by showing how it both incentivizes *and* constrains artists, inspiring them to adapt, react, embrace, critique, and resist these laws through their creative practices.

Visual Art and IP

Although it's hard for many of us in the twenty-first century to imagine, paintings and other forms of visual art weren't always seen as the unique expression of a single creative visionary. In fact, as mentioned briefly in chapter 1, it wasn't even very common for European painters to sign their names to their work until the Italian Renaissance gave rise to modern notions of authorship, in turn creating the cultural preconditions for the birth of intellectual property. This absence of ownership, both cultural and legal, was visible in the aesthetics of the paintings themselves in a variety of ways.

First of all, European paintings up through the late Renaissance rarely featured intimate portraits, landscapes, or still lives, let alone abstract or conceptual themes.[6] Instead of these see-life-through-the-artist's-eyes subjects, most paintings during this time depicted well-known scenes from religious or classical texts, especially stories from the Bible and Greco-Roman mythology, as well as formally commissioned portraits of public figures. There are countless pictorial versions of the Annunciation, the Crucifixion, and the Pietà spanning hundreds of years, but far from being seen as evidence of unoriginality or derivativeness on the part of the painters, these depictions were understood to express and augment the shared values, experiences, and beliefs of those living in a culture dominated and defined by Christianity. Moreover, anyone could paint the Crucifixion because *no one owns the Bible.* True, the church might punish an artist whose depictions were viewed as heresy, blasphemy, or apostasy, but this was a matter of dogma, not property.

Visual artists in the days before IP were also less likely to use idiosyncratic methods or styles in their work, and the rare artists whose styles *were* celebrated were more likely to inspire copying by their peers than to discourage it. Broadly speaking, the aim was to represent a theme or subject as clearly and accessibly as possible, without calling attention to the artist's role in the process. Consequently, it was not only acceptable but commonplace for painters (even the most celebrated masters of the era) to copy brazenly their own past work or the work of others, using a variety of elaborate methods to transfer faces, figures, and other pictorial elements from one canvas to another. In the words of twentieth-century painter Mark Rothko, "The Renaissance artist appropriated everything from everywhere, making no distinction between the innovations of his next-door neighbor and those from across the continent."[7]

This tradition began to draw criticism only with the rise of more individualistic and idiosyncratic visual art around the early sixteenth century (though it continued to be employed widely, especially in arts education, at least through the early twentieth century).[8] One of the first litigations over authorship in the visual arts took place during this period, when Albrecht Dürer, the celebrated painter and printmaker, discovered that his work had been copied masterfully by a Venetian artist named Marcantonio Raimondi, and that the Italian's patrons were selling his work at a premium, possibly as original Dürers, in their home city.

The German artist traveled to Venice and pursued a lawsuit against Raimondi, which he lost, in part because the defendant had added his own signature (in addition to Dürer's) to his reproductions—meaning they weren't forgeries. After returning to Germany in anger and defeat, Dürer oversaw the reprinting of one of his most popular prints, adding a proto-copyright notice to the new edition in which he warned "pilferers of other men's brains" against laying their "thievish hands" on his work—or else face "mortal danger" at his own hands. In other words, the law didn't yet protect Dürer's right not to be copied, but he was willing to assert and protect this right himself, by any means necessary.[9]

As intellectual property laws, notions of authorship, and visual art coevolved over the next few centuries, each influenced the others in a variety of ways. Not long after it invented modern copyright in 1710 with the Statute of Anne, the British Parliament extended the law to cover visual prints with the Engraver's Act of 1735. This law was—and is—often referred to as "Hogarth's Act" because of the central role played by the famous printmaker William Hogarth in lobbying for its enactment. Among other aspects of what we would now call his "public awareness campaign," Hogarth printed and disseminated a pamphlet entitled *The Case of Designers, Engravers, Etchers, etc*, in which he argued that copyright was essential to engravers' livelihoods—not just because it protected them against copying by other artists but because it protected them against copying by unscrupulous publishers, whose cheap copies could rapidly devalue a work. In other words, the justification for the law was rooted in the rhetoric of artists' rights, and it was intended to play a role in mediating artist/industry relationships.

Hogarth's Act, as it was eventually written, protected only original designs, thus drawing a legal distinction between artist engravers (who developed new material) and craftsmen engravers (who merely reproduced material and were therefore not entitled to protection for their work).[10] While the Engraver's Act came about far too late (and too far from home) to help Dürer press his cause against Raimondi, it did have the effect of changing the norms and practices within the world of printmaking in a way that Dürer would have approved. No longer would one printmaker have to threaten another with "mortal danger" for copying his work without permission—he could simply take the alleged infringer to court.

Printmaking was the first visual art to warrant copyright in part because it was so similar to book publishing from an industrial stand-point: individual authors' work was acquired and widely reproduced by publishers using presses in exchange for up-front payments and/or royalties on sales. Yet once Hogarth's Act had established the validity of original visual design as a copyrightable artifact, it was only a matter of time before other, less industrially produced visual arts were covered as well. And once such laws were enacted, these newly covered art forms would also see rapid changes in both their norms and aesthetics.

Copyright coverage was extended to both photography and painting in the UK in 1862, while in the U.S., photography was covered in 1865, with drawings and paintings following in 1870. With the passage of the Berne Convention in 1886, a growing number of countries around the world followed suit. The highly individualistic logic of these laws reflected and reinforced the era's visual art, which culminated in the birth of impressionism (usually dated by art historians to 1870), characterized by painters and sculptors such as Claude Monet, Pierre-Auguste Renoir, and Edgar Degas. These artists didn't merely ignore but flat-out *rejected* the notion that art should reproduce objective reality or focus on Very Important Subjects. Instead, they depicted their intimate surroundings in highly original ways. You'd never have to ask who painted Monet's water lilies or Renoir's *A Girl with a Watering Can*—although these artists did typically sign their work, their styles were so individualized it was virtually unnecessary. Another way to put it is that the real subject of the impressionists' work wasn't the world that surrounded them but rather the inner lives of the artists themselves.

In the twentieth century, many leading visual artists took the lessons of the impressionists to the extreme, abandoning the representation of the "real world" altogether (in the case of cubism and abstract expressionism) and even questioning and challenging the very concept of "representation" (in the case of Dadaism, minimalism, and conceptualism). For many of these artists, all that existed was the author's interior world and/or the material reality of the artwork itself. And for some of these artists, this hyper-individualism had its corollary in a hyper-possessive relationship to their work.

Rothko, for instance, never allowed anyone, including his own assistants, to witness, let alone learn, his painting techniques. Even once the resulting works had been created and sold, this bond persisted; according to his close friend Herbert Ferber, Rothko "had 'an umbilical attachment' to his work, as if he were mother to these 'children.' "[11] Rothko himself, an avid scholar of art history, was perfectly aware of how historically unique this relationship was. In fact, he drew a direct parallel between the propertization of culture and the proprietary relationship he had to his work, praising "that laudable individualism which is the basis of our life here. Pride in acquisitiveness and ownership." To Rothko, this ethic represented the pinnacle of artistic liberty and success, and consequently he encouraged art educators to "nurture" the same acquisitive, proprietary desires in their students.[12]

Despite the modernist focus on individual vision and achievement, artists in the twentieth century appropriated just as much as from other creators as their predecessors had. Painters and sculptors like Pablo Picasso, Henri Matisse, and Francis Picabia, for example, took a great interest in what at the time was derogatorily referred to as "primitive" art, drawing on cultural traditions from Africa, South America, and Asia to inspire new ways of seeing and representing the world around them. Although these artists saw such methods as fundamentally liberatory, an antidote to the formalism and rigid conventions of Western art and society, today most cultural scholars view primivitist art as an act of "cultural imperialism," an extension of the economic and political imperialism that Europeans had imposed on the people and societies of these regions for centuries. Regardless of broader cultural politics, it's certainly the case that the work these artists drew upon was not protected by copyright, and it seems more than likely that the turn from local to global appropriation in the early years of the new century was a direct result of the extension of copyright protection to visual art in the Western world at the end of the previous century.[13]

Of course, the modern fascination with appropriation didn't stop with primitivism. In fact, it was just getting started. After World War I, artists like Marcel Duchamp, Hannah Höch, and Kurt Schwitters began to make appropriation a central aspect of their aesthetics, calling into question the Romantic notions of authorship and artistry that had justified copyright for visual artworks in the first place. As with the primitivists, most of the work that these artists drew upon was safely beyond the scope of copyright protection. A vital source was the public domain; one of the Duchamp's most celebrated pieces is *L.H.O.O.Q.*, a postcard of Leonardo da Vinci's *Mona Lisa* on which he had drawn a beard and moustache. It was a powerful attack on an icon of creative individualism and artistic genius, but not one that was likely to inspire a lawsuit. Similarly, Duchamp's experiments with readymades—industrial objects like urinals and bicycle wheels transformed into art by virtue of being signed, titled, and placed in a curatorial setting—continued to undermine the concept of artistic originality but without appropriating anything that *belonged* to another artist or rights holder.

Höch and Schwitters were pioneers of collage and installation art, in which various objects—including pieces of copyrighted work like newspapers and photographs—were cobbled together into two- or three-dimensional artworks that sought to reproduce the multifaceted and often confusing cultural experience of life in an industrialized, media-saturated society. While some of these pieces may possibly have infringed copyright (depending on how you interpret the fair use and de minimis doctrines—there were neither laws nor lawsuits to establish meaningful guidelines at the time), any infringement was incidental to the aesthetic. In other words, the works weren't *about* appropriating intellectual property; such materials were merely caught in the dragnet of aesthetic inclusivity.

This began to change in the mid-twentieth century with the rise of "pop" artists like Andy Warhol, whose best-known work is a reproduction of a highly recognizable trademark—a Campbell's soup can. Unlike the Dadaists and collagists, Warhol was intentionally tweaking the concept of cultural ownership and inviting debates about the appropriate role of intellectual property in art and in commerce. A former advertising illustrator, Warhol was very aware of the fine line separating the two fields, and he sought to show that the aura and glamour surrounding art was the only thing that distinguished it from more commercial, instrumental forms of expression.

Following Warhol's lead, artists in the later twentieth century took greater and greater liberties with the limits of intellectual property. When art scholar Erle Loran published a book containing a somewhat reductionist black-and-white diagram of a famous painting by Paul Cézanne, the painter Roy Lichtenstein lampooned his efforts by painting a reproduction of Loran's diagram and including it in a major exhibition, ultimately prompting a lawsuit and provoking a heated public debate about plagiarism and the appropriate uses of appropriation (which was, of course, Lichtenstein's aim in the first place).

Twenty years later, the artist Sherrie Levine pushed Lichtenstein's approach to its logical conclusion, taking pictures of prints by celebrated Depression-era photographer Walker Evans and making her own identical prints from them. She then displayed the collected photos, for which she claimed full attribution and copyright ownership, in an exhibition titled *After Walker Evans*. Instead of embarking on a risky and expensive infringement lawsuit, the Evans estate simply bought the entire set of photographs in order to keep them off the market. To this day, Levine still holds the copyrights in these "rephotographs," and her work is celebrated (and sometimes derided) as "a deliberate provocation" that "challenges the authenticity of a work of art, the nature of authorship itself, and the sanctity of copyrighted material" while striking a feminist blow against "male artistic eminences."[14]

In more recent decades, the tactics embraced by Lichtenstein and Levine have coalesced into a recognizable genre, often referred to as "appropriation art." Although this is, by now, well-worn aesthetic terrain, it continues to generate public controversy and provoke lawsuits, occasionally resulting in a major judicial decision. Contemporary artists like Jeff Koons, Damien Hirst, and Richard Prince have made a (lucrative) cottage industry out of exploiting the gray area at the intersection of art, law, and technology, leaving a trail of admirers, imitators, and enemies in their wakes. Yet for all the litigation, there is still very little clarity as to what kinds of creative appropriation constitute infringement and what kinds do not. For instance, the recent appeals court ruling in *Cariou v. Prince* (centering around collages made partially from copyrighted photographs) concluded that some—but not all—of the appropriative works at issue in the case constituted fair use, leading some law scholars to lament that the precedent "forces a judge to engage as a critic" and creates "an uncertain legal landscape likely to discourage the creation of certain art."[15]

If courts can't clarify the ineffable line between legitimate and illegitimate appropriation, they can hardly be blamed, as artists themselves have consistently equivocated on the issue. In fact, appropriation artists have sometimes been among the most litigious in the art world—even to the point of jealously protecting works that they themselves have been accused of lifting from others. Such was the case in 2008 when Hirst threatened a sixteen-year-old artist with a copyright infringement suit for making collages that incorporated a photograph of his sculpture *For the Love of God*, a crystal-

encrusted skull. Using the threat of litigation, Hirst forced the teen-
ager to turn over all of his allegedly infringing artwork, plus a fee,
to the UK's Design and Artists Copyright Society. Ironically, when
Hirst had first produced the sculpture, he had himself been accused
of plagiarism by his (former) friend, the sculptor John LeKay, who
had been making jewel-encrusted skulls since the early 1990s.[16]

This ambivalence among artists about the role of copyright in
art is perhaps most evident when the copyright symbol itself plays
a visual role in the artwork. This has been a remarkably durable
theme for the better part of a century, and although it means different things in different contexts for different artists and audiences, it
always indicates a complex relationship between notions of artistry,
authorship, and ownership.

An early example is Lichtenstein, who began affixing the copyright symbol to his work, sometimes in conjunction with his signature or other identifying marks, around the time he started producing pop art in 1961. While this may at first glance seem like a
simple, cover-all-bases attempt to protect his work from infringement, it was anything but; Lichtenstein was a canny student of both
art and commerce, and he viewed the visible symbol as a talismanic
touchstone connecting the two. As art historian Michael Lobel explains: "Lichtenstein was attempting to find a motif with which to
mark his work yet which would at the same time suggest a connection to commercial culture. However, it was the copyright symbol's
very connection to commerce that made its use problematic; like
the trademark, it signified a network of economic, social and jurid-
ical relations that were carefully policed and controlled. . . . A close
examination of his paintings provides evidence that the very am-
biguity of the artist's claim to authorship came to be embedded in
his work in material form."[17] As an example of this material embed-
ding, Lobel cites Lichtenstein's appropriative 1961 painting *Popeye*,
in which the top of an open can of spinach visually echoes and am-

Figure 8: Roy Lichtenstein's *Popeye*, 1961.

plifies the copyright symbol painted just beneath it, perhaps suggesting that IP, like canned spinach, is a source of power, a store-bought commodity, or both.

A few decades after Lichtenstein began affixing the copyright symbol to his work, Warhol acolyte Jean-Michel Basquiat exploded into the art world with an innovative fusion of graffiti, expressionist, pop, and neo-primitivist styles. As a teenaged street graffiti artist in New York in the late 1970s, Basquiat had often paired his tag (the nom de plume, or nom de spray paint, of graffiti writers) SAMO with a copyright symbol and/or a crown. These icons have since been analyzed ad nauseam by critics, scholars, and historians, and though there are many ways to interpret them, to me (a dabbler in street graffiti as a teenaged New Yorker in the mid-1980s) they clearly connote an ironic but aspirational relationship to both political and commercial authority. Even as an unknown youth, Basquiat was aware of the mechanisms of cultural power, evincing a begrudging desire to engage with those mechanisms in order to become powerful himself.

As Basquiat's fame and success grew, so did his interest in the aesthetic implications of IP; copyright and trademark symbols appeared in both the titles and the visual fields of many of his later works. Yet while Lichtenstein had used the symbol in conjunction with his signature, referring only obliquely to these themes in his actual work, Basquiat directly confronted IP and all of its cultural implications, bringing it front and center both literally and figuratively. A good example is the piece *Untitled* (1984), in which the text "ABORIGINAL GENERATIVE©" is superscribed over the prominent figure of a woman giving birth. There is no way an observer could mistake the use of the symbol here as an attempt by Basquiat to protect his work from infringement; instead, in the words of art critic Louis Armand, "The copyright symbol here serves to ironise the exploitative 'ownership' of both indigenous peoples and natural resources by colonial powers and Western capital, including the very process of generation."[18]

In the years since Basquiat's death in 1988, many other visual artists have engaged with intellectual property in and through their work, with differing degrees of critical distance, ambivalence, enthusiasm, and success. Prominent examples run the gamut from neo-psychedelic artist Takashi Murakami's ©*MURAKAMI* retrospective exhibition to middlebrow kitsch powerhouse Thomas Kinkade's legal trademark for the self-appellation "Painter of Light™" to the sculptor Anish Kapoor's exclusive license to use the light-absorbing Vantablack pigment. If anything, the number and variety of examples have continued to grow in recent years as IP has emerged from policy backwater to the forefront of debates over technology, politics, and culture in the wake of the internet boom. Thus, it seems

Figure 9: Jean-Michel Basquiat's *Untitled*, 1984.

likely that visual art and intellectual property will continue to co-evolve in fascinating and unexpected ways for many years to come.

Music and IP

The trajectory of Western music's coevolution with intellectual property shares many similarities with that of visual art, beginning in the medieval era. Although there were celebrated composers prior to the Renaissance, they tended to be either church musicians (such as Hildegard von Bingen and Petrus de Cruce) or court musicians and troubadours (such as Adam de la Halle and Guiraut Riquier). Just like the pre-Renaissance painters, these early musicians served a primarily functionary role, facilitating and commemorating religious and political events rather than expressing their individual perspectives on the world around them.

This began to change with the rise of ars nova in the early fourteenth century, "the first full manifestation of a pure musical art, freed from the service of religion or poetry and constructed according to its own laws."[19] With this liberation from institutional constraints, new Renaissance notions of individual authorship began to be applied to musical composition just as they were to painting and sculpture in the same era. This philosophical change bore aesthetic fruit; in some cultures, such as France, "mannerist" secular music began to outstrip religious music in complexity and sophistication by the turn of the fifteenth century.

With the widespread adoption of the printing press in the sixteenth century, European music began to see a formal division of labor between the creative, intellectual work of composing and the more mundane, physical work of performing (similar to the distinction between "artistry" and "craftsmanship" reflected in Hogarth's Act). This helped to set composers—and their compositions—apart from the immediate circumstances of performance and to spread their names and works broadly for the first time. The following century saw the birth of opera, the first musical form underwritten by bourgeois ticket buyers instead of wealthy court and church patrons. These two developments helped to accelerate the widespread demand for printed scores, laying the industrial and cultural foundations for what we today typically refer to as "popular music" and creating a marketplace primed for the introduction of copyright.

In the seventeenth and eighteenth centuries, the baroque and classical eras were virtually defined by their "great" composers, who produced much of the music that we still venerate today. This was the epoch of Bach, Handel, Haydn, and Mozart. Although these composers were, and still are, revered for their ingenuity and originality, they also routinely engaged in the kind of creative "borrowing" that would today be considered grounds for a copyright infringement suit. According to *The Oxford History of Western Music*, "Every church and theater composer indulged in the practice," especially Handel, who copied "both his own works and those of other composers in unprecedented numbers and with unprecedented exactness," even recycling old material for two choruses of his best-known work, *Messiah*.[20]

Indeed, it's hard to find any composers in the Western classical tradition who did not make similar borrowings, even for their most celebrated compositions. In Mozart's *The Magic Flute*, Papageno's signature song is lifted note-for-note from an aria written by his Viennese contemporaries for *The Beneficent Dervish*, an opera whose libretto was even based on the same source material as Mozart's.[21] Mozart himself was frequently copied by Beethoven, who used a series of arpeggios from *Don Giovanni* as a harmonic and rhythmic scaffolding for his beloved "Moonlight Sonata" and who lifted a theme from "Misericordias Domini" to form the central melody in his "Ode to Joy."[22]

Although music historians today debate the degree to which these borrowings were considered ethical or plagiaristic by musicians and audiences at the time, they were clearly well within the scope of normal creative and commercial practice. This was partly because musical works didn't have the same aura of sacrosanctity and finality that they would acquire a few decades later with Romantic notions of genius and authorship; for instance, it was common at the time for publishers to edit or "fix" the works of even the most celebrated composers before printing and selling their scores.[23] But it was also due to the fact that there was no copyright yet for musical works, and thus there was neither the proprietary philosophy that justifies IP nor the legal means or financial incentive to prosecute borrowings in court. The price of overstepping the line between influence and theft was reputational: a composer who borrowed too much "frequently drew sharp censure" from his peers.[24]

Musical scores were granted copyright coverage decades *before* paintings—probably because they were, like books and engravings, printed on presses by publishers and because there was already an economic and political model for IP rights based on these analogous (and to a certain degree co-controlled) print industries. Although there had been a few very early examples of musical composers receiving monopoly rights for the publication of their own work, such as lutist Guillaume Morlaye's ten-year license from Henri II in 1552, comprehensive copyright coverage didn't apply to printed musical scores until 1777 in Britain, 1793 in France, and 1831 in the United States.[25]

Just as the introduction of IP in the visual arts world can be correlated with the onset of impressionism, copyright for printed scores emerged at the same cultural moment as musical Romanticism, characterized by an "emphasis on individuality and peculiarity, which became over the course of the nineteenth century an ever more pressing demand for originality."[26] Again, it's not merely that intellectual property and individualistic art share a common philosophical foundation, it's that, with the ability to litigate, concerns about plagiarism become concerns about infringement, creating a financial incentive for composers to effectively distinguish their work from one another's. On the one hand, this is exactly what the U.S. Constitution says IP should be about—inspiring artists to create and share innovative work with the public. On the other hand, these new legal mechanisms upended centuries of established creative practice based on copying that had given the world the innovative works of Handel, Mozart, and Beethoven, among countless others.

As in the case of visual art, musical composers in the copyright era didn't simply stop appropriating other people's work once these laws were passed—they just switched the focus of their appropriation from contemporary Western composers to noncopyrighted sources, such as Eastern and "folk" traditions. For the first hundred years of musical copyright, European and American composers exhibited a growing fascination with Eastern music, integrating melodies, rhythms, and even instruments from a variety of Asian traditions into their work. Examples of this "Orientalism" run the gamut from Mozart's 1782 opera *Die Entführung aus dem Serail* to Camille Saint-Saëns's *Samson et Dalila* a century later.

During this same period of time, Western composers also became increasingly interested in mining the public domain for new material, integrating the ubiquitous, authorless, ownerless melodies from their local and national traditions into their own work. Sometimes multiple composers would even recycle the same material, as when Beethoven and Mussorgsky both used the song "Slava" (published in a 1790 folk song anthology) for the "Razumovsky" string quartets (1806) and *Boris Godunov* (1868–73), respectively.

There are a great many reasons that Western composers chose to begin appropriating Asian and folk musics in the late eighteenth and nineteenth centuries that have nothing to do with copyright or intellectual property. This was an era marked by expanding trade and conquest abroad, growing nationalism in Europe, and the development of a globalized culture, accelerated by new electronic communications networks in the form of first telegraphy and then telephony. In this context, it makes sense that Western artists and audiences would be interested in telling stories about, and reconciling their art with, the Eastern cultures and modes of expression with which they were confronted. Likewise, it makes sense that newly unifying nations like Germany and Italy would look to folklore for some sense of national identity rooted in the premise of a common heritage. Whether these depictions of "Oriental" and "folk" were accurate—or even respectful—is almost beside the point; they were the musical manifestations of popular narratives, repeated and shared for purposes related to tectonic changes in the European sociocultural landscape at the time.

And yet we cannot ignore the power dynamics inherent in intellectual property law, nor can we discount the role of copyright in inspiring and supporting these stylistic shifts. Just as the new democracies and republics of the modern era offered citizenship and enfranchisement to some while leaving others without rights or representation, the advent of copyright provided protection to a privileged group of creators while simultaneously giving them free rein to appropriate from others. To the classical composers of the nineteenth century, these unprotected works were simply a natural resource waiting to be exploited, like iron ore or coal. As Robert Schumann, a leading composer and musical scholar of the era, advised his peers and readers, "Listen attentively to all folk songs. They are mines of the most beautiful melodies."[27]

This double standard became visible only in those rare instances in which it was violated. A classic example is Georges Bizet's 1875 opera *Carmen*, for which the composer borrowed what he believed was a Spanish folk song in composing the melody of the "Habanera," one of the opera's signature arias and an instant international sensation. There was no shame in this; early printed copies of the score acknowledged frankly that the melody was "imitated from a Spanish song." Yet it turned out that the melody wasn't a folk song at all—it was copyrighted in 1863 as "El Arreglito" by a contemporary Spanish composer named Sebastián Yradier. This revelation sparked years of international litigation and legal debate, further complicated when the Berne Convention copyright treaty was signed a decade later. Ironically, the legal wrangling was all undertaken by those with commercial interests in the sale of the sheet music rather than by the composers themselves. Both had already passed away— Yradier in 1865, and Bizet in 1875, a few months after the opera's premiere.

A final kink in this story: although he published and copyrighted the tune first, it is likely that Yradier was not its composer either. Prior to writing "El Arreglito," he had traveled from his native Spain to Latin America and "collected" the melodies he heard there for future use in creating "pseudo-folk" compositions with a Spanish flavor.[28] Had Bizet done the same, going straight to the source rather than appropriating an appropriation, there would have been no lawsuit and no outcry. The original source of Yradier's musical inspiration has never been credited or compensated, nor was there any call for it.

Despite the *Carmen* imbroglio and the shifting ethics and aesthetics of appropriation, musical copyright in the 1800s typically wasn't used to police "borrowings" by one composer from another but rather to prevent one publisher from selling wholesale copies of a song controlled by another. In the U.S., in fact, there appears to be only one case during the entire nineteenth century in which one song was found to infringe on another based on substantial similarity—and both songs in this case were essentially variations of the public domain tune "Danny Boy."[29]

This dynamic changed in the twentieth century, a far more litigious period in which the economic stakes grew considerably with the advent of the musical recording and broadcasting industries as well as the revisions to copyright that both anticipated and reflected these technological and economic developments. During the early part of the century, there was a virtual gold rush among composers and publishers to lay ownership claim to melodies both old and new. The epicenter of this frenzy in America was the popular music industry, exemplified by the publishing powerhouses of Tin Pan Alley and the booming market for what was then called "race music" —African American styles such as blues, jazz, and ragtime. Savvy composers of the time, such as W. C. Handy, Jelly Roll Morton, and George M. Cohan, published and copyrighted hundreds of songs, many of them minimally differentiated from the public domain material their work was drawn from, and others more or less lifted directly from less savvy composers who lacked the expertise or means to file for copyright themselves.

By midcentury, copyright infringement cases were so common in the music industry that several prominent law firms specialized in this subfield. Although the vast majority of suits (as always) were settled privately, the number of judicial decisions increased drastically, from fifteen in the first full century following the creation of American musical copyright to thirty in the next *quarter* century. After the creation of the phonographic "master" copyright in 1972 and the significant extensions to copyright coverage and power in the 1976 revision to the law, litigation went into overdrive: between 1975 and 2000, there were fifty-six judicial opinions on music copyright cases, many of them setting the bar for infringement lower and lower. One well-known example is *Bright Tunes Music v. Harrisongs Music*, the infamous 1976 suit in which former Beatle George Harrison was found by a federal judge to have "subconsciously" plagiarized "He's So Fine," a song made famous a decade earlier by girl group the Chiffons, in his solo hit "My Sweet Lord."[30]

Yet even as music copyright was becoming stronger, more assiduously policed, and consequentially more influential in shaping and constraining the sound of commercial music, composers and performers pushed back increasingly against these constraints. While visual artists were experimenting with new techniques like collage and readymades that undermined the philosophical foundations of authorship (and, by extension, challenging the legitimacy of intellectual property), musical artists in both the U.S. and Europe began to apply similar principles to their own work.

In the years after World War II, innovators like John Cage, Pierre Schaeffer, and Pierre Henry used the recording and copying capacities of newly developed magnetic tape to develop *musique concrète*, a kind of sonic collage, while they and others experimented with chance-based or "aleatory" composition, in which randomly generated numbers are used to determine pitch, rhythm, and other aspects of the music. As with their painter and sculptor peers, these composers didn't typically risk facing a copyright infringement suit, but their work still served to highlight some of the central tensions surrounding the role of IP in their creative and commercial environment.

A generation later, the cutting-and-pasting techniques used in musique concrète began to filter into popular music. Early examples included the Beatles' self-consciously avant-garde "Revolution 9" and the brilliant postcolonial experimentalism of Jamaican dub reggae innovators like Lee "Scratch" Perry and King Tubby. Yet these techniques remained somewhat arcane curiosities for most artists and audiences until the late 1970s, when a Jamaican-born DJ named Kool Herc based in the Bronx began to integrate these aesthetics into his live performances, building the musical foundations for what would soon come to be called hip-hop.

Within a decade, hip-hop had become a major musical force in American media culture and around the world. Innovative DJs and producers in this field soon expanded beyond turntable-based scratching and beat juggling, exploiting new technologies like the Roland TR-808 drum machine (released in 1980) and the Akai MPC series of digital audio samplers (released in 1988) to create dense, complex tapestries of sound, merging both recognizable and unrecognizable snippets of song, speech, and industrial noise with sequenced beats and synthesized tones. Many artists, critics, and scholars hailed hip-hop both as a challenge to established Eurocentric pop music aesthetics and as a slap in the face of the regimented, cartelized industry that promoted them.

At first, as with visual collage, most hip-hop DJs weren't intentionally confronting copyright so much as ignoring it altogether. As Hank Shocklee, a founding member of the pioneering group Public Enemy, explained in an interview, "At the time, it wasn't even an issue. . . . The copyright laws didn't really extend into sampling until the hip-hop artists started getting sued."[31] This was technically true; with neither legislation nor case law addressing the matter, music sampling existed in a legal gray area between fair use and infringement. Yet after two prominent hip-hop artists—Biz Markie and De La Soul—lost infringement suits for sampling in 1991, industry practice changed entirely, and every sample had to be precleared and licensed from whichever label owned the rights to the source material. This had two significant effects. First, it consolidated this radical, independent new art form within the existing cartels; for the most part, major labels would clear samples only for and from other major labels, and at the rates they charged (thousands of dollars or more per sample), no one else could afford to use them. Second, it changed the music. As Public Enemy's Chuck D explained, "Public Enemy's music was affected more than anybody's because we were taking thousands of sounds. If you separated the sounds, they wouldn't have been anything—they were unrecognizable. The sounds were all collaged together to make a sonic wall. Public Enemy was affected because it is too expensive to defend against a claim. So we had to change our whole style."[32]

This wasn't merely an aesthetic change—the inability to create sonic collage on the same scale and with the same freedom as before blunted the political and cultural bite of the entire genre. In Shocklee's words, "If you notice . . . by the early 1990s, the sound has gotten a lot softer."[33] Music critics and historians have acknowledged this fact as well; in the 2010s, this bygone era of uninhibited sampling in the 1980s and early 1990s is often referred to nostalgically as the "golden age of hip-hop," spoken of in the same reverent tones as the "pre-code" era before Hollywood began to self-censor its films.

The 1991 ruling against Biz Markie, in which Judge Kevin Duffy directly cited the Ten Commandments ("Thou shalt not steal") as an "admonition followed since the dawn of civilization," effectively chilled fair use claims for sampling.[34] A decade later, the decision in the *Bridgeport v. Dimension* case against "gangsta" rap group N.W.A. established that not even de minimis claims could be made in the case of tiny, unrecognizable samples.[35] Today, universal sample clearance is still the norm, and though commercial hip-hop remains a lucrative market, its decline has been lamented at least since Nas proclaimed in the title of a 2006 album (the year after the *Bridgeport* ruling), "Hip Hop Is Dead."[36] This claim is, of course, debatable, and there are several reasons to believe that the genre may yet have some life in it.

First of all, at the time of writing, some of the most popular and successful new hip-hop artists, such as Kendrick Lamar, use backing tracks that harken back to the dense, collagist soundscapes of De La Soul and Public Enemy (unfortunately, Lamar has also been sued for infringement for uncleared samples). Second, although sampling remains unaddressed in copyright legislation, there is evidence that today's courts, populated by many judges and clerks who have a cultural relationship to hip-hop, may be more sympathetic to fair use and de minimis claims than their predecessors in the previous generation.

For instance, in 2014 (as we discussed in chapter 2), rapper and impresario Jay-Z successfully defended an infringement case for his song "Run this Town," which used a one-syllable sample from "Hook and Sling—Part I," a 1969 funk hit by Eddie Bo. In his memorandum dismissing the suit, Judge Lewis A. Kaplan argued that the plaintiffs had "not stated a plausible claim" because the sample had "essentially no quantitative significance" to the original work, and because the complaint had "improperly conflate[d] factual copying and actual copying."[37] Similarly, and even more promisingly for sample-based musicians, a 2017 legal decision in the same court found that the rapper Drake's use of a spoken word recording by jazz organist Jimmy Smith constituted fair use. This was the first legal decision ever to establish fair use for sampling beyond the scope of parody. In his opinion, Judge William H. Pauley III argued that Drake's song "Pound Cake" didn't compete in the market with Smith's spoken word piece and that, because Drake's purpose was "sharply different" than Smith's, his use of the sample was "highly transformative."[38] Thankfully, when it comes to hip-hop, today's judiciary exhibits a level of cultural and legal sophistication that far outstrips "Thou shalt not steal."

To summarize, musicians have always "borrowed" from one another, from Bach to Bizet to Biz Markie. Countless musical histories and analyses have documented this practice, and few people with any degree of musicological expertise would argue that music can be created, out of whole cloth and from scratch, without any reference to what's come before. On the other hand, the ethical distinction between "borrowing" and "plagiarism" seems to predate copyright law, and overstepping has always carried a significant reputational (and thus economic) risk for musicians.

As in the case of visual art, the introduction of copyright to musical cultures and economies radically altered the stakes and power dynamics surrounding creative expression, with repercussions that significantly changed the aesthetics of the work itself. In the nineteenth century, Romantic artists strove for originality and innovation in their work, reinforcing the model of individual creation underpinning newly enacted IP laws, while many composers simultaneously mined the unprotected works of Asian and "folk" composers in search of novelty, inspiration, and risk-free commercial success. In the twentieth century, the avant-garde pioneered the use of recorded sound as source material for new work, yet these same techniques were effectively outlawed once they became staples of hip-hop expression.

Though this brief overview cannot possibly capture the richness or complexity of musical culture or the many-faceted relationship it has with intellectual property laws, it should offer compelling evidence that IP necessarily changes the ways in which artists relate to their own work, to one another, to institutions, and to audiences, and thus plays a significant role in reshaping cultural expression on a broad scale. Whether these changes are good or bad is, of course, in the eye of the beholder; unlike the issues of revenue and remuneration introduced at the outset of this chapter, cultural impact can't be meaningfully quantified.

Although we have focused on visual art and music, this chapter could just as easily have explored the role of IP in countless other cultural fields, from literature to design to cinema. In the twenty-first century, there is virtually no cultural practice anywhere on the globe that is not influenced in some way by copyright, patent, trademark, or a combination thereof. Yet this totalizing presence is anything but monolithic in its effects. The relationships between law and culture are subtle and powerful: they both enable and constrain creative expression, and they are both embraced and resisted in myriad ways by creators and audiences alike. The challenge for those of us who live within a culture shaped and circumscribed by IP is to recognize it as an invisible source of gravity, tugging this artist that way, pushing that one this way. And once we do see it, hiding in plain sight, like the copyright symbol on Popeye's lid, we must decide: does it empower us like the spinach, or commodify us like the can?

FIVE

The Politics Behind Intellectual Property

As we have seen, intellectual property plays a central role in both business and culture, reflecting and shaping the interests and behaviors of every social stakeholder, from creators to consumers to corporations and other large-scale institutions. This makes IP a powerful political tool and the subject of many high-stakes political battles. In this chapter, we will explore some of the political machinery behind IP law and policy, charting the flow of money and other forms of influence between major stakeholders and the public officials who are responsible for creating and enforcing our copyright, patent, and trademark laws. As we will see, transparency laws allow us to document many of the lobbying and campaign finance relationships between the private and public spheres, yet there are other forms of influence and persuasion that may be glimpsed only through inference and deeper investigation.

Lobbying and Legislation

Intellectual property laws are not born in a vacuum. In the introduction, we noted that in the U.S. alone, hundreds of companies

126

lobby the federal government on copyright, patent, and trademark issues each year, employing thousands of lobbyists and spending about $700 million annually to shape these laws. Given how much they spend and how long they've been spending it, those footing the bill must believe it's worthwhile and that the resulting shifts in policy provide enough help in generating new revenues to offset the considerable costs. These general practices and the calculations behind them have been analyzed and evaluated by many political scientists, and their impact on national politics has been decried in recent years by reformist candidates, such as Zephyr Teachout and Bernie Sanders.[1]

But while it's one thing to problematize lobbying as a whole and to make generalized claims about its economic incentives and political consequences, the more granular details are still worth examining. Which companies and industries are lobbying, and for what specific IP policy agenda items? To what degree do they coordinate, cooperate, and conflict? How successful is the process, and what counts as a victory? To what extent are other interests, such as the public's, represented in these deliberations? These are big thorny questions. Although a satisfying set of answers would require a book of its own (as well as some extensive investigative research to get beneath the story told by publicly available data), this chapter will provide a deep enough glimpse into the IP lobbying/legislation process to give the reader some indication of its complexity and a sense of the motivations, methods, and means behind the multiplicity of diverse stakeholders who participate in it.

To many people, the very concept of lobbying may seem shady or dishonest: do corporations and other moneyed interests actually spend billions of dollars a year to convince legislators to make laws that suit their needs and interests, helping them to generate more profit and ultimately enabling them to spend more on influencing the laws? It can sound more like the plot of a late night cable television potboiler than the everyday business of elected officials and the stuff of banal federal and state paperwork. Yet it is both everyday and banal; although there is no official tally of one-to-one meetings between lawmakers and lobbyists, numerous analyses have shown that legislators in the U.S. spend anywhere from one-quarter to half their time each day on fund-raising, often in the company of lobbyists or on premises owned by lobbying firms.

Thanks to government transparency initiatives like the Lobbying Disclosure Act of 1995 and its follow-up, the Honest Leadership and Open Government Act of 2007, these activities generate a long and detailed paper trail, manifested in thousands upon thousands of publicly available reports filed with federal and state governments, detailing the lobbyists involved, the clients' names, the amount of money spent, the issues discussed, and the governmental bodies (but not the specific lawmakers) targeted. The data in these reports are then cataloged and made searchable via the internet thanks to the efforts of nonprofit organizations such as the Center for Responsive Politics, the National Institute on Money in State Politics, and the Sunlight Foundation. If you haven't ever visited their websites (such as Opensecrets.org and Followthemoney.org), it's well worth doing; you can learn a *lot* about your own federal and state representatives, where they get their funding, and where their policy interests and political allegiances most likely lie.

If all of this still sounds shady to you, despite the transparency, you're not alone; lobbying and other forms of paid persuasion in the legislative process are widely and routinely criticized as a form of legal influence peddling—that's what led to the transparency laws in the first place. Every few years, some news organization (or, more recently, some satirical news show, such as Jon Oliver's *Last Week Tonight*) publishes an exposé on the issue, spurring public awareness and generating calls for reform. Yet actual reform is very rare, and there are good reasons for this.

First of all, like it or not, lobbying is a form of speech, and speech is protected under the First Amendment in the United States. Every citizen has the right to say what she likes and to "petition the Government for a redress of grievances." Whether we each have the *means* to exercise this right is a different matter; it's a lot easier to gain access to a congressperson's time and attention if you're providing office space for his or her Washington-based fund-raising activities than if you're working the night shift at a Denny's in Akron, Ohio.

Second, legislators *need* both the information and the funding that lobbyists provide. Thousands of bills are introduced in Congress each year, and even the most diligent representative couldn't possibly be expected to educate himself adequately on every issue at a level necessary to justify binding law. One lawmaker may know a lot about education but very little about agriculture, while another is deeply involved in defense but clueless on the subject of women's reproductive rights. The educational overviews and policy proposals provided by lobbyists, though often partisan and paid for, help to fill these holes in legislative expertise (and ideally, each legislator is exposed to several sides of each issue by competing interests).

This is especially true in the case of arcane issues such as intellectual property. While a great many laypeople hold well-informed and deeply passionate views on subjects that play heavily in the news media, such as war, immigration, and healthcare, only a handful of very geeky people know or care much about copyright, patent, or trademark (it's probably safe to say that the average person doesn't even know the difference between them). Thus, very few elected officials enter office with even a shred of interest or expertise in the subject of intellectual property. It's not sexy enough an issue for either campaigning or fund-raising, so there's also little incentive or opportunity for legislators to become better educated than they were as laypeople, which means that by the time most of them vote on IP-related legislation, much of what they know about the issue has been learned from lobbyists.

This education, of course, comes hand in hand with funding and campaign support of various kinds. Sadly, these are at least as necessary to the legislators as the information they receive. For a variety of reasons, it has become largely impossible in this era to run a campaign of any size without a significant external source of funding, and thus lobbyists play a crucial role for any legislator hoping to gain and keep office.

IP and Lobbying: Who, What, and How Much

Who actually lobbies for intellectual property laws and policies, and how does this process work? Thanks to the transparency laws noted above, we have fairly clear data on lobbying for the last two decades or so. According to the reports generated by lobbying firms and analyzed by the Center for Responsive Politics, between 200 and 500 companies and organizations have paid for IP-related lobbying at the federal level each year since 1998. While the numbers vary annually depending on the economic and political climate, the trend is generally upward; between 1998 and 2006, an average of 274 companies lobbied each year on IP-related issues, and that average climbed to 410 for the years from 2007 to 2015.

As you might expect, the companies most involved in lobbying for IP laws tend to be either copyright-driven entities (for example, the media and communications sectors) or patent-driven ones (such as the pharmaceutical and tech sectors). Over the years, this distinction has blurred as mergers, acquisitions, vertical and horizontal integration, industry consolidation, and "convergence" between media, communications, and technology have created mega-corporations with a stake in virtually every IP-related business sector (a good example is Alphabet, best known as Google's parent company but also a growing force in cutting-edge health and wellness research).

In 1998, the earliest year for which such data are available, the top ten companies paying lobbyists for IP-related work accounted for about 13 percent of the 692 reports generated by lobbyist firms related to this issue. The list includes four organizations from the media and communications sectors (the Recording Industry Association of America; BSA, also known as the Software Alliance; performing rights organization BMI; the Motion Picture Association of America) and four pharmaceutical companies (Schering-Plough, now part of Merck; Pharmaceutical Research & Manufacturers of America [PhRMA]; Roche; Bristol-Myers Squibb). As this list shows, both individual titans and trade groups representing industry consortia (some of which technically count as lobbyists themselves) ranked among the chief spenders on lobbying.

In 2015, the most recent year for which we have complete data at the time of writing, the top ten clients lobbying for IP laws and policies accounted for about 11 percent of the 2,759 reports related to this issue. The list includes five organizations from the media and communications sectors (Comcast; Intel; iHeartMedia; Microsoft; BSA), four from the pharmaceutical and biotech sectors (PhRMA; Biotechnology Industry Organization; AstraZeneca; Amgen), and one that represents both (Alphabet—the top lobbying client of the year). Again, the list includes a mixture of individual companies and industry trade groups, with some consistent contributors, such as BSA and PhRMA.

While lobbying reports work well as a general indication of the amount of money flowing between the private sector and government officials related to broad areas of interest, they lack the granularity or specificity to tell us exactly *how much* an organization is spending to lobby *whom* for *what*. Though a report will cite a specific dollar figure received by a given firm from a given client, it may list several issues covered by that figure, several individual lobbyists at the firm, and several targets for lobbying, generalized by

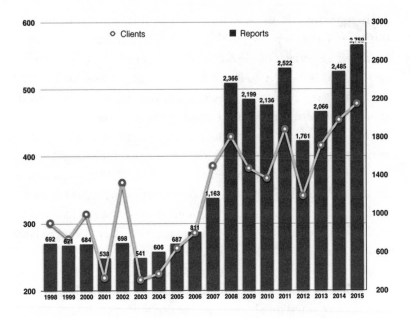

Figure 10: Federal lobbying clients and reports
for intellectual property, 1998–2015.

governmental division rather than broken out by individual law-makers or regulators.

For instance, one of these thousands of reports shows that Google paid lobbying firm Capitol Legislative Strategies $50,000 at some point in the first quarter of 2016. The money was related to lobbying efforts by two employees at the firm, Charles Mellody and Jenna Hamilton. The figure covered several specific lobbying issues, including immigration, business competition, privacy, and cybersecurity. The form indicates that the targets of these lobbying efforts were both the Senate and the House of Representatives. Some of this money may possibly be related to IP ("cybersecurity" bills typically contain provisions related to policing IP infringement). Then again, it may not. Even if it is, we have no way of knowing what percentage of the $50,000 is related to that specific issue, what Google's actual position on the issue was, or which specific senators and congresspeople received the benefits of Capitol Legislative Strategies' education and largesse.

All told, according to analysis conducted by OpenSecrets.org, lobbying clients spent a little more than $3.6 billion from 2011 to 2015 on reports that explicitly mention copyright, patent, or trademark issues. Though we can't ascribe this whole figure to only IP for the reasons cited above, it's reasonable to conclude that at least $1 billion of this total was spent by these clients during this five-year period specifically to influence intellectual property law and policy at the federal level.

While there is no way to track who received these IP-related lobbying funds, it is possible to assess how much a given lawmaker has received overall in lobbying support during a given election cycle. During a presidential election year, non-sitting presidential candidates typically receive the most by far. During a midterm election, it's often the most influential lawmakers who collect the highest figures. In the 2014 cycle, for instance, the top three recipients were Mitch McConnell (the Senate minority leader), Arkansas senator Mark Pryor (who himself became a lobbyist the following year after losing the election), and John Boehner (the Speaker of the House of Representatives). As we will see below, these somewhat detailed but still maddeningly vague findings become a little more concrete when we examine the individuals involved in lobbying, their methods, and the related outcomes in terms of actual legislation and policy.

There are more lobbyists than lawmakers in Washington, by orders of magnitude. Like lawmakers, they may specialize in certain areas of policy, have differing levels of economic power and prominence, and may bring different social and institutional connections to the table. A single client may employ dozens of lobbyists in a single year, each with a different expertise or set of connections vital to the client's particular interests.

In 1998, the top lobbying client related to copyright, patent, and trademark issues was the Recording Industry Association of America (RIAA) which, as its name suggests, is a trade group representing the interests of record labels. That year, the organization employed thirty lobbyists, of whom twenty had what are often referred to as "revolving door" profiles. As the Center for Responsive Politics describes it, the revolving door process "shuffles former federal employees into jobs as lobbyists, consultants and strategists just as the door pulls former hired guns into government careers."[2] In fact, one of these lobbyists, Dennis DeConcini, had himself been a senator for Arizona from 1977 to 1995 (after being investigated as one of the "Keating Five" in a major corruption scandal in the early 1990s, DeConcini declined to run for reelection). While there are no available records regarding the issues or bills he lobbied for that year, more than half of his thirty-nine clients in 1998 were in the pharmaceutical and health sector, and several more were in the media and communications fields, suggesting that intellectual property law was one of his specialties.

In 2015, the top lobbying client for IP-related issues was Alphabet. Out of the eighty-four lobbyists hired by the firm that year, sixty-five of them had revolving door profiles, including David T. Murray, whose two-decade lobbying career was punctuated by a stint at the Commerce Department from 2005 to 2011, and Susan Molinari, a congresswoman from New York between 1991 to 1997, who had a brief career as a television journalist on CBS following her resignation from the House. Of the sixty-six lobbyist reports from 2015 bearing Murray's name, sixteen of them specifically cite intellectual property as an issue, and fifteen of them (probably an overlapping subset) cite specific pending IP legislation—in this case, both House and Senate bills related to cybersecurity and patent reform. While Murray appears to be an issue-centric lobbyist, representing more than a dozen firms with shared concerns about IP and telecommunications, Molinari is a client-specific one, solely representing Alphabet as an in-house lobbyist on dozens of issues ranging from IP to taxes to immigration. Like Murray, she also lobbied specifically on the issues of patent reform and cybersecurity in 2015.

Lobbying at the state level is very similar to the process at the federal level: professional firms representing the interests of corporations and other stakeholders provide education, finance, and additional perquisites to lawmakers and other government employees, with the expectation that their spending and efforts will influence policy. Because most IP law is federal, most IP lobbying happens at the federal level. Yet IP-centric companies do spend a significant amount of money on lobbying state governments, and some of that is related to state-level IP policy and enforcement (for instance, state attorneys general sometimes play a key role in targeting alleged infringers, and certain forms of IP law, such as rights of publicity, are based on state rather than federal statute). According to data made available via the website followthemoney.org, the pharmaceutical and health sector and the communications and electronics sector spent over half a billion dollars—$541,138,782, to be precise—lobbying state agencies between 2002 and 2015, with an average expenditure of over $10,000.

The biggest spenders on state lobbying in 2015 include companies that have been very active in IP lobbying at the federal level, including telecommunications giants like AT&T, Verizon, and Comcast; pharmaceutical interests like Pfizer, GlaxoSmithKline, and PhRMA; and media-oriented clients such as the RIAA and the Motion Picture Association of America (MPAA). And, of course, Google. Unfortunately, publicly available databases of state lobbying expenditures don't include details about the issues attached to the checks, so there's no way for us to know what portion of these funds went toward IP-related policy, but given its central importance to companies in these sectors, the figure is no doubt significant.

Lobbying in the Lawmaking Process

So far, most of this chapter has been dedicated to documenting the facts and figures of lobbying, giving us a sense of the specific clientele, lobbyists, governmental targets, and dollar figures at work behind the scenes of IP policy. But how does all of this money and effort actually turn into law? While the details of lobbyist-lawmaker interactions don't appear on the dotted lines of federal paperwork, they have been studied fairly extensively over the years by political scientists, law scholars, and other researchers. One law scholar who has written both widely and persuasively about this process as it applies to intellectual property is Jessica Litman, a professor at the University of Michigan Law School. As she discusses, the lobbying efforts behind copyright law are preceded by an "inter-industry negotiation process." In her words, "For the past 100 years, Congress has relied on lobbyists for copyright-affected industries to get together with each other and negotiate the language for any new copyright legislation. When all the lobbyists have worked out their disagreements and arrived at language they can all live with (commonly with some House and Senate Report language to accompany it), they give it to Congress and Congress passes the bill, often by unanimous consent."[3]

Thus, according to Litman, the deliberation that's ideally supposed to take place between publicly elected representatives on the floor of the House or the Senate actually takes place between paid representatives of private interests in closed-door meetings, and the negotiated results are then passed on to the legislature to be rubber-stamped and made into law. A quick glimpse at legislative history supports these claims: the Copyright Act of 1976 passed the Senate with a vote of 97-0 and the House with a vote of 316-7. Both major revisions to the law enacted in 1998, the Digital Millennium Copyright Act and the Copyright Term Extension Act, passed the Senate with unanimous consent and passed the House with voice votes (the specific tallies of such votes are not recorded).

Furthermore, as Litman observes, because this inter-industry negotiation ultimately shapes the laws that will be passed by Congress, one of the major factors influencing the outcome of these negotiations is the decision about *who* gets a seat at negotiating table, both literally and figuratively. In the case of the DMCA, which included "anti-circumvention" provisions making it a felony to bypass encryption placed around content by its distributors (even if bypassing such encryption is the only way to exercise fair use), the negotiating table conveniently lacked any representatives from either libraries or universities, which rely heavily on fair use rights. Instead, as Litman describes, they "were shunted off into a special, topic-specific negotiation about library copying and distance education, and excluded for a time from the talks that led to the overall strategy of the bill."[4]

This was not a coincidence or an accident but rather the direct result of lobbyist oversight of the negotiation process. In Litman's words, "A lot of lobbyist energy has gone into questions of who gets to play."[5] These days, lobbyists don't merely help to draft bills and convince legislators to pass them—they actively play a role in including and excluding interests from the negotiating process to begin with. Stakeholders that lack the funds or connections to engage in lobbying at the level of large media, communications, and pharmaceutical companies, from universities to libraries to nonprofit organizations representing the public interest, tend to get left out in the cold.

Given the growing number of lobbyists, clients, and dollars spent on this process over the decades and the intimate role that lobbyists play in nearly every stage of the legislative process, it seems self-evident that lobbying *works*—that is to say, it accomplishes actual policy changes that positively benefit clients' bottom lines and strategic positions in their markets. Although no one has yet published research that empirically shows this to be the case with respect to IP laws and policy, several recent studies have shown that this is true for lobbying in general or for specific case studies examined by researchers. A 2009 study, for instance, found that not only did companies receive a 220:1 economic return on investment for their lobbying expenditures, but "corporations that lobbied received the lion's share of the available benefits and those corporations were concentrated within a fairly small group of industries." At the top of the list were several IP-centric companies in the pharmaceutical, tech, and communications industries; Pfizer, Merck, and Hewlett-Packard occupied the top three positions.[6]

Lobbying is such a reliable indicator of a company's long-term financial success that Strategas, an institutional brokerage firm, has assembled a "lobbying index" tracking the fifty companies spending the most money on lobbying year by year. This index, which includes several pharmaceutical firms, has outperformed traditional market indices like the S&P every year for well over a decade. In lay terms, this means that the biggest lobbying clients are consistently worth more than companies of similar sizes in the same industries that don't spend as much on lobbying.[7]

IP and Campaign Finance

Lobbying isn't the only way in which interested parties can flex their economic and political muscles to help shape IP laws and policy. Another major conduit of money and influence flowing from the corporate sector to the legislature comes in the form of campaign finance. While lobbying is technically a form of education, conveniently paired with various perquisites and financial incentives, there are no such ambiguities about campaign contributions—they are straightforward expressions of financial support for legislators and other elected officials, who are then expected to vote or govern in a way that is beneficial to the contributing party.

While lobbying reports typically mention specific issues or even specific legislation about which the lobbyists are intended to help educate, inform, and influence their beneficiaries, there is no such explicit correspondence between campaign contributions and the policies they are intended to affect. AT&T or Comcast may donate money to a Senate candidate, for instance, but the check doesn't come with a note attached to it saying, "Please deregulate the telecommunications industry." Instead, such expectations are usually communicated via lobbyist intermediaries—thus, lobbying and campaign finance work hand in hand as a multifaceted approach to influencing policy.

As with lobbying activities, campaign contributions in the U.S. are regulated and monitored by federal and state governments in order to minimize the potential for corruption. There are limits on how much an individual or organization can donate to a candidate or committee and reporting requirements for recipients of donations, which vary according to a range of factors as well as from state to state. The result is a vast morass of semi-transparent data, much of which can be searched via the same nonprofit websites that make lobbying records available.

Searching through these data looking for the role of campaign finance in shaping IP law and policy is even more challenging and less fruitful than searching the data from lobbyist reports. Without any indication of which dollars correspond to which intended outcomes, we can make only circumstantial claims. Based on data made available by the Center for Responsive Politics, we can ascertain that, as of the time of writing, companies in the pharmaceutical industry and the communications and electronics sector donated a combined total of about $2 billion to federal candidates between 1989 and 2016.

This total includes individual donations from company employees or organizational members, donations from affiliated political action committees (PACs), and "soft money" from corporate and union treasuries. During this same time period, according to the National Institute for Money in State Politics, the same sectors and industries contributed $1.22 billion to state and local candidates.[8] As with lobbying expenditures, the stakes have grown higher over the years, and the vast majority of these campaign contributions have taken place over the past decade.

How much of this roughly $3 billion spent by media, communications, tech, and pharmaceutical interests was related to IP law? Perhaps the best way to answer is to look at the top donors and compare their spending habits to their lobbying agendas. If we compare a list of the top twenty campaign donors in the communications and electronics sector and the top twenty in the pharmaceutical industry with a list of the top forty-eight clients lobbying on copyright, patent, and trademark issues in 2015, we see a considerable overlap: eighteen companies appear on both lists.[9] The correlation becomes even higher when we consider that several top contributors belong to trade groups that lobby on their collective behalf. For instance, the list of the twenty top pharmaceutical donors includes ten companies that aren't top lobbying clients themselves but are members of PhRMA, which is currently the second-largest lobbying client on IP-related issues at the federal level.

All told, the vast majority of top campaign funders in IP-centric business sectors are also among the top lobbying clients for copyright, patent, and trademark issues, either singly or via industry trade groups. Thus, it seems more than likely that a significant portion of the billions of dollars they've contributed to local, state, and federal

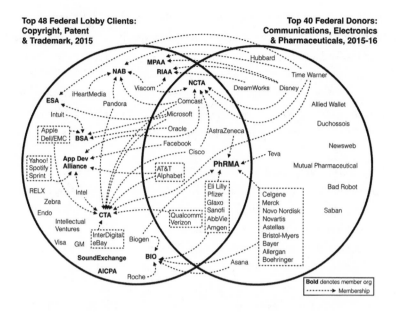

Figure 11: Top IP-related lobby clients and campaign donors, 2015–16.

campaigns over the past few decades was spent with the expectation that it would help influence intellectual property policy in a way that directly benefits their businesses.

As with lobbying, there is strong evidence suggesting that campaign finance achieves strategic policy goals on behalf of contributors and creates measurable profit for donor companies above and beyond what they could otherwise expect in the marketplace. A 2010 study in the *Journal of Finance*, which analyzed twenty-five years' worth of Federal Election Commission (FEC) data as well as financial filings from publicly traded companies, found "a strong and robust correlation" between companies that supported a greater number of candidates and "a firm's future abnormal [greater than expected] returns" as well as "a positive link between the number of supported candidates and the firm's future earnings." The authors conclude by arguing that their findings strongly suggest political contributions are motivated primarily by profit rather than patriotism. In their words, "Our results are consistent with the idea that firms participate in the political system not from the standpoint of consuming a patriotic consumption good ... but rather from the standpoint of creating positive net present value investments."[10]

Off the Grid: Dark Money and Secret Negotiations

Above and beyond the traceable flow of money from interested parties to political candidates and officeholders, there are a number of other ways in which stakeholders can use their money and other forms of leverage to influence IP law and policy. One method that bears many similarities to campaign finance, but without even the semi-transparency of this practice, is the use of "dark money." Broadly speaking, this term refers to a variety of legal technicalities that enable individuals, corporations, and organizations—both within the U.S. and around the world—to fund American political campaigns without either the spending limits or the disclosure requirements that are typically obligatory under campaign finance laws.

There are two major components of the dark money process. First of all, nonprofit organizations (which fall under section 501(c) of the United States Internal Revenue Code) may raise as much money as they like, without revealing their donors, and then spend the funds on political activities, so long as such activities are not their "primary purpose." In many cases, this simply means they spend 49.9 percent—a technical minority—of their funds on political contributions. Second, so-called Super PACs (a relatively new species of political action committee) are permitted to raise an unlimited amount of money from nonprofits and shell corporations, neither of which is required to reveal its own membership or donor list, then spend the money to support or attack a political candidate. The

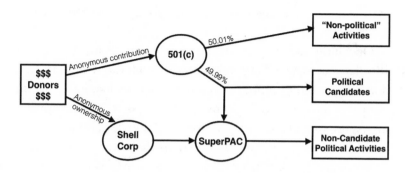

Figure 12: The flow of dark money from donors to campaigns.

only limitations on Super PACs are that they must not directly fund or coordinate with a given candidate, and that they must report their donors (the anonymously funded nonprofits and shell corporations) to the FEC.

The net result, of course, is that interested parties can funnel as much money as they like into political campaigns without revealing their identities or intentions. While they are prohibited from coordinating directly with candidates, this problem may be solved through the use of lobbyists as intermediaries. This new system, which was strengthened through a series of court decisions in recent years (most notably the 2010 U.S. Supreme Court decision in *Citizens United v. FEC*), has led to a sudden influx of untraceable dollars into the political campaign process. In the 2012 election cycle, according to an analysis of FEC data by the Center for Responsive Politics, $308.7 million was spent by untraceable donors —three times the amount spent during the 2008 cycle and *fifty-two times* as much as in 2004.[11] The official tally for the 2016 cycle dropped significantly to $178.4 million, although at the time of writing, there are several simultaneous scandals unfolding about potentially illegal and unethical forms of influence peddling and even collusion between campaigns and foreign governments during this election.

Obviously, ascribing a portion of dark money expenditures to IP-related law and policy is even more difficult than connecting the dots in the case of more transparent processes like lobbying and campaign finance spending. There are no reports conveniently listing issues, funders, and targets compiled and searchable via nonprofit websites. Yet there are indications that intellectual property is part of the agenda when it comes to this form of influence as well. In both the 2014 and 2016 election cycles, the top spender of funds from undisclosed donors was the U.S. Chamber of Commerce, a 501(c)(6) nonprofit organization that, according to its website, represents "the interests of more than 3 million businesses of all sizes, sectors, and regions."[12] The chamber is an active lobbying client as well, hiring firms to educate and influence lawmakers and other public officials on dozens of issues relating to American business interests. Among these dozens of issues, IP policy has risen in the ranks over the years, entering the chamber's top five most lobbied issues in 2008 and remaining in the top five almost every year since then.

In fact, most if not all of the major IP-related laws and treaties that have been proposed and/or enacted over the past decade have been promoted with lobbying funds from the chamber. This includes legislation and policy documents such as the PRO-IP Act (2008), which instituted a federal "copyright czar"; SOPA (2012), which sparked widespread protests over its potential to weaken free speech and user rights in its efforts to strengthen online copyright; and the IP section of the Trans-Pacific Partnership (2016), a controversial trade accord that we will discuss in greater detail in the next chapter. While there is no paper trail explicitly connecting the chamber's continuing investment in lobbying for IP policy to its role as a conduit for untraceable campaign contributions, it is reasonable to conclude that the two agendas are linked.

Another data point that bolsters this conclusion is the evident relationship among dark money, lobbying, and specific candidates and campaigns. In the 2014 election cycle, the candidate who won office with the most support from dark money was North Carolina senator Thom Tillis. According to records compiled at OpenSecrets.org, Tillis's campaign was aided by about $48 million in untraceable funds, two-thirds of which were spent campaigning *against* his opponents rather than directly supporting his candidacy. The top source of nonprofit dark money in Tillis's race was the U.S. Chamber of Commerce, which spent over $5.6 million to influence his election.

Since winning, Tillis has sponsored or co-sponsored several IP-related bills (some successfully enacted) for which the chamber has actively lobbied. One recent example is the Defend Trade Secrets Act of 2016, which creates "a private civil cause of action for trade secret misappropriation," strengthening this historically limited form of intellectual property protection. The bill passed in May 2016 after two years of extensive lobbying by a variety of interested parties. The second most aggressive lobbyist was the U.S. Chamber of Commerce, which appears as a client in seven different lobbying reports that specifically cite the bill.

While these connections between dark money and IP law are admittedly tenuous and circumstantial, there are two good reasons to give them credence. First of all, under current U.S. law, it's impossible to find an actual paper trail or "smoking gun" linking the two; in the absence of such documentation, these inferential connections are the best indication we can come by that dark money leads directly to specific policy outcomes. Second, these aren't random data points; the connections we have explored here are typical. The number of bills and other policy documents that correspond to dark money sources and lobbying records is overwhelming, suggesting a widespread role for dark money as a form of influence across all party lines, geographic boundaries, and political issues, up to the highest levels of government. To cite one relatively recent example, investigative journalists at the *Telegraph* revealed that a Donald Trump–related Super PAC directly agreed to grant "influence" to donors purporting to represent a Chinese billionaire.[13] In short, our analysis of the role of dark money with respect to intellectual property could just as easily have been reproduced for laws related to agriculture, defense, or healthcare.

Parties seeking to influence IP policy without leaving a paper trail have additional options beyond dark money. In some cases, when legislative efforts haven't been successful, stakeholders have worked directly with regulators and other enforcers to make de facto changes to policy without the force of law behind them. This is exactly what happened in the case of the Copyright Alert System (CAS). For years, the MPAA and other representatives of America's copyright-centric industries lobbied for a "graduated response" approach to stopping unlicensed sharing of content over the internet. Under such a system, internet service providers would be required to keep track of their own customers' online behaviors. If an ISP suspected one of its customers of accessing or sharing copyrighted materials without permission, it would be required to send the customer a warning note. If the customer ignored the note, she would face a gradual throttling of her internet service, until after several alleged infringements she would finally be blocked from using the internet altogether.

Other nations, such as the UK and France, have passed similar laws (at the urging of American business and political interests, as we will explore in the next chapter), but the idea never received enough legislative support to become law in the U.S. This fact is due in part to the serious implications for free speech and due process that such a law would entail—not to mention that the policy ignores fair use altogether. Seeing the futility of a legislative approach in the near term, the MPAA and its allies switched their focus from Congress to the federally appointed "copyright czar" (technically, the intellectual property enforcement coordinator, or IPEC), Victoria Espinel.

With Espinel's unofficial help (in some cases via emails sent from her personal Gmail account rather than her official government account), representatives of the film and music industries met with executives from the country's largest ISPs and hashed out a secret deal to begin a graduated response program in the U.S. The deal was officially announced in 2011, but not before the vice president's office and the Justice Department had weighed in on the negotiations (again without leaving any official paper trail). The resulting CAS, which gave ISP customers five alerts regarding their suspected infringement before "mitigation measures" such as bandwidth throttling were implemented, went into effect in 2013. It was discontinued in 2017 after failing to achieve many of its stated goals.

Despite the integral role played by several branches of the federal government in these negotiations, the government was not a technical signatory to the agreement, and its role would have remained secret and invisible were it not for privacy researcher Christopher Soghoian, who filed a Freedom of Information Act (FOIA) request for access to the relevant emails, then shared his findings with *Wired* magazine, which published a exposé.[14] The active role of lobbyists in the process may be inferred from the fact that the term *graduated response* appears in over a hundred lobbying reports over the past decade, the vast majority of them listing the MPAA and National Amusements (an international cinema chain and parent company of both CBS and Viacom) as the clients. A great many of these reports, most of which date from the years 2009 to 2012, also cite IPEC as an issue (suggesting Espinel's role without explicitly stating it) and document lobbying efforts targeted at the Justice Department, the Office of the Vice President, and other federal agencies.

As with dark money contributions, there is no way for us to know the full scope of these kinds of secret negotiations because they are, by definition, off the record. Nor is there any way to gauge to what extent federal and state governments are involved in brokering such deals without filing a great many more FOIA requests. Yet there are enough data points obtained via leaks, whistleblowers, and investigations like Soghoian's to suggest that, like dark money contributions, the practice is fairly widespread. Indeed, a great many of the technical obstructions built to prevent us from using and sharing copyrighted work without permission have no basis in copyright law itself. Ever wonder why your eBook reader won't read books out loud to you, why you can't easily copy songs from an iPod to a laptop, or why you can't watch a DVD purchased in Asia on a machine purchased in the U.S.? It's not because any of these activities are illegal but rather because the technology is intentionally limited to restrict you from exercising your full scope of legal rights over the content. In many of these cases, such restrictions are the result of inter-industry negotiation processes hashed out between rights holders and tech manufacturers in secret or closed-door meetings, with or without the participation of government agencies and officials.

This chapter has focused on the role of lobbying, campaign finance, and other forms of persuasion to shape IP law and policy *within* the United States. As complex and confusing as these processes may be, they tell only half the story. Equally important is the role of intellectual property as an aspect of international relations, including the role of lobbying, finance, and other forms of persuasion in shaping the treaties and accords that govern those relationships. This will be the subject of our next chapter.

SIX

Intellectual Property in the Global Arena

In the previous chapter, we delved into some of the political mechanisms behind intellectual property law and policy in the U.S. As we discussed, powerful stakeholders in copyright- and patent-dependent industries spend billions of dollars a year via lobbying, campaign finance, and other channels to help shape the contours of domestic IP, with a well-founded expectation that their investments will pay off by creating markets in which they exercise greater influence and reap bigger benefits over the long term.

As complex as this process is, the relationship between private interests and public policy becomes exponentially more convoluted when we consider the role of intellectual property in the global arena. Because IP is so deeply entwined with culture, with industry, with markets, and with the political process itself, it comes to play a role in almost every aspect of international relations, from friendly trade to cautious protectionism to outright warfare. And because each sovereign nation has its own laws and each culture has its own traditions and worldviews, there are inevitably points of friction in even the friendliest relations.

Whose version of copyright and patent should govern international sales and licenses? Which authorities should regulate the global markets, and which courts should adjudicate disputes? Whose cultural traditions will be deemed legal, and whose will be prohibited? And what about nations that refuse to accept the terms of these negotiations? Are they outlaws, rogues, or merely independent sovereignties entitled to their own way of conducting their internal affairs? In the case of intellectual property, such tensions aren't merely difficult to navigate, they're nearly impossible to define and distinguish.

As Thomas Jefferson pointed out centuries ago, ideas aren't like other forms of property. They don't stay in a person's closet or a nation's vaults, waiting to be exploited once by a single person for a single purpose. Instead, they leap from mind to mind, from town to town, from nation to nation. Books, movies, songs, and software—the expressions of these ideas—behave in much the same way, traveling around the globe literally at light speed along fiber optic cables and high-bandwidth satellite links. Inventions and discoveries are much the same. A molecule can be replicated, a mechanism can be reverse engineered, a design can be copied and improved upon—and then reintroduced into the marketplace—with greater ease and faster speed in each passing year.

Although the speed of transmission may have changed since Jefferson's day, the underlying tensions of IP in a global context have not. In fact, not only were these tensions present from the very birth of copyright and patent, they were part of the genesis for intellectual property in the first place. As historian Adrian Johns demonstrates in his book *Piracy: The Intellectual Property Wars from Gutenberg to Gates*, "The invention of copyright itself was largely a response to a piracy feud overflowing with national resentments, namely the attempt of Scottish reprinters to compete with London's book trade in the first generation when both lived in a 'united kingdom.' "¹ Thus intellectual property doesn't so much create tensions between nations as it illuminates, exacerbates, and formalizes them within a matrix of international law and trade obligations.

In this chapter, we will examine some of the ways in which these tensions arise and are either resolved or not, depending on the state of diplomatic relations between allies and rivals in the global marketplace. We will consider the logic of "harmonization," the effort to develop a unifying set of IP principles that apply across national and regional boundaries. We will also review some examples of cultural stakeholders who lack the power to participate in these high-stakes games of international negotiation and brinkmanship, and explore the fate of cultural traditions whose norms, ethics, and/or aesthetics do not match the increasingly stringent delineations of a harmonized global IP system.

IP Treaties: The First Century

Even though the earliest copyright laws were intended, in part, to ward off market competition *from* neighboring countries, the notion of trying to influence intellectual property laws and policies *within* other countries—or, for that matter, respecting the IP rights *of* other countries—is a somewhat newer idea. For instance, as we touched upon briefly in chapter 1, the U.S. didn't recognize the copyrights of foreign authors until 1891, more than a century after the nation passed its first copyright law.

This wasn't a mere oversight but rather a calculated decision that benefited the bottom line of American publishers while making it easier for the richer and more diverse universe of European public culture to reach American audiences swiftly and cheaply. It simply didn't make sense for America to give up these substantial benefits only to send a percentage of book sales revenue back to publishers in England, the very monarchy from which the nation had just liberated itself politically and economically. Better to keep the money "in the family," providing an economic boost to America's homegrown publishing industry and thereby generating more economic incentives and market opportunities for American authors and ideas.

Yet this omission was just as much a matter of protocol as it was of pragmatism. Even if America had *wanted* to pay royalties on English books to their copyright holders, the domestic industry would have expected some form of reciprocity—an assurance that English publishers would also pay royalties to American ones for use of their work. This would have required not only some kind of formal trade agreement but also the mechanism for policing the terms of the agreement, ensuring that rules were followed and dues were paid. In short, it would have meant a lot of international cooperation between two nations with a recent history of war (fomented, in part, by American publications) and tentative diplomatic relations.

In those early years of IP, even countries with strong alliances and trade relationships didn't engage in any kind of reciprocal recognition of rights. The first such agreements, bilateral copyright accords hashed out on an ad hoc basis, emerged during the early 1800s. Later in the century, European and American inventors began to raise a call for reciprocal recognition of patent rights—largely due to the increasingly central role of international exhibitions in the sharing of new discoveries and devices. But it was only at the very end of the 1800s that the first stable, binding multilateral international intellectual property treaties were developed between industrialized nations with a shared interest in developing a global marketplace for publications and inventions.

The first major international IP accord was the Paris Convention for the Protection of Industrial Property, signed in 1883. Under the terms of this treaty, each signatory nation respects the patents, trademarks, and related IP of each other signatory, treating foreign inventors and designers the same as domestic ones and granting priority to the first filer for a given patent or mark, regardless of the nation of origin. While the treaty doesn't unify the terms of the patent and trademark laws in the signatory states, or force one nation to grant a patent just because another nation has, it does provide "common rules" that each signatory must follow. Seven European nations and Brazil signed the initial treaty in 1883. By the end of the nineteenth century, the number of "contracting parties" (nations agreeing to the treaty's terms) had doubled to sixteen, including the United States. As of 2018, the treaty is still active and has 177 contracting parties.

Shortly after the Paris Convention, in 1886 another major international IP treaty was signed: the Berne Convention for the Protection of Literary and Artistic Works. The terms of this treaty are similar to those of the Paris Convention but refer to copyright rather than to patent and trademark. According to the treaty's original terms, each contracting party was required to grant the work of foreign authors and creators the same protection as it granted to its own nationals, for a period of ten years. The agreement has been amended significantly since then—for instance, a clause covering moral rights was added and the minimum term of protection was extended to an author's life plus fifty years. Seven European countries and Tunisia signed the treaty initially, and as of 2018 there are 176 contracting parties, including the United States, which signed on in 1988.

In the century and a half since the Paris and Berne conventions, there have been dozens of additional treaties and accords governing the use of intellectual property in the global arena, all of them further extending the scope and increasing the strength of protection while deepening the level of international collaboration in the policing and prosecution of IP infringement. Yet each of these agreements represented an incremental step—a little ratcheting up here, a little tightening up there—until a new species of IP accords emerged in the 1990s.

Modern IP Treaties: TRIPS and Harmonization

The modern history of international IP agreements begins with something called the Uruguay Round—an eight-year effort from 1986 to 1994 by 123 contracting parties to develop a new general framework for international trade that would bring previously separate issues, such as international finance, agriculture, and intellectual property, under one umbrella. This unification of function was a clever move by the more powerful parties to the accord: they could make one aspect of trade contingent on all the others (kind of like saying, "You can come to my awesome birthday party but only if you wear a funny hat, dance the whip and nae nae, and buy me an iPad"). Smaller and less powerful nations could no longer pick and choose which aspects of international trade they wished to participate in—from now on, it would be all or nothing.

One of the major accomplishments of the Uruguay Round was to create a new intergovernmental organization called the World Trade Organization (WTO for short; watch out, this section will have a lot of acronyms). To continue our birthday party analogy, the WTO is like the grownup who plays host to all of the partygoers; the organization provides a home for international trade agreements, plans events, structures relationships, and resolves disputes between members ("Ecuador pulled my hair!" "No, Thailand started it!"). At the time of writing, the WTO has 164 members, with another 23 states currently in the process of joining. It is not an understatement to say that in the twenty-first century, it is impossible to have a thriving national economy without being a WTO member; as of the time of writing, 49 of the 50 wealthiest nations ranked by gross national income are members, and the remaining country (Iran) is in the process of joining.[2]

Along with establishing the WTO, the Uruguay Round also created the first intellectual property accord to be administrated under the new organization. This was called the Agreement on Trade-Related Aspects of Intellectual Property Rights, or TRIPS for short. The agreement which, like many other aspects of WTO-administered policy, is *mandatory* for all member states, goes far beyond any previous IP treaty or pact. In the words of law professor Susan K. Sell, who wrote the definitive legal history and analysis of TRIPS, it represents "a dramatic expansion of the rights of IP owners and a significant instance of the exercise of private power."[3]

What does this "dramatic expansion" consist of, and what does "private power" have to do with deals made between state governments? In a nutshell, TRIPS and the international treaties that have followed in the past two decades represent a significant break from history because they (1) impose new laws on parties rather than building a consensus from existing laws; (2) expand the scope and strength of IP coverage drastically compared to previous levels for most members; (3) use the leverage of the WTO to impose trade sanctions against states that don't comply; (4) create a foundation for "harmonized" intellectual property policy, applying a one-size-fits-all approach to lawmaking that is virtually unprecedented in international law; and (5) represent the interests and agendas of a few specific industries above the national interests of the broad citizenry in member states.

To be a bit more specific, the new laws imposed by TRIPS included new forms of intellectual property (such as semiconductor chip rights), new categories of protected expression (such as software, databases, and sound recordings for copyright and "virtually all subject matter" other than living organisms for patents), longer minimum terms for both copyrights (life plus fifty years) and patents (twenty years), mandatory enforcement protocols within member states and at borders, and mandatory criminal punishment, including imprisonment, for some forms of infringement (historically, IP has been considered more of an issue for civil law, which seeks compensation rather than punishment from those who have violated it).[4]

The role of the WTO as compliance watchdog is also unprecedented in the world of intellectual property. According to the terms of agreement, the Council for TRIPS, comprised of representatives of WTO member states, has fairly sweeping power to "monitor" member compliance with the agreement and to authorize trade sanctions by one member state against another in the case of noncompliance.

It is hard to overstate how new and transformative this power is. To return to our earlier analogy, imagine if the host of the birthday party had the right to follow the partygoers home, peek through their windows, and make sure they shared the contents of their goody bags with their brothers and sisters; the right to authorize other partygoers to exclude them from future parties and activities; and even the right to demand candy and toys from them as a punishment for not sharing equitably. This is a great arrangement if you prioritize fairness and following the rules above privacy and autonomy, but a painful pill to swallow if your priorities are different.

Thus TRIPS represents a significant departure from earlier IP agreements by requiring all WTO members to adopt new, more stringent laws and by installing a nongovernmental authority above member states that supersedes sovereign power in some ways. Yet the most radical element of the accord is in its shift away from negotiation, interpretation, and consensus as the basis for international agreements and toward a top-down, harmonized approach to policy making. This is not merely a new method for managing international trade relations, it's a new philosophy.

Both supporters and opponents of IP harmonization agree that this approach to coordinated lawmaking and enforcement lowers the old barriers between sovereign states, reduces "friction" in trade, and creates a single globalized (or, at the very least, international) marketplace for information-based goods and services. They differ only on the question of who benefits from this arrangement, and whether these benefits are worth the costs.

One of the major arguments in favor of harmonized IP laws is that they help to globalize every other form of economic activity. Companies in one nation can do business with companies in other nations or delegate work to laborers in other nations, secure in the knowledge that their copyright, patents, trademarks, and trade secrets will be protected just as much abroad as they are at home.

Another, related argument is that many innovative goods and services, such as pharmaceuticals, blockbuster movies, and cutting-edge technologies, require a significant amount of time and capital to develop before they yield a product that can be patented or copyrighted. The movie *Pirates of the Caribbean: At World's End* cost over $300 million to produce, and that was before a single cent was spent on marketing and promoting the film.[5] As we discussed in chapter 3, the cost to develop a new medicine can be even greater.

Proponents of harmonization argue that with price tags this high, the only way a big company feels secure enough to invest in a new product is if it has a reasonable expectation that the product will sell just as well abroad as it does in the company's home country, and that it won't be "pirated," counterfeited, or otherwise undermined by IP infringement once it passes national borders. It also follows, according to this argument, that harmonization benefits the citizenry as much as it does the commercial sector because consumers might not have access to entertaining films or life-saving medicines without international products in their local markets.

The main argument against harmonization is that it stacks the deck unfairly against smaller and "developing" nations, forcing them into long-term economic and cultural subservience to bigger, more powerful countries. This is because not every WTO member has an equal amount at stake in protecting IP rights and exploiting intellectual property internationally. The people of Croatia and Ghana watch a significant number of American movies and television shows, and consume a significant volume of Swiss pharmaceuticals (Novartis, the largest pharma company by market capitalization at the time of writing, is based in Basel). Yet there is virtually no market for Croatian movies or Ghanaian pharmaceuticals in the U.S. or Switzerland.

This one-way flow of information goods and services from wealthier to poorer nations means that harmonizing IP laws, then compelling Croatia and Ghana to enforce them or face steep trade sanctions puts those smaller countries between a rock and a hard place. Either they must try to thrive without access to international goods and markets (take a look at Cuba to see how well that works out), or they must agree to act as enforcers for foreign interests, to the detriment of their own citizens.

To put it another way, these governments are forced to ensure that for every dollar a Ghanaian or a Croatian spends on media, medicine, technology, or other IP-based goods, several cents flow *out of the country* and into the coffers of companies based in their larger, richer neighbors. To add insult to injury, recall that the United States—the greatest proponent and economic beneficiary of harmonization—consciously refused to recognize foreign copyrights when it was itself a developing nation, declining to join the Berne Convention until a century after it was drafted.

Critics of harmonization cite several other reasons to oppose such laws and treaties above and beyond their wealth-siphoning function: they undermine national sovereignty; they contribute to global cultural homogenization; they ignore the diverse and divergent moral, ethical, and aesthetic systems from nation to nation and region to region; they create the economic conditions for global oligopolies led by multinational corporations that are larger and more powerful than some nations themselves.

Intellectual property professor Peter Drahos, one of the most consistent critics of harmonization over the past few decades, has even suggested that after the ratification of TRIPS by WTO members, we have entered a whole new era of international relations. In this new "global period," national sovereignty and identity take a back seat to corporate bottom lines, and the less powerful must develop "strategies" to mitigate the political and cultural effects of harmonization (we will explore these "political and cultural effects" more later in the chapter).[6]

Yet despite the considerable debate and backlash surrounding harmonization, it has become the touchstone for international intellectual property relations over the past quarter of a century. Although the process began with the Uruguay Round and the establishment of WTO and TRIPS, it has continued since then. In 1996, the World Intellectual Property Organization (WIPO; a United Nations agency that administers IP treaties and has a "mutually supportive" relationship with WTO) brokered a major copyright treaty.[7] This treaty cemented many aspects of TRIPS but added extra forms of copyright protection, such as making it illegal for consumers to circumvent digital encryption in order to copy or access copyrighted material, even if that copy or access is completely within the consumers' rights. The WIPO treaty became the basis for the DMCA in America and for several similar laws in the European Union.

In the decades since then, dozens of bilateral and multilateral trade accords have been negotiated around the world, each of them ratcheting up IP protection and many of them advancing harmonization. Policy wonks often refer to both specific treaty provisions and the general global state of IP law and enforcement as "TRIPS Plus"—meaning that contracting parties are consistently expected to agree to levels of IP protection that go above and beyond the levels set by TRIPS, for instance, by extending patent terms, limiting compulsory licenses, or restricting market competition from the public domain.

The WTO and WIPO have acknowledged that TRIPS threatens to exacerbate power imbalances between wealthier and poorer countries, leading to both public health crises (based on access to medicine) and cultural ones (based on the privatization of folk culture and traditional knowledge). These concerns were addressed in an agreement signed in 2001 called the Doha Declaration, which clarified that IP laws should take care to protect public health and cultural diversity. Yet public health organizations from Oxfam to Médecins Sans Frontières have consistently warned that TRIPS Plus standards don't deliver on the promise of Doha when it comes to access to medicine, and as we will discuss more below, many "developing countries" continue to lament that their cultural and political sovereignty are under assault from harmonized IP laws.

At the time of writing, these issues are still very contentious and very much in play; for instance, they were sticking points in the prolonged (and largely secret) negotiations over controversial trade accords like the Trans-Pacific Partnership (TPP) and the Transatlantic Trade and Investment Partnership (TTIP). In the words of law professor Peter K. Yu, the world is still in the midst of "TRIPS Wars," and the current episode might be called "Developing Countries Strike Back."[8]

The Politics Behind TRIPS

As the brief history of modern IP treaties outlined above suggests, these agreements (and disagreements) are political in every sense of the word—they are created, negotiated, and enacted through political channels, and they have profound consequences for diplomatic relationships between contracting parties as well as for the relationships between parties and nonparties. In the rest of this chapter, we will explore some of the specific ways in which states use IP as an instrument of international relations and as a tool for political ends that are fairly distant from the rhetoric of artists' rights and incentivized invention that gave rise to copyrights and patents in the first place.

The politics of harmonization begins with America—a latecomer to international IP treaties, though the country has more than made up for lost time. The U.S. was the driving force behind TRIPS and continues to be one of the staunchest advocates for TRIPS Plus policy around the globe. Where did this new philosophy come from, and why did America embrace it and export it to the rest of the world? As with domestic IP policy, the answer lies in the private sector. As Sell demonstrates in her exhaustively researched history of these negotiations, "TRIPS resulted from lobbying by twelve powerful CEOs of multinational corporations who wished to mould international law to protect their markets."[9]

These twelve men, chief executives of U.S.-based pharmaceutical, media, and software companies, gathered together a few months before the Uruguay Round to form the Intellectual Property Committee (IPC), an ad hoc group dedicated to framing intellectual property primarily as a "pro–free trade" issue (before this, IP had been understood widely as an *obstacle* to free trade because it was an instrument of state-sanctioned monopoly) and to developing domestic and international support for harmonized, highly protectionist IP laws.

Support within the U.S. was built largely through an "extensive lobbying campaign" that not only streamlined the concerns of diverse industries reliant on copyrights, patents, and other forms of IP under one shared umbrella but also promoted IP protection abroad as a central element of America's economic health with respect to trade.[10] A significant portion of the lobbying dollars discussed in chapter 5 was dedicated to this ongoing project, and millions of dollars were spent by the IPC and its allies specifically on one lobbyist during these years—Jacques Gorlin, who was also formally an adviser to the IPC.[11]

Support for the IPC agenda was developed overseas through personal relationships between executives. According to Sell, "The IPC member executives bypassed their industry associations and directly engaged their European and Japanese private sector counterparts" —a masterful tactic that, by all accounts, was far more successful than anyone involved expected it to be.[12] Together with these international allies and with the full support of the American government, the IPC submitted a proposal to the treaty organization overseeing the Uruguay Round, and the results were overwhelmingly positive; as Gorlin told Sell, "The IPC got 95 percent of what it wanted" in TRIPS.[13] As she neatly summarizes the situation, "In effect, twelve corporations made public law for the world."[14]

Although the TRIPS Plus regime reflects the targeted interests and agenda of a handful of private companies, the political uses of IP law and policy are far too broad and diverse to be reduced to the wholesale subversion of state power by corporate interests. In fact, each contracting party to a treaty—and each holdout that balks at signing or enforcing one—has its own agenda and interests at stake, informed both by its own internal politics and by its diplomatic relations with the other nations involved. While it is true that the IPC and its allies have spent millions to lobby the U.S. government in support of TRIPS Plus, it is equally true that these efforts would have been unsuccessful if the lobbyists hadn't been able to make a compelling argument that the policy would dovetail well with existing American interests.

This framing has been remarkably durable since then; twenty years after TRIPS, presidential candidate Donald Trump took pains to discuss the "outrageous theft of intellectual property" in China as a significant threat to American interests in his acceptance speech at the Republican National Convention.[15] The fact that he did this in the same breath as he criticized multilateral trade deals like the TPP is extraordinary; it shows that the political rationale for TRIPS can outlast support for such deals, and may even be used to argue against them!

IP and Cultural Protectionism

Thus far, we have discussed the politics surrounding harmonization and the efforts to lower barriers to international trade by streamlining IP laws. Yet there are also political functions in taking the converse approach: many countries, including the U.S., have also strategically *limited* trade in IP by erecting barriers, resisting the demands set forth in multinational accords, or excluding parties from these agreements.

One of the oldest forms of strategic obstruction to globalized IP trade is called "cultural protectionism." This is a complex term with a long history and a lot of baggage attached to it. It is based on the belief that, by opening its doors to foreign cultural products, a nation risks losing its own unique voices, styles, and identity. These concerns have been raised at least since Europe's colonial era and have often accompanied debates over international trade and IP accords.

Sometimes cultural protectionism is used as a basis to reject trade agreements, but at other times, secondary measures are put in place to limit the cultural effects of such deals. For example, nations may add extra tariffs or taxes to nondomestic products, impose import quotas on foreign cultural goods, or require retailers and programmers to ensure that a minimum percentage of the cultural material they distribute comes from within the country. In the post–World War II era, for instance, when American culture rose to new levels of dominance throughout the Western world, the General Agreement on Tariffs and Trade (GATT) allowed European nations to legislate strict quotas limiting the importation of Hollywood films. During the Uruguay Round half a century later, France continued to lobby aggressively for these protectionist powers. As a result, the WTO, which technically bans import quotas, contains some loopholes allowing what's widely referred to as a "cultural exception" to this ban.

At the time of writing, negotiations over the newest multilateral treaties continue to stumble over the irreconcilable tension between harmonization and protectionism. For instance, France threatened not to support TTIP if it erodes the cultural exception any further, and some newer members of the EU have proposed similar exceptions in response to efforts to create a "digital single market" for internet streaming services in Europe.

The prolonged wrangling between the U.S. and the EU, and within the EU itself, demonstrates how cultural protectionism can complicate relationships even between the closest of allies and the most similar societies. These tensions can be even greater when the nations involved have a more distant relationship. A good example is China (a WTO member since 2001), which in recent years has taken significant steps to limit Western cultural influence by canceling several high-profile cultural events and by developing sophisticated mechanisms to censor and shape the internet consumption habits of its citizens.

A 2013 Chinese Communist Party publication called *Document 9* made it clear that these measures were taken specifically to limit access to "Western ideas and values, [which] are cultivating so-called 'anti-government forces.'" The document concludes with the exhortation that "we must reinforce our management of all types and levels of propaganda on the cultural front, perfect and carry out related administrative systems, and allow absolutely no opportunity or outlets for incorrect thinking or viewpoints to spread."[16] In other words, the Chinese government has concluded that cultural protectionism is a national security matter, and that it therefore supersedes any obligations related to its WTO membership.

France and China are wealthy and powerful nations with the ability to either influence or ignore trade deals when it's deemed important enough to national interests. But what of the less powerful countries bound by the dictates of TRIPS Plus, and what of the less powerful cultural groups within treaty-bound nations, such as indigenous and folk cultures?

Despite the resolutions set forth in the Doha Declaration, many representatives of these nations and groups continue to call for greater cultural protection in the face of free trade, sounding the alarm about harmonization. As the celebrated Australian novelist Tim Winton recently wrote in an op-ed article for the *Sydney Morning Herald*, international IP treaties threaten to "usher in a new colonial era of publishing" ruled by a "beige business model that reduces every human endeavour to monoculture," threatening Australians' "own voices, their unique sound, their irreplaceable stories."[17]

Although copyright is the branch of IP typically associated with cultural expression, concerns about trade agreements as an instrument of cultural imperialism by stronger groups and nations over weaker ones can extend to patent laws as well. A widely discussed example is the case of "biopiracy," in which commercial interests file patents on folk remedies and other uses of biological resources such as plants, bacteria, and fungi. This practice is technically legal according to the terms of TRIPS, which allows WTO members to exclude "plants and animals" from patentability but requires them to protect "plant varieties."

In her book *Biopiracy: The Plunder of Nature and Knowledge*, Indian activist Vandana Shiva catalogs several examples of multinational corporations privatizing the shared heritage of her own national culture, from a patent for neem (a staple of traditional Indian medicine) to one for basmati rice (a staple of traditional Indian cuisine) to one for *Bacillus thuringiensis* bacteria (a naturally occurring element of Indian agriculture). These claims were not only insulting but injurious; once patents have been granted, rights holders often use the power of the WTO and binding trade deals to prevent traditional users of the newly patented life forms from continuing their practices, or to saddle them with crippling licensing obligations.

As a popular aphorism puts it, "To a man with a hammer, everything looks like a nail." That is to say, when we have one powerful tool in our possession, we look for a way to solve every problem with it. The TRIPS Plus regime gives every member state a giant hammer in the form of harmonized IP laws. Thus, while some nations and groups see copyright harmonization as an instrument of cultural imperialism, others view binding multilateral treaties as a weapon of defense *against* the appropriation of their cultures and traditions by larger, more powerful interests.

There are numerous examples of developing nations and indigenous or folkloric cultures invoking copyright, patent, or trademark to defend themselves against the perceived theft of their heritage, with mixed degrees of success. For instance, the Ethiopian government, which is highly dependent on its coffee crops as a source of income, decided to trademark the names of its most famous coffee-growing regions, such as Harrar, Sidamo, and Yirgacheffe. Once it had obtained these trademarks, it was able to license them to coffee distributors and sellers around the globe, who could charge more on their end for beans that were certified as originating in a single district.

Yet there is also market value in exploiting the folkloric connotations of these regional trademarks. Today, for instance, Starbucks advertises its Organic Ethiopia Yirgacheffe™ coffee beans on its website with the following text:

It was here that the first coffee trees flourished, where the first beans were roasted and ground to a fine dust, where the first cups were poured from a clay jebana centuries ago.

You can taste those centuries of tradition in a cup of this legendary coffee. Organic Ethiopia Yirgacheffe™ is most noted for its intensely floral aromatics that complement an elegant acidity and a dense, fruity sweetness. It also has undertones of exotic spice, with peppery or cinnamon notes.[18]

These "exotic" flavors and "legendary" beans generate real market value, some of which actually flows back into Ethiopian coffers. According to a case study written by WIPO, Yirgacheffe farmers' income doubled the year after these licenses were negotiated.[19]

Some other efforts to use IP as a bulwark against market exploitation and cultural imperialism have not worked out quite as well. For instance, in 2012 the Navajo Nation filed a trademark infringement lawsuit against apparel retail chain Urban Outfitters for using its name, along with its distinctive textile patterns, on a number of dubiously tasteful products, such as "Navajo Hipster Panty" underwear and a "Navajo Liquor Flask." After a set of judicial rulings in 2016 denying an important motion by the plaintiff and dismissing two of the counts in the complaint, the parties agreed to settle out of court for an undisclosed amount.

You may be wondering why an obvious case of cultural appropriation like Navajo Hipster Panty would face such challenges in court. The answer is very simple: IP laws aren't formulated to protect indigenous and folk cultures, and despite the Doha Declaration, they still do a very poor job of it. To return to our earlier analogy, not all problems are nails, so not every solution can be a hammer. Indige-

Figure 13: Advertisement for Starbucks Ethiopia Yirgacheffe™ Chelba.

nous rights advocate and global studies professor Greg Younging has identified three "main problems" in the current global IP system that prevent it from serving effectively as a shield against unpermissioned commercial exploitation of traditional knowledge (TK):

1) that expressions of TK often cannot qualify for protection because they are too old and are, therefore, supposedly in the public domain;

2) that the "author" of the material is often not identifiable and there is thus no "rights holder" in the usual sense of the term;

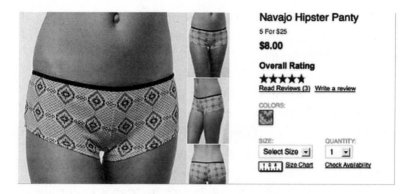

Figure 14: Advertisement for Urban Outfitters Navajo Hipster Panty.

3) that TK is owned "collectively" by Indigenous groups for cultural claims and not by individuals or corporations for economic claims.[20]

These three concerns are not mere technicalities that can be addressed by a simple update to the letter of the law; instead, they point to a fundamental philosophical mismatch between the idea of culture enshrined in intellectual property law for the past three hundred years and the basic contours of traditional culture. IP exists to protect novelty and innovation, while traditional cultures are premised on the preservation of ancient knowledge. IP is based on the theory that culture is produced by individuals who can be incentivized via the promise of monetary reward, while traditional cultures often lack basic concepts of original authorship; cultural artifacts are collectively produced for reasons that tend to be more ritual than commercial.

Of course, there are countless cultural traditions around the world, each with its own ethics and aesthetics, and each one corresponds with IP in some ways and diverges from it in others. By and large, however, the vision of cultural production that is protected by IP law is one rooted in the modern, industrialized European and American context and fundamentally biased against other modes of production, distribution, and reception.

Strategic Opposition to TRIPS Plus

In addition to cultural protectionism, there are also political and economic reasons for nations to both resist and enforce IP laws in the TRIPS Plus global regime. One important and growing movement is encapsulated in the word *access* and in the philosophy of human rights. While protectionists seek to prevent local cultures and values from being dissolved in a globalized marketplace aided by frictionless trade in IP, supporters of the "access to knowledge" (A2K) movement seek to increase local access to global information by dropping the barriers introduced by IP laws. Although these might sound like fundamentally opposite philosophies, there are many who advocate both cultural protectionism *and* A2K. The unifying theme is restoring power to developing nations, traditional cultures, and other parties without a major stake in IP-centric industries by giving them more leverage to restrict, enable, and shape the flow of information into and out of their communities.

The A2K movement isn't merely about abstract notions of power or about the cultural value of information—often human lives are on the line. One particularly vocal and volatile dimension of this movement is in the push for access to medicine. In the words of India's ambassador to the United Nations, Ajit Kumar, the TRIPS Plus patent regime has "resulted in skyrocketing prices for lifesaving vaccines and medicines, promoted discriminatory access to medicines based on geographical location or economic status and has further widened health inequities."[21]

These concerns are among the most contentious in the field of intellectual property today. Recently, the Human Rights Council (HRC), an intergovernmental body within the United Nations system, adopted a resolution to reevaluate international trade deals and IP agreements in light of their impact on access to medicine. The language of this resolution was hotly contested. For instance, it argues for "the primacy of human rights over international trade, investment and intellectual property regimes"—text adopted by consensus among a core group of nations that included Brazil, China, Egypt, India, Indonesia, Senegal, South Africa, and Thailand. Unsurprisingly, several states objected to the inclusion of this language in the resolution, including the EU, the U.S., Switzerland, Japan, and Australia.

At the time of writing, these matters are still very much in play, and these tensions are unresolved. The HRC will be addressing them further in an access to medicines panel at its next session.[22] Whether and to what degree the HRC's resolutions and conclusions will have an impact on WTO- and WIPO-administered IP treaties—and ultimately, on access to medicine and information in developing nations—is an open question.

The A2K movement is primarily an altruistic one. As the language of the HRC resolution makes clear, it's widely understood as an effort to prioritize human rights over corporate profit, to balance the inequities between nations and peoples that are exacerbated by the TRIPS Plus vision of global IP harmonization. Yet other acts of resistance against these treaties are not so well intentioned. In fact, some governments treat IP infringement as a form of economic and political warfare, calculated to undermine the financial and cultural dominance of the U.S. and other IP-exporting countries. And when they do recognize IP rights, some nations enforce treaty obligations only selectively as a justification for censorship and repression within their own nations.

An excellent example of both of these dynamics is the Russian Federation. In the first decade after TRIPS, Russia was considered to be a safe haven for high-volume commercial media piracy. During this period, the Russian government turned a blind eye to most infringement of foreign copyrights, even providing state protection for CD, DVD, and software replication factories. Some of these factories were hosted at sites already meriting state protection (and closed to the watchful eyes of the international community), such as military industrial manufacturers and nuclear power plants.[23]

The effects of this industrial piracy were considerable; according to estimates by the U.S. Trade Representative (USTR), two-thirds of the CDs and four-fifths of the DVDs in the Russian market in 2006 were produced without the permission of, or any payment to, rights holders. In addition to illicit media reproduction, Russia was also considered to be one of the global leaders in counterfeit drug production, causing an alleged $250 million in market harm to pharmaceutical companies.[24]

Beginning around 2006, Russia began to update its laws and to crack down on many of its largest piracy and counterfeiting operations. These moves were made as part of a larger bid to join the WTO (the country became an official member in 2012). Today, IP infringement is still a widespread commercial and cultural activity within Russia, despite periodic efforts by the government to shut down major manufacturers and distributors. This limited success may be attributed to the fact that the crackdowns are often motivated by politics that are neither pro-WTO nor pro-A2K. Instead of trying to protect the economic interests of its trade partners comprehensively, for instance, the Russian government uses piracy investigations selectively "as a means of harassing political activists and journalists."[25]

Russia is by no means unique in its complex, selective, and far from altruistic relationship to IP rights and treaties. China, a WTO member since 2001, continues to have a thriving market for counterfeits of global brands. As media professor Fan Yang discusses, the government tacitly supports this counterfeit market even as it simultaneously invests in developing a thriving national and international trade in trademarked brands and copyrighted products from China. While this represents a difficult balancing act from a policy stand-point, Yang makes a compelling argument that both sides of the coin are ultimately acts of "nation-branding," elevating China's pro-file in global media and commodity culture.[26]

China is also a major sponsor of corporate espionage and the hacking of trade secrets (a form of intellectual property discussed in the introduction). According to a U.S. government report pre-sented to Congress in 2015, "China's increasing use of cyber espio-nage directed against commercial targets . . . has already cost U.S. companies tens of billions of dollars." These activities are not merely the work of sophisticated criminals. According to the report, "The largest and most sophisticated cyber attacks have been traced to government-sponsored or government-run teams of hackers in China," and often the stolen trade secrets are "turned over to Chi-nese government-owned competitors" who undersell the American companies that were the sources of the trade secrets to begin with.[27]

Sometimes the U.S. and other WTO members take direct judi-cial action against infringers. For instance, in 2014, the U.S. De-partment of Justice (DOJ) indicted five officers of the China's Peo-ple's Liberation Army on counts related to the theft of trade secrets over the internet, from companies and unions including Westing-house Electric, Alcoa, Allegheny Technologies Incorporated, U.S. Steel, the United Steelworkers Union, and SolarWorld. Rhetoric from the White House and the DOJ suggest that the government is going to increase its efforts to prosecute these crimes as a form of diplomatic pressure on China, Russia, and other state sponsors of cyber espionage and IP infringement. Yet given the scope and frequency of these operations, such measures are likely to have a limited effect.

A more all-encompassing tool used by the American government to police and retaliate against state-sponsored infringement is an annual publication called the *Special 301 Report*. This document, prepared by the USTR in consultation with a range of government agencies and corporate rights holders, is basically a "most wanted" list of nations that either ignore or sponsor infringement on a broad scale. Nations that rise to the top echelon of infringement, in the USTR's estimation, are designated "Priority Foreign Countries" (PFCs), and their placement on the list may trigger trade sanctions. For smaller nations, such sanctions can be economically crippling and politically destabilizing. Even for larger nations, such sanctions represent more than a mere inconvenience, amounting to a major political and economic liability.

Because of these sizeable effects, it is rare that the USTR designates countries as PFCs—this is reserved for the most drastic cases. More frequently, they are placed on the "Priority Watch List" (PWL) or the "Watch List" (WL). These designations are essentially used as warnings to nations in danger of being upgraded to PFCs. While getting put on the PWL doesn't trigger immediate sanctions, it can be a justification for the U.S. to initiate formal dispute settlement proceedings with the WTO, which can lead to other economic and political consequences.

In 2016, China, Russia, and nine other countries were designated PWL, while twenty-three additional nations were designated WL. No countries were designated PFC (Ukraine was only recently downgraded from this designation to PWL after the nation agreed to create a special unit of its national police force just to investigate and enforce IP violations).

Yet, while the *Special 301 Report* is a very effective tool of diplomatic persuasion, it is not always used in ways that are either altruistic or in accordance with the principles of equity and fairness espoused by the WTO. As critics of the USTR frequently allege, the U.S. has used the report as a weapon to bully other, less powerful nations into adopting laws and policies that are not in their own national interests, and to further the priorities of the same narrow commercial interests that lobbied for TRIPS Plus in the first place.

According to an analysis of the 2016 *Special 301 Report* by the Electronic Frontier Foundation (EFF), a public advocacy organization focused on digital law and policy, it "calls out numerous countries for a range of perfectly lawful practices," such as prioritizing the free speech and privacy of their own citizens over the demands of American rights holders.[28] Secret international diplomatic cables leaked by American soldier Chelsea Manning and published by Wikileaks in 2010 provided further insight into how the threat of PFC designation has been wielded as an instrument of coercion in specific instances, leading countries such as Spain and Sweden to adopt laws that were opposed not only by many citizens but by the governments themselves.[29]

Thus, there are no "good guys" and "bad guys" in the world of international IP, only shades of gray and a complex mixture of methods and motivations, ranging from altruistic to strategic to self-serving to criminal. Even "rogue" nations like China and Russia have sophisticated and often justifiable reasons for their selective enforcement of IP, while champions of harmonization and the TRIPS Plus regime like the U.S. have recourse to unethical methods of coercion and enforcement at times.

Only rarely, in the midst of these international negotiations, threats, and skirmishes, does any party actively recognize the ostensible rationale for IP—the incentivization of creation and the enrichment of the public sphere. Instead, by framing expression as property and communication as trade, IP policy in the TRIPS Plus era often reduces the universe of arts and ideas to little more than a set of pieces to be moved around a sheet of cardboard imprinted with a map of the world, like toy soldiers in a game of Risk.

SEVEN

Copyright Piracy

One of the greatest challenges in writing about intellectual property (and, I concede, in reading books on the subject) is in the language itself. Like many other arcane fields of scholarship and expertise, IP has its own lexicon, full of words and phrases that are hard to spell, pronounce, and remember. This is partially because IP is a matter of law, and as such, it's inflected with the same kind of "legalese" that pervades the literature on tax policy, mergers and acquisitions, and other matters conducted exclusively within boardrooms, courtrooms, and congressional and judicial chambers.

Some may suspect this legalistic language exists for the same reason that Sleeping Beauty's resting place was surrounded by briars and brambles—to ward off outsiders and protect the sanctity of the chambers within. While there is no doubt some truth in this, there are also some very practical reasons for the tortured verbiage that characterizes publications and discussions about IP.

First of all, because so much is at stake for so many different parties, the language needs to be very precise. For instance, determining whether an act of infringement was "willful" or not, or whether a case of secondary liability is "contributory" or "vicarious," can have serious implications, ranging from the amount of money owed to the possibility and duration of imprisonment.

Second, as we have reviewed throughout this book, the law at any given point is inevitably the result of negotiation and compromise between multiple parties over many years in a range of different venues, from state to state, nation to nation, and legislature to courthouse. Thus, many of the law's most contorted terms and phrases are not the pure expression of one person's bizarre vision but rather the end product of prolonged haggling between disparate interests, each with its own more straightforward ideas. Nobody is happy with the resulting language, but most are willing to live with it. Think of it like a high school band name: the drummer wants to call the band Lordz of Sound and the lead singer wants to call it Firewater. So they end up with Lordz of Water. It might not make a lot of sense to the audience, but both bandmates feel that their interests were served.

This brings us to the subject of the current chapter: "piracy." I put the word in scare quotes because in a field as precise and convoluted as intellectual property, a term this simple and seemingly straightforward is an anomaly, and we should view it with extreme caution. I have tried my best to avoid the term thus far, putting the word in quotation marks in chapter 1 and using more well-defined and contextualized settings of the term, such as "industrial media piracy" and "biopiracy," in chapter 6. I hope you have picked up on some of these cues, and that you have waited patiently for me to explain them. If so, you're in luck.

Piracy: A Definition

The word *pirate* carried a lot of cultural baggage before it had anything to do with copyright or intellectual property. Just as it is today, the ancient Mediterranean was dependent on international trade via cargo ships, and as far back as thirty-two hundred years ago, historical records from a variety of coastal nations recorded assaults by mysterious "Sea Peoples" who would attack port cities and sea-farers, raiding goods and killing civilians. In ancient Greece, perpe-trators of such deeds became known as *peirates* (brigands), a word that evolved from the verb *peiran* (to attack or attempt). By the time this word had further evolved into the Latin *pirata*, philosophers had developed a complex approach to understanding piracy that ex-tended beyond its immediate impact on ships and shores.

The Roman philosopher Cicero (106–43 BCE) defined pirates as "the common enemy of all" because they conducted crimes not just against civilians but against the social order itself, operating outside the scope of national sovereignty and beyond the pale of accepted rules of commerce and warfare. From this era on, "piracy" has been understood as a negative category defined not by specific deeds or actors but rather in opposition to the ever-changing norms and expectations of organized society. Thus, what made ancient sea-faring brigands "pirates" wasn't so much their habit of stealing or killing but rather the fact that they did so without any official ca-pacity as agents of a government or state.[1]

As a matter of fact, it was very common up until the modern era for "privateers" to conduct exactly the same kinds of raids, for ex-actly the same kinds of reasons, under the aegis of state sponsor-ship. In its early years, the United States was an enthusiastic spon-sor of privateering, for instance, granting ships permission to attack and plunder hundreds of British vessels during the Revolutionary War and the War of 1812. When dozens of nations signed a treaty outlawing privateering in 1856, the United States declined to sign, ceasing support for this practice only a decade later during the Civil War.

This brief history sheds a little light on the term *piracy* as it has been applied to intellectual property. Just as in the maritime context, the word doesn't refer to a specific set of actions or actors so much as it connotes an absence of legitimacy and a threat to the established order. And, even more than in the case of maritime piracy, the identities and actions of so-called copyright pirates have changed drastically over the years, as both the established order and the nature of the threats against it have continued to coevolve with technology, culture, and commerce.

Piracy in the Age of Print

The concept of textual piracy is actually older than copyright itself. As historian Adrian Johns has shown, the term *wit-pyrat* was used by the poet John Donne as a metaphor for plagiarism (still a relatively new concept itself during this first blush of modern authorship) in 1611.[2] By the mid- to late seventeenth century, the terms *pirate* and *piracy* were used widely within the book publishing trade to describe the reprinting, without permission, of a work published and controlled by another party. By the beginning of the eighteenth century, this definition appeared in dictionaries across much of western Europe (published, of course, by booksellers with an interest in promoting the use and legitimacy of language sympathetic to their own business interests).

Yet, despite becoming a bona fide dictionary definition, this vision of piracy had its critics and opponents. Recall that, prior to the invention of copyright, many nations employed patents to grant exclusive publishing rights to private individuals and groups—usually nobility who enjoyed the crown's favor. Proponents of this older system viewed the rise of stationers' companies and profit-driven booksellers as a threat, both to their source of wealth and to the aristocratic political order that had given rise to it. Thus, while booksellers were busy defining piracy in terms of unpermissioned reproduction, patent holders and supporters of the older system accused *the booksellers themselves* of being "pirates," of commodifying the world of ideas solely for the purposes of profit (rather than for the noble, aristocratic reasons they ascribed to their own actions).

The booksellers came up with a novel counterargument: the notion of authors' rights. Rather than conceding their role as avatars of self-interest, they reinvented themselves as the champions of creators and promoters of the public good. It was this vision that ultimately won out and was enshrined in the Statute of Anne and later in American copyright law. As Johns summarizes, "Authorial property and piracy were thus being forged in contest with each other. Each rested on highly contentious grounds, and neither was intrinsically credible."[3] To put it another way, textual piracy is neither a violation of copyright nor an economic challenge that made copyright necessary—rather, it's one of several competing notions of piracy that exists in order to bolster the concept of copyright as it was first written into law.

Once the booksellers had won out and modern notions of copyright, promoted in the name of authors' rights, had fully eclipsed the old-fashioned printing patent, the definition of piracy also became more stable: it referred to unauthorized reprinting of copyrighted work. Yet acts of piracy were still often in the eye of the beholder.

As we have discussed in previous chapters, the United States did not recognize the copyrights of foreign authors during its first century of nationhood. Early American publishers like Matthew Carey and Robert Bell (Irish immigrants who had participated in Dublin's reprinting trade) took advantage of this fact, building a thriving, and technically legal, international business based on reprinted European books and essays. While British authors and publishers complained loudly that this business amounted to wholesale state-sanctioned piracy, the American publishers framed their reprinting practices as not only legitimate but patriotic and even revolutionary. At the same time, American booksellers tried repeatedly to organize their own domestic trade into "companies" (trade associations similar to the Company of Stationers in Britain), explicitly for the purpose of preventing piratical reprinting of the works they controlled by other domestic publishers. These companies, in turn, were excoriated as cartels, cast by critics as the enemies of authors and as impediments to the free flow of knowledge and information. Thus, the creation of copyright did little to stem accusations of piracy; if anything, it only intensified the finger pointing among authors, printers, and booksellers on both sides of the Atlantic.

Over the course of the nineteenth century, as the number of successful American authors and the size of the American publishing industry grew, and as copyright law expanded to encompass music, art, and other forms of expression, concerns about both domestic and foreign piracy became more pointed and more explicitly connected to the project of internationalizing intellectual property.

Prominent American authors became vocal advocates for stronger IP protection and enforcement, all in the name of combating piracy. In 1868, celebrated poet William Cullen Bryant gave a talk at a New York meeting of the International Copyright Association in which he lamented that "we have . . . so framed our laws that the foreigner is robbed of [literary] property here and our own citizens plundered abroad."[4] Mark Twain took up the cause as well, spending decades lobbying and advocating for steeper copyright laws and inveighing against the "pirates" in Canada and Europe that reprinted his books and stories with impunity.

In 1875, Twain even started a campaign to bring together America's greatest literary figures to petition Congress to outlaw the piracy of foreign books by American publishers—an act of goodwill that he hoped would lead foreign nations to reciprocate in kind. The influential clergyman and short story author Henry van Dyke gave this movement some religious momentum, publishing a sermon in 1888 titled *The National Sin of Literary Piracy*. These efforts were ultimately successful; though the U.S. would not become a party to the Berne Convention for another century, in 1891 Congress passed the International Copyright Act, extending copyright protection to certain works by foreign authors.

Piracy in the Electronic Age

As we reviewed in chapter 1, both media culture and copyright law changed considerably in the twentieth century. New technologies like radio, sound recording, cinema, and television became dominant platforms for the distribution of creative works. New laws created new categories of rights, such as public performance and mechanical reproduction, and extended copyright protection for longer terms. Later in the century, even more exotic forms of copyright would emerge, such as phonographic master rights and software copyright, while the Copyright Act of 1976 would drastically extend both the term of protection and the range of works covered by eliminating the requirement for registration.

Throughout these many changes, the definition of piracy would continue to evolve, both anticipating and reflecting these legal and technological shifts. As in previous eras, the term didn't refer to a single set of actors or actions, or even reflect the technical legality of these actions, so much as it conferred a sense of illegitimacy and threat to established business and social interests.

One concept that emerged early in the twentieth century and still reverberates today is the notion of *pirate radio*. Over the years, this term has been used to refer to many different practices—some of them explicitly related to intellectual property and others more broadly related to the use of the airwaves themselves. When radio transmission was first developed at the turn of the twentieth century, the airwaves were understood as a free public resource. By the end of the century's first decade, over a hundred thousand amateur American radio enthusiasts had purchased or built their own sets and were both sending and receiving transmissions, sharing news, gossip, music, and other forms of sound in a nationwide, unregulated peer-to-peer network.

Although there was not yet any law to break, these amateurs were increasingly seen as a threat to both economic and national security because of their unwitting (and occasionally intentional) interference with commercial and military signals. As early as 1907, an article in *Electrical World* magazine decried the "wireless and lawless" state of amateur transmissions and proposed that the government "declare a state of war" to prevent further threats.[5] Congress didn't declare war, but it did begin to regulate the airwaves in 1912, progressively cutting back on the ability of amateurs to broadcast freely over the next two decades.

By the early 1930s, two kinds of piracy were routinely discussed with respect to radio: "wave-length piracy," conducted by "wave-pirates," concerned the use of assigned frequencies by unlicensed parties, while "news piracy" and "music piracy" were terms used to describe the interception or rebroadcasting of unlicensed content over the airwaves (although as one law professor conceded in a 1930 article entitled "Piracy of Broadcast Programs," "the word 'piracy' is much too strong a term properly to be applied to many of the practices" it described).[6]

As with textual piracy in earlier times, the concept of radio piracy was coined not to describe copyright infringement but rather to argue that these actions *should* be seen as infringement under the law. Only in 1932, after a ten-year battle between the National Association of Broadcasters (NAB) and the American Society of Composers, Authors and Publishers (ASCAP) involving lawsuits, public relations skirmishes, and congressional hearings, was it finally established that radio stations needed to pay royalties to songwriters for the use of their work on the air.

Shortly after this historic agreement, a fawning profile of ASCAP

president Gene Buck in the *New Yorker* called him "the greatest ex-
terminator of piracy since Decatur."[7] Yet despite this victory for
songwriters and publishers, recording artists and record labels were
left out of the equation altogether. By ASCAP's logic, they continue
to be "pirated" by radio broadcasters today, though at the time of
writing this contentious issue is once again being reconsidered by
Congress.

One example of pirate radio that involved both "wave piracy"
and "music piracy" yet remained technically legal was Radio Caroline, a station launched in 1964 that transmitted from a ship in
international waters, beyond the political borders of the UK but
not outside of its broadcasting range. The founder of Radio Caroline, Ronan O'Rahilly, was a London music promoter and manager
who represented up-and-coming artists such as Alexis Korner and
Georgie Fame. After trying and failing to get several commercial
radio stations to play one of Fame's records, O'Rahilly concluded
that record label "payola" (the practice of paying promotional fees
to radio stations and DJs in exchange for airtime) created an anticompetitive marketplace in which deserving artists without the funds
or the stomach to engage in such practices were systematically excluded.

O'Rahilly launched Radio Caroline explicitly as a form of protest against the market dominance of American record labels and
major European broadcasters. The station was, unquestionably, a
"pirate" in that it was a threat to the established order. This threat
was not merely symbolic in nature; it directly attacked the traditional industry's bottom line; according to some tallies, pirate radio
in the 1960s accounted for the majority of UK radio listening hours.
Yet because Caroline was based in international waters, there was
nothing technically illegal about its use of either the airwaves or the
copyrighted materials it broadcast.

The UK Parliament set about to remedy this situation, passing a law in 1967 that outlawed offshore radio as well as advertising on such stations. Radio Caroline's brief stint as the UK's most popular pirate station ended, although its story continued through many twists and turns over the next fifty years, always skirting the edges of legality while retaining the disruptive spirit of piracy. Today, the station is still broadcasting via various channels, including online at radiocaroline.co.uk.

Another form of piracy that emerged in the twentieth century was the unlicensed reproduction of recorded materials such as music and films. This phenomenon took many forms. The most unequivocally illegal versions of this activity involved the industrial copying and resale of copyrighted films and music, both for commercial use (for example, showing a pirated film in a theater) and for consumer use (such as selling a pirated record in a store), without obtaining permission from, or paying royalties to, the copyright holders.

Yet beginning around the middle of the century, a new form of behavior emerged that, like pirate radio, was disruptive without being explicitly infringing: home taping. Advances in magnetic tape technology after World War II gave consumers access to electronic devices like reel-to-reel tape decks, audiocassette recorders, and VCRs that, unlike traditional "passive" media devices such as radio receivers, television sets, and record players, could be used for production, storage, and retrieval of audiovisual information. In a way, it was almost a pendulum swing back to the early days of radio, when nearly every set was both a transmitter and a receiver.

These technologies caught on like wildfire, and consumers in large number began to engage in behaviors that gave them a new degree of power over the media in their lives (and, by extension, over the companies that produced and distributed the media programming). *Time-shifting* allowed radio and television fans to record their favorite shows and watch or listen at their leisure instead of being bound by the dictates of the programming schedule. *Space-*

shifting allowed consumers to record shows and bring them to new venues, such as work, school, or the homes of friends. *Librarying* allowed consumers to make recordings of shows, and copies of albums and films, then watch or listen to them over and over again. And *home recording* allowed consumers to become producers in their own right, either making videos and recordings from scratch or editing together pieces of existing footage to make new, transformative work, like cut-ups, mixtapes, slash, and fanvids (more on this in the next chapter).

Of course, in addition to all of this self-empowering creative behavior, consumers were also using magnetic tape to make copies of other people's media collections, such as friends' record albums and rental movie cassettes—in many cases, using copying as an alternative to purchasing. While the behaviors cited above merely challenged the organizational dominance of big media companies, this particular behavior threatened their bottom line by potentially undermining the retail market for records, movies, and other electronic media.

When consumer taping practices first emerged, there were no laws clearly allowing or prohibiting them. This didn't stop the film and music industries from sounding the alarm about the pernicious new threat of "home piracy"—especially after 1972, when American copyright law first gave recording artists and their labels a new copyright for their phonorecordings.

Jack Valenti, then the head of the Motion Picture Association of America, testified before Congress in 1983 that "the VCR is to the American film producer and the American public as the Boston strangler is to the woman home alone." Around the same time, the British Phonographic Industry (BPI), a record label trade association, launched a massive public awareness campaign warning, "Home taping is killing music, and it's illegal," accompanied by an image of a cassette tape recast as a skull and crossbones. BPI's message was

Figure 15: Logo for the anti-taping campaign launched by BPI in the 1980s.

somewhat misleading, given the fact that there was no actual evidence of economic harm (elsewhere, BPI acknowledged that the UK had the lowest "piracy rate" in the world) and that there were no laws expressly prohibiting such behavior.[8]

Despite the alarmist outcry about home taping from traditional media companies, onlookers in both the legal and business communities were skeptical about whether it amounted to a form of piracy and whether it should be outlawed. As late as 1979, record industry trade publication *Billboard* ran an article in which it referred to "so-called 'home piracy,'" emphasizing the fact that noncommercial home taping was not necessarily equivalent to the usual understanding of piracy as a commercial behavior.[9] For its part, Congress had explicitly declined to criminalize home taping in its 1972 law creating phonographic copyrights, and four years later, it codified fair use exemptions to copyright infringement that applied to many of the most common use cases for home taping.

The coup de grâce came in the form of the lawsuit *Sony v. Universal*, often referred to as the "Betamax case."[10] Sony (not yet a major film studio owner) had introduced the Betamax, its proprietary VCR format, in 1975. At the time the suit was brought, there was still a format war in the marketplace between Betamax and VHS (which ultimately won out). In the suit, a group of major film studios claimed that Sony was liable for the infringing behaviors of its VCR users, and also engaging in "unfair competition" with the studios. The lawsuit eventually made its way to the U.S. Supreme Court, where a 5-4 majority found that, due to the "substantial noninfringing uses" of the device, Sony was not liable for any infringing actions of its customers. Furthermore, the court also absolved users of any liability in taping television shows, clarifying that "home time-shifting is fair use."

Following the Betamax ruling, home taping flourished for two decades, and the term *piracy* tended to be used exclusively in the context of unlicensed commercial copying and redistribution rather than in reference to noncommercial consumer behaviors. It was assumed, of course, that a certain percentage of home taping was fundamentally substitutional—that is to say, people dubbing tapes instead of buying them. Yet any economic costs associated with these behaviors were miniscule compared to the burgeoning multibillion-dollar market in VCR movie sales and rentals as well as the unprecedented growth in the recorded music market. It would not be an exaggeration to say that some of the entertainment industry's most profitable years in history coincided with the golden age of home taping.

Piracy in the Digital Age

In the 1990s, a variety of technological and social developments contributed to some profound changes in the relationship between media and culture, and between media industries and their customers. Foremost among these was the sudden popular adoption of the internet, spurred by the creation of the World Wide Web and the free availability of web browsing software. Underpinning this trend was the development of graphical operating systems such as Windows and Macintosh, and the widespread diffusion of personal computers in the home. Previously seen as a business appliance or a hobby for geeks, the home computer rapidly became understood as essential for schoolwork, domestic tasks, communication, and entertainment.

Another important development was the entertainment industry's embrace of optical media platforms (such as CDs and DVDs) and their efforts to migrate consumers away from the magnetic tape formats that had dominated for the past few decades. This move can be understood both as a means of inflating profit (by encouraging consumers to buy content they already owned on cassette in new, more expensive, digital disc formats) and as a method of countering both legal and illegal unlicensed duplication (by replacing the read/write capabilities of tape decks with the purely "passive" capacities of disc readers).

Yet this would prove to be a miscalculation: beginning in the mid-1990s, most new desktop computers came equipped with optical readers, allowing consumers to copy effortlessly the contents of CDs onto their hard drives. A few years later, those optical drives would be upgraded to both read and write CDs and DVDs. In conjunction with freely available "ripping," "burning," and editing software and increasingly fast internet connections, this endowed media consumers with a degree of power and autonomy that far outstripped anything they had experienced in the days of cassette decks and VCRs.

This newfound consumer power was justifiably understood as a threat to established business practices and the commercial interests behind them. From about 1994 onward, hand-wringing over the dangers of "internet piracy" permeated both the popular press and the congressional record. Yet these technologies and practices were still in their infancy, such that few people had a sense of what the piracy consisted of. Did it apply to both commercial and noncommercial, both large-scale and personal? Did it include the digital equivalents of time-shifting, space-shifting, librarying, and home recording? Did such distinctions even make sense in the context of a networked platform like the internet?

The media industries and consumers diverged on these issues. While the former busied themselves lobbying for stronger, digitally focused copyright laws and attempting to limit consumer behaviors with the use of encryption technology (as we will discuss further in the next chapter), the latter busied themselves exploring a wide range of emerging expressive and communicative possibilities, many of them drawing on the cut-and-paste aesthetics of tape culture in a new networked digital context.

Despite these changes and tensions, there was not much of an actual threat to established media industries from digital piracy during this period. A consumer on a fifty-six kilobits-per-second dial-up internet line would have to wait fifteen minutes or so to upload or download a single MP3, and sending or receiving an entire movie over the internet was still virtually unthinkable. With speeds this slow, and platforms built for text and images rather than videos and songs, there simply wasn't much audiovisual content, either licensed or unlicensed, available on the internet at the time. Even as late as the spring of 1999, the recording industry itself estimated that there were about half a million unlicensed music files available on the internet in total. Then, suddenly, everything changed.

On June 1, 1999, a college student named Shawn Fanning released a free software program called Napster, which allowed any user to share her personal library of MP3s directly with any other user over the internet. Because there was no intermediary and no need to upload a file to an internet server before it could be downloaded, this software was referred to as a "peer-to-peer file sharing network," or P2P for short. Virtually overnight, Napster gained millions of users and dozens of imitators. Online music fans, who were still not able to purchase MP3s over the web, freely exchanged billions of song files with one another.

Was Napster piracy? As with the historical examples we reviewed above, it depends on your definition and point of view. Like pirate radio and home taping, P2P represented a new paradigm in media distribution and conferred new powers on consumers and outsiders, threatening the dominance—and potentially the bottom line—of the major media companies. On the other hand, it wasn't clearly illegal. In the wake of the Betamax case, librarying, time-shifting, lending, and other noncommercial forms of copying and distribution were generally understood to be fair use.

Seen from one perspective, Napster merely provided a digital equivalent to these traditional consumer behaviors. Users could become "buddies" with one another on the service and listen to one another's digital music libraries, much as they might go to a friend's house and raid his vinyl collection. Furthermore, nobody profited from the exchange. Seen from another perspective, however, Napster represented a commercial piracy operation on a scale never seen before, enabling the unlicensed copying and redistribution of billions of protected works and effectively cutting retailers and broadcasters out of the equation altogether.

Further complicating the issue was the fact that P2P didn't have a clear impact on the market, either negative or positive. Since the year 2000, dozens upon dozens of researchers have published empirical studies examining the links between P2P usage, purchasing behaviors, and profitability. Amazingly, no consensus has emerged from these studies. Some conclude that P2P helps media industries and creators because it informs and excites consumers, ultimately causing them to spend more, and to spend more wisely. Others conclude that P2P hurts media industries because it gives consumers access to anything they want for free—hence, no need to pay for anything. Finally, many studies have found no discernable impact of P2P on media industries, concluding that the ups and downs in the music, film, and software markets have more to do with economic and cultural trends—and the industry's ability or inability to adapt to those trends—than they do with the unlicensed sharing of content over the internet. With reputable research from so many scholars and analysts leading to so many incompatible findings, P2P has become something of a Rorschach test: what you see in it says more about your state of mind than it does about the state of the marketplace.[11]

This indeterminacy didn't stop the copyright-based industries from doing everything they could to classify P2P as piracy and to put a stop to it via legal challenges and by any other means necessary. The first major challenge came in the form of a lawsuit against Napster, filed only months after the service first launched. Ultimately, a panel of federal judges found that the Betamax precedent didn't apply to Napster because, unlike Sony, the company had the ability (and thus the responsibility) to police the actions of its users. This was due to an architectural quirk of the software; although users shared files directly with one another without passing through Napster's servers, the information about which files each user had to offer and the search interface that depended upon this information were part of a centralized database operated by Napster. A year after this ruling effectively shut down and bankrupted the service, its assets were acquired by media company Bertelsmann, which was then the parent company of major record label BMG.

After the Napster shutdown, P2P continued to thrive. Like the mythical hydra, each time the industry cut off one of its heads, two more seemed to grow in its place. Following the logic of the Napster decision, several file-sharing platforms emerged that lacked the centralized search architecture that had brought down their predecessor. Like Sony's Betamax devices, P2P technologies such as Gnutella, eDonkey, FastTrack, and BitTorrent lacked the technological capacity to police their users. They also enabled many of the "substantial noninfringing uses" that had contributed to Sony's fair use win. Yet several P2P software providers using these protocols were still sued by media industry rights holders and were ultimately found liable for infringement.

In 2005, the U.S. Supreme Court handed down a historic decision against P2P software provider Grokster, which used the decentralized FastTrack protocol to allow its users to share files directly with one another without policing or oversight. Although the service met all of the "safe harbor" conditions that had provided immunity to Sony in the Betamax decision two decades earlier, the court ultimately decided that the company was liable anyway.

In order to reach this conclusion, the justices relied upon a novel new standard for secondary liability, arguing that because Grokster had "induced" its users to infringe upon copyright through its marketing materials and its software's capabilities, the company was itself liable for their infringing actions. Five years later, the operator of P2P service LimeWire (which used both Gnutella and Bit-

Torrent networks) was found liable under the inducement standard as well.[12]

The music and film industries' court victories over these and other P2P networks were widely covered by the press, which frequently framed the cases in the language of piracy. For instance, when the Supreme Court ruled against Grokster in 2005, *CNN/ Money* covered the story with the headline "Hollywood Wins Internet Piracy Battle."[13] This framing was neither proof positive that P2P amounted to "piracy" in the minds of the public at large nor a happy accident for the media companies that wished to portray it in those terms. Rather, it was the result of an "intense global information campaign" by the recording industry beginning in 2003, which aimed at having a "decisive impact in raising public awareness" about the dangers of P2P.[14]

Immediately following the launch of this campaign, press coverage of the issue shifted drastically. In the first year, according to the news archive Westlaw, the number of stories using the phrase *illegal downloading* quadrupled, and the number using the term *music piracy* nearly tripled. By 2005, when the Supreme Court decided that even decentralized P2P was illegal, the use of this framing in the press had reached an all-time peak. After five years, funding for the campaign was cut, and the use of these terms in the press diminished considerably.[15]

These years also coincided with a different kind of campaign aimed at influencing public opinion and consumer behavior: between 2003 and 2008, the recording industry sued over thirty-five thousand Americans for engaging in P2P. The film, software, and adult entertainment industries soon followed suit. By 2010, there were one hundred thousand lawsuits *per year* against American citizens for unlicensed sharing of content over the internet.[16]

Very few of these suits have ever gone to trial, let alone ended in a decision; instead, the plaintiffs typically ask for, and receive, a cash

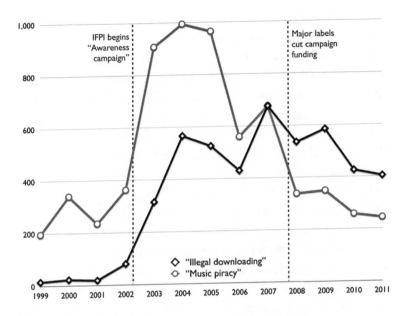

Figure 16: Incidence of terms promoted by music industry awareness campaigns in news sources, 1999–2011.

settlement of a few thousand dollars per defendant. Over the years, these settlements became a significant revenue stream for copyright-based industries, yielding hundreds of millions of dollars or more for rights holders. These litigations have also given rise to a new cottage industry, often referred to as "copyright trolls"—companies that specialize in identifying and litigating against possible online infringers.

In their efforts to classify P2P definitively as piracy, the media industries and courts have both largely overlooked fair use which, as you may recall, was an integral dimension to the Betamax ruling establishing that VCRs were legal. While the earlier ruling took great pains to emphasize that many consumer uses of tape copying technology were noninfringing, there was no such acknowledgment in the Grokster decision, which used the word "fair" only once, in reference to VCRs rather than to P2P.

Of course, many people do use file-sharing technology for the same purposes they once applied to VCRs—for instance, downloading TV shows and movies to which they already have legal access, because Blu-ray discs and cable television set-top boxes don't easily enable copying to a laptop or tablet. Yet, in the wake of the Grokster case, these and *all* uses of P2P to access copyrighted materials are presumed to be infringing, and carry the risk of litigation.

In recent years, as technology, culture, and industry have continued to coevolve, digital copying and the piracy debates have moved beyond traditional P2P networks. In the 2010s, the commercial market for media and entertainment has shifted away from retail-based downloading (like iTunes) toward subscriptions and advertising-based streaming (like Netflix and Spotify) as the dominant business models for copyrighted content. Similarly, unlicensed copying has taken a range of new forms, from digital "storage lockers" (like Megaupload and Putlocker) to BitTorrent streaming services (like PopcornTime and Auros) to rebroadcasting via "livestreaming" platforms (like Periscope and Facebook Live). Although a number of these platforms and many of their users have been branded as pirates and targeted in infringement suits, there has been little if any consideration of the fair uses such technologies might enable.

The shifting definition of piracy, accelerated by the widespread adoption of digital technology in recent decades, has contributed to a growing crisis in contemporary media culture. In the days of print, there were only a handful of "pirates"—those with the means to print unlicensed books and articles and distribute them commercially in large volume. In the electronic era, pirate radio typically entailed an expensive broadcasting apparatus, and often a seaworthy ship to keep it in international waters, while commercial media piracy required a factory for the mass replication of tapes and discs. By contrast, noncommercial, small-scale consumer copying and broad-casting escaped the taint of piracy through the legal recognition of fair use for home taping, and regulatory approval for low-power community radio. Actual, bona fide copyright pirates were still few and far between.

Today, instead of a handful of pirates plying their wares to a largely law-abiding consumer base, large swaths of the internet are classified as piratical, and the untold millions of users who engage in digital copying practices are treated as pirates. Media industries have turned mass litigation against their own customers into a boom-ing business, and the courts have backpedaled on recognizing non-commercial duplication as a definitively fair use.

The upshot is that two main factors—the divergence between the fundamental worldviews of media industries and their audiences and the criminalization of normative behavior—have helped to turn copyright into a mainstream political issue and have contributed to an unprecedented level of animosity among citizens and consumers toward rights holders and regulators. In the next chapter, we will explore this growing "copyfight" and examine some of the possible solutions to this crisis promoted by industries, governments, critics, and communities.

EIGHT

Copyleft and Copyfight

Throughout most of its first three centuries, copyright was a fairly arcane issue, more the domain of boardrooms and courtrooms than of the popular press and protest marches. The reason for this is simple: except in very rare instances, copyright law didn't play a direct role in the lives of ordinary citizens beyond appearing in small print at the beginning of a book or the end of a TV show. Most people never held a copyright in anything they themselves produced (remember that, until 1978, obtaining a copyright required registration with the federal government), and thus they had very little invested in the contours of the law itself.

By the same token, most copyright holders were more concerned with competition and "piracy" by other industrial interests than they were with the potentially infringing actions of their customers. Without printing presses, broadcasting towers, recording studios, or editing bays, let alone well-oiled relationships with major television networks, radio conglomerates, and retail chains, what threat could a mere civilian pose to media titans like New York book publishers or Hollywood film studios? Thus, just as consumers rarely concerned themselves with the restrictions posed by copyright in their daily lives, producers rarely concerned themselves with the limitations to their monopolies posed by small-scale duplication and distribution among the general populace.

All of this has changed over the past four decades or so as new laws, new technologies, and new cultural trends have brought traditional producers and consumers into greater competition and conflict, causing battles over copyright to erupt into mainstream public consciousness and making it more difficult for both everyday citizens and media industries to go about their business unhindered by one another's practices and demands.

The seeds of these changes were sown in the 1970s, when both copyright law and media technology began to move in profoundly new directions—trajectories they continue to follow to this day. As we have discussed, copyright law became far more ambitious in its scope, jettisoning registration requirements and applying automatically at the moment of creation to all works of original authorship in a fixed, tangible medium, and for far longer a duration than earlier laws had provided. In the same revision to the law, Congress codified fair use for the first time, creating a definitive statute supporting noncommercial uses—and creative reuses—of copyrighted materials by third parties. Thus, with one sweep of President Carter's pen, hundreds of millions of Americans simultaneously were given both ownership over their own cultural expression and exemption from liability for some uses of materials owned by others.

At the same time, as we reviewed in the previous chapter, new tape-based technologies like cassette decks and VCRs gave everyday people an unprecedented degree of power over their cultural experiences and a new level of independence from traditional media companies. These technologies allowed consumers to time-shift, space-shift, and library their electronic media, disrupting business practices and economies based on the regimented broadcasting and retail distribution of movies, songs, and shows. Additionally, they gave consumers the ability to become producers, taping and distributing their own creations as well as cutting and pasting bits of commercial material into new works.

One important example of this new cut-and-paste cultural aesthetic was the fan-produced video, or "fanvid" for short. Although there are many types of fanvids, one of the most popular and durable genres is "shipping" (an abbreviation of "relationshipping"), which may often also fall under the category of "slash" (homoerotic fan-produced stories named for the slash between two characters' names, such as Kirk/Spock). These fanvids created counternarratives challenging and deepening the stories shown on television by recombining broadcast materials in ways that brought new meanings to the surface. Thus, while Captain Kirk and Mr. Spock were merely good friends on the popular 1960s science fiction TV show *Star Trek*, they became (literally) star-crossed lovers in thousands of slash fanvids created and distributed among innumerable VCR owners during the 1970s, '80s, and '90s.

These videos rarely relied on any new materials. Instead, they took scenes from *Star Trek* episodes and movies out of their original context and, by juxtaposing a tender glance from one episode with a gentle bit of physical contact from another, overlaid by an appropriately syrupy love song from the pop charts, told a new story that, to many close observers, seemed to have been lurking just beneath the surface the entire time. The videos were then shared and sold via "zines" (amateur magazines, usually produced with photocopiers), which augmented the video-based narratives with erotic fiction, art, discussions, and other ruminations on the private lives of popular fictional characters.

Thus, these new consumer behaviors didn't merely challenge the

Figure 17: Cover of *Naked Times*, a *Star Trek* fanzine, 1978.

authority of media companies as industrial suppliers of entertainment, they also challenged their roles as the official gatekeepers of popular narratives. In the 1960s, Kirk and Spock belonged to NBC. In the 1980s, they belonged to the fans, especially those who took the time to produce vids, slash, zines, and other examples of "fan culture," altering and recirculating popular narratives in an underground network that paralleled the official channels of the airwaves and Blockbuster rental shelves.

With the growth of personal computers in the home and the rise of first desktop publishing in the 1980s and then the World Wide Web in the 1990s, these tape-based cultural practices evolved to become some of the foundational elements of what we often refer to today as "digital culture." At the same time, many of the political and industrial tensions engendered by tape culture emerged to become full-fledged political, economic, and legal crises as media companies and their newly empowered audiences faced ever greater degrees of conflict over the ownership and control of cultural information.

Once independent authors began using desktop publishing technology to lay out, print, copy, circulate, and sell their articles, stories, and books without the aid of commercial partners, finding global audiences for their work via the web, and once readers and fans recirculated previously published work via the same channels, the New York publishing titans no longer seemed quite so safe in their office towers. And once aspiring musicians and filmmakers began to produce and distribute their own work using little more than an internet-connected laptop, while legions of fans copied, mixed, and shared commercial music and video over the internet, the Hollywood heavyweights began to feel the ground give way beneath their feet.

The media industries responded to these new threats to their dominance by doubling down on copyright as an instrument of control. In the past, high production costs, cartelized markets, and limited airwaves and shelf space had served as an ample bulwark against outside competition, especially from noncommercial actors and independent creators without the means to participate on equal terms. As digital platforms and networks lowered costs, opened up markets, and enabled consumer choice and supplier competition on an unprecedented scale (consider the tens of millions of musicians on YouTube compared to the dozens featured on contemporary pop radio), copyright control over the most popular movies, books, and songs became one of the few unique assets of the traditional media companies, and thus it became the linchpin of their strategy to retain control over their markets.

At the same time, the legacy copyright industries hoped to slow or even reverse the tide of barbarians by closing and barring as many of the gates around their walled city as possible. In practical terms, this meant persuading lawmakers, internet services, and hardware and software manufacturers to rethink and reengineer digital platforms, making it more difficult for everyday people to edit, copy, and share cultural information. This would be a difficult pill for technology companies to swallow, given that ease of use and empowering media audiences were the main selling points for their products and services. Even more difficult would be getting independent creators and newly empowered audiences to agree to accept fresh limitations on their digital cultures and practices; once people have tasted the freedom to produce, how could they be content merely to consume?

Part of the media industries' strategy, as we discussed in the previous chapter, came in the form of adapting and amplifying "piracy" rhetoric, both to win legislative concessions and to build sympathy and support among the larger consumer base. A complementary approach has been using the metaphorical carrot in addition to the stick—for instance, making it easier and safer for people to stream music and movies legally than to download them illegally. Yet despite these efforts, there has been a continuing—and by some measures growing—resistance among the general population to both legislative and technological limitations on digital cultural practices. While this resistance takes many forms and varies from community to community and context to context, it is often referred to in general terms as "the copyfight."

In the rest of this chapter, we will take a closer look at these dynamics, exploring some of the specific ways in which media industries have strategically used both copyright law and digital barriers —often in conjunction with one another—to limit competition and neutralize threats from outsiders and from their own customers. We will also examine some of the innovative ways in which different digitally rooted communities have resisted these efforts, using legal, technological, and cultural means to present alternative visions of copyright, industry, and creativity. Finally, we will examine the current state of the copyfight and consider its political significance in our era.

Blocking the Gates: The Battle over Source Code

Professional prognosticators and commentators often treat the development of media technology as a one-way street, an inevitable series of magical innovations leading to an equally inevitable set of disruptions in business, culture, and society. In reality, of course, the process is far more complex. Technology developers and media programmers must constantly navigate a dense and contradictory web of expectations and obstacles presented by consumers, suppliers, partners, competitors, investors, legislators, regulators, creators, and their own human and material resources, and thus what ends up being offered to the public is often very far from what a given creator, designer, or marketer may have planned at the outset of the process.

Even once they've introduced their new products and services to the marketplace, businesses can never fully anticipate how interested consumers will be, which set of consumers might show an interest, or what uses those consumers will ultimately find for the things they choose to spend their money on. Why did the VHS videocassette format win out over the technically superior Betamax? Why did FM radio gain dominance over AM technology half a century after its invention, decades after it had been written off by many as a waste of the electromagnetic spectrum? Why did the television cartoon franchise *My Little Pony*, initially targeted at young girls, gain a massive fan base among adult men? Plenty of ink has been spilled explaining such phenomena in retrospect, but few people, if any, anticipated these developments beforehand.

The coevolution of media, technology, and markets rarely follows a straight line, let alone a clear trajectory toward some vision of progress or perfection. One of the ways in which this process frequently defies conventional wisdom, mystifying and bedeviling many creators and consumers, is when media technology becomes *less* useful over time, making it more difficult for people to access, edit, store, and share information with one another. An excellent case in point is computer software, which has become much more difficult to copy and build upon than it was a few decades ago.

A nonprogrammer might be excused for being unaware of this trend or, if he is aware of it, for considering it to be an inevitable consequence of Moore's law and the geometric growth in computer capacity and complexity over the years.[1] Yet there is nothing remotely inevitable about it; the truth is that computer programs have become more difficult to access and edit because software publishers have engineered it that way, mostly for the purposes of forestalling competition and preventing unlicensed sharing.

In the early days of computers, there were no screens or keyboards as we now know them, and programs existed in paper form as stacks of cardboard cards with holes punched in them reflecting the 1s and 0s of binary computer code. A programmer would create a sequence on paper, then very carefully feed it, card by card, through the computer to run the program itself. At this point, copying programs was still logistically difficult—it meant reproducing the thousands of cards in a stack flawlessly and in the correct order, or re-creating the stack of cards based on detailed instructions.

By the 1960s and '70s, computer programming languages, and the programs themselves, had evolved considerably. Instead of keying 1s and 0s directly into a machine, software developers could use a text-based screen interface, writing code that would tell the machine itself where to put the 1s and 0s. This is how most programming is done to this day, with the programmer writing *source code* (legible to humans) and special software converting it into *machine code* (also known as binary code; these are the 1s and 0s legible to computers).

Even though computer programs became copyrightable as literary works in the U.S. beginning in the late 1970s, there was no technical reason they couldn't be copied or edited by an end user, either for legal or illegal purposes. That's because every software publisher, from individual hobbyists to big businesses, included the source code along with the machine code, allowing anyone to tweak and tinker with the programs they ran, optimizing them for their individual needs and idiosyncratic machines.

This began to change drastically in 1983, when IBM—one of the biggest names in the computer industry at that time—started distributing machine code without source code attached to it, so programs could be run by machines but not edited or copied by humans. This move was seen as an affront to the computer programming community, both because it prevented users from accessing software they had bought and rightfully owned and also because untold numbers of programmers within the community had contributed to the open commons of shared code that was now being privatized and severed from its source. Furthermore, the move made it harder for third-party companies to develop innovative products and services based on IBM's hardware and software; now, any such efforts would require permission and participation by IBM.

The move was also seen as a massive business risk; even by the late 1980s, mainstream tech publications like *Computerworld* openly wondered whether IBM's anticompetitive strategy would be worth the bad will it engendered among the company's customer base and the impediments to innovation it erected for the industry at large. Yet, within a few more years, IBM's closed-source strategy would become the norm for commercial software, contributing to the massive industry consolidation that would elevate companies like Microsoft to dominance.

The programming community didn't sit idly by while Congress transformed its previously public domain of code into a privatized market of copyrighted goods, or while IBM and its followers started shipping private software, built on the foundations of that public domain, without its source code. Tectonic changes of these magnitude meant there was no more neutral ground; coders were either for privatization or against it, and very few people could comfortably remain in the widening chasm between the two positions.

Plenty of programmers supported these changes, of course. More privatization meant more investment, which meant more jobs and more opportunities to make money. After decades of hobbyist hacking at home with little or no financial remuneration, there were many coders who welcomed a paycheck and a cubicle in an air-conditioned office building. Others relished the chance to turn their passion into a profession by launching their own software companies, taking advantage of the same laws and practices used by IBM to achieve similar market effects on a smaller scale.

Yet there were also many programmers who resented these legal and technological obstacles to sharing code freely, and some who actively resisted the new regime of privatized code. Chief among these was a programmer named Richard M. Stallman, a veteran of the artificial intelligence lab at MIT, which was a hothouse for computer innovation in the 1970s and widely considered to be one of the birthplaces of "hacker culture." Frustrated and morally appalled at the implications of copyrighted, closed-source software, Stallman set out to create legal and technological alternatives to the "proprietary and secret" products, services, and business practices that he believed were coming to dominate computer programming. In 1983, Stallman announced plans to start work on a new, open-source operating system called GNU (the acronym stands for "GNUs Not Unix," a recursive joke calculated to appeal to those with an appropriately nerdy sense of humor).[2] As he explained two years later in a manifesto published in the hacker periodical *Dr. Dobb's Journal*, "Copying all or parts of a program is as natural to a programmer as breathing, and as productive. It ought to be as free."[3]

Later, Stallman would coin a widely repeated slogan defining freedom in the context of the "free software" movement. In his formulation, software should be free as in *speech*, not as in *beer*. In other words, Stallman wasn't advocating that tech laborers simply give away the fruits of their labors or toil without the benefit of a paycheck. To the contrary, he expressed hopes that software would thrive as an industry and a community not only despite having open source code but because of it. Yet he also believed that free-as-in-speech software would be one of the keys to achieving what he called a "postscarcity world," in which well-engineered, universally accessible software programs would help to liberate humanity from the drudgery of labor and the privations of poverty, allowing everyone to "devote themselves to activities that are fun."[4]

Creating an open-source operating system and laying the ideological foundations for the free software movement were both impressive and influential interventions, earning Stallman an important place in hacker history. Yet these technical and philosophical efforts would become far more durable and powerful when he added a legal component to the mix. In 1989, Stallman wrote the GNU General Public License (GPL), a new species of legal instrument that would help to change the way that people thought about copyright and technology for decades to come.

As we have discussed throughout this book, the history of copyright is one of increasingly broadly defined powers to restrict access to an increasingly wide range of artifacts for an increasingly long duration. For better and for worse, copyright exists explicitly for the purpose of monopolizing cultural expression, at a cost to free and open discourse that is calculated to be worth the corresponding boost in incentive for creators to share their work. The GPL reversed this trend and inverted this power dynamic in a way that no other legal technique had ever done in the previous two and a half centuries.

Stallman accomplished all of this primarily through the use of two clever legal requirements in the GPL. First of all, any software published under this license would have to include the source code along with the machine code, allowing any user to edit and adapt the program to suit his individual needs. Second, anyone who adapted code released under the GPL into something new would also have to use the GPL if she released it, whether commercially or not. Thus, for the first time in legal history, the power of copyright was leveraged to enforce openness and access rather than exclusivity and exclusion. This concept came to be called *copyleft*—a play on words that served to call attention to copyright's historically one-sided role in the marketplace of ideas while providing a quick and easy term to encapsulate the premise that the law could be used to liberate creative expression rather than to restrain it.

In the years following the launch of the GPL, both open licenses and the free software movement caught on like wildfire. Alternative licenses like Berkeley Software Distribution (BSD) and Apache, which defined freedom and openness in slightly different ways than the GPL, also gained widespread traction (although by many measures GPL remains the free software license with the widest use to this day). In the meantime, countless free and open-source software initiatives were launched, building on the success of GNU and the legal foundations of the GPL.

Perhaps the best-known and most widely used free software initiative is Linux, an open-source operating system first proposed and developed by a Finnish student named Linus Torvalds in 1991. Over the following decades, thousands of programmers would contribute their time and expertise to the Linux project and, with the aid of a GPL license, it would come to dominate many of the largest computing markets in the world, including (at the time of writing) over 95 percent of all internet servers and over 80 percent of all smartphones (in the form of Android, which is based on the Linux kernel).

True to Stallman's vision, Linux is also responsible for tens of billions of dollars in annual revenues for a variety of companies large and small, from Red Hat, which makes over $2 billion per year providing open-source software and services to the business community, to IBM itself, which currently generates billions of dollars per year by selling and servicing hardware that runs on Linux. Ironically, it seems IBM's decision to switch to closed-source software in 1983 paid off for the company over the long term—by inspiring Stallman, Torvalds, and thousands of others to invest in developing better, cheaper, open-source alternatives!

Closed-Source Culture: DRM and the DMCA

In the 1990s and 2000s, as digital devices and networks increasingly supplanted tape and broadcast technologies in people's homes, the cut-and-paste aesthetics and do-it-yourself ethics of tape culture blended with certain elements of hacker culture to give rise to a new set of digital communication practices and creative forms. While small communities of enthusiasts once had shared fanvids, mixtapes, and zines via the postal service and face-to-face meet-ups, now millions of people around the globe were using the web and other digital platforms such as Usenet and peer-to-peer file sharing to exchange mash-ups, remixes, memes, machinima, video game mods, anime music videos, and countless other new types of art and expression.

Like their cultural antecedents, these new digital forms were largely based on taking bits and pieces of commercially distributed mainstream culture and giving them new meanings by combining and juxtaposing them in new ways. Yet the internet's size and speed meant that many more people could participate in the process and that creative communities could react to world events and emerging trends instantaneously, rather than waiting weeks, months, or decades (in the case of *Star Trek* fanvids) to put a new spin on an old idea. Empowered audiences could now challenge the official narrative about any subject, from politics to celebrity gossip, by mashing it up and remixing it, just as they had once challenged "master narratives," such as heteronormativity, by creating homoerotic shipping vids. To put it another way, now it wasn't merely the authority of the major television networks that was being challenged but the very concept of authority itself.

Another important respect in which digital culture differed from tape culture was in its recursion. To make slash from a television show in the 1980s, a creator would have to record several episodes from her television onto a magnetic tape, then use multiple VCRs and additional audio equipment to edit the footage into something new, then make a duplicate copy of the finished product and send it through the mail to its intended recipient. Digital technology collapsed this process; a single internet-connected laptop could serve as the source for all materials, the editing tool to create the new work, and the distribution platform to share it with the world at large. This technological convergence meant not only that creators could act more quickly, they could poach more omnivorously from a broader range of sources—including other mash-ups and remixes!

Thus, while tape culture began with commercial media and ended with a mixtape or fanvid produced by a single creator, digital networked culture has neither beginning nor end, nor even necessarily distinct authors. Instead, an ocean of digitized cultural information from a variety of commercial and independent sources is continually published, remixed, reinterpreted, and recirculated by billions of participants, blurring the traditional lines distinguishing producer from consumer, art from entertainment, and mass publication from interpersonal communication.

To social scientists, cultural theorists, and legal scholars, these changes have been fascinating to watch. During the first decade of the twenty-first century, countless books and articles were published attempting to make sense of these rapid developments, using terms like *remix culture, configurable culture*, and *convergence culture* to describe the new forms of power and influence wielded by media audiences and consumers, the new economies and business practices developed by media producers and distributors, and the new legal conundrums surrounding copyright concepts like fair use, derivative works, and authorship. Uniting many of these disparate theories and arguments was the observation that the world's cultural information, digitized and accessible to billions of internet users, constituted a kind of digital commons—a shared collective heritage from which all had the power to draw, and to which all had the power to contribute, with a degree of fluidity and on a scale never before conceived.[5]

To the traditional media industries themselves, these changes were equal parts terrifying, tantalizing, and confusing. In a way, mainstream culture was becoming more and more like software, with different versions of each song, movie, and game tailored to different audiences and platforms, and with members of an increasingly technology-literate consumer base willing and able to take the official products apart and reconfigure them to suit their own needs and interests. This meant that movie studios and record labels had the opportunity to enlist their own customers as their allies in producing, marketing, and distributing new work geared toward ever more targeted audiences. But, as we discussed above, it also meant losing the absolute control over products and narratives that had been the cornerstone of media industry strategy since the days of the printing press.

The media industries responded to the challenges of digitization, and the increasingly software-like qualities of cultural expression, by taking a page from the software publishers' playbook: in order to regain control over their products and their customers, they would separate the source code from the machine code. Of course, they couldn't do this literally; a movie needs to be seen and a song needs to be heard, so there's no significant difference between the version a producer hears in the studio and the one a fan hears on her earbuds. There's no cultural equivalent of machine code. But beginning around the turn of the century, many commercial media products were made to behave *as though* they were closed-source through the use of a technology called "digital rights management," or DRM.

DRM has many different variations and uses. At its most basic, it is a kind of digital padlock that, when wrapped around another file such as an MP3, prevents people from copying, editing, and/or distributing the file in question. You have no doubt experienced the limitations imposed on your own media by DRM in your daily digital life. When you download a movie from Apple's iTunes store and can't play it on your Android tablet, that's DRM. When you buy a video game for your PlayStation and can't make a backup copy of the disc (in case your dog eats the original), that's DRM.[6] When you buy a DVD in Japan and can't play it on your American DVD player, that's DRM. In all of these cases, the outcome is parallel to what happens when you ship computer software without the source code: people can use the product exactly as the manufacturer intended but can't adapt it to their own particular needs as consumers or use it as an element in their own creative production.

Even when it is used well, DRM has several drawbacks. First of all, the technology makes it extremely difficult for consumers to exercise their fair use rights, from time-shifting to librarying to creative transformation. It's also annoying—often consumers won't even become aware of DRM until it prevents them from doing something they want to do with the media they've purchased, leading to bad will and dissatisfaction.

There are challenges from a business standpoint as well. For one thing, DRM doesn't really do much to prevent unlicensed sharing because even if nearly every copy of a digital file remains secure, only one copy needs to be "cracked" (stripped of its protective wrapper) in order for it to be seeded to the internet and shared countless times. For another, the obstacles introduced by DRM are actually a good incentive for consumers to shun commercial media formats and seek out unlicensed, DRM-free versions instead. Many a time I myself have resorted to P2P networks to find a copy of a movie, game, or album I already owned legitimately, simply because it was too much trouble for me to make my own copy based on the DRM-protected version.

In the worst-case scenarios, DRM can destroy millions of dollars worth of goods owned by consumers, or even invalidate every single sale ever transacted by a given merchant. This has happened several times in the past, for instance, when Yahoo! and Microsoft decided to close down their digital music download stores. In both cases, the companies had to choose between either keeping their DRM servers running indefinitely to service their past customers (at an ongoing cost) or shutting them down, which would make all the music people had previously bought from them unusable. In both cases, the companies chose to shut the servers down, destroying countless consumers' music collections in the process. As *Wired* magazine wrote about the Yahoo! shutdown, "If you bought DRMed, copy-protected music, you are an idiot."[7]

Despite the many well-documented technological, legal, and economic problems caused by DRM, it has continued since the 1990s to be one of the primary means used by media and software companies to protect their work from unlicensed copying. This is partly because, despite its many drawbacks, it *works.* When Apple wraps DRM around a movie from the iTunes store, it makes consumers more likely to buy an iPad than an Android tablet, which means more money for Apple. And if a consumer does buy an Android device after all, he'll need to pay a second time to watch the movie, which means more money for the film studio. There is little question that DRM effectively puts obstacles in the way of consumers' efforts to copy and edit their media, and that those obstacles present business opportunities to both media and technology companies (of course, these opportunities may or may not be worth the costs to goodwill and future consumer spending).

Yet there is a second, equally important reason that DRM remains a primary tool used by media companies to control the distribution of cultural information: it's baked into international copyright law. The WIPO Copyright Treaty of 1996, which we discussed in chapter 6, requires all contracting parties to "provide adequate legal protection and effective legal remedies against the circumvention of effective technological measures that are used by authors in connection with the exercise of their rights . . . that restrict acts, in respect of their works, which are not authorized by the authors concerned or permitted by law." In plain English, this means that all treaty members have to create laws making it illegal for people to bypass DRM. In legal circles, this is called the "anti-circumvention provision."

In the United States, this provision is enshrined in the Digital Millennium Copyright Act, which we discussed in chapter 2 in relation to safe harbors. When the DMCA first passed, it was criticized widely by free speech advocates for privileging protection over expression. Although the original text of the law explicitly states that its provisions would not "affect rights, remedies, limitations, or defenses to copyright infringement, including fair use," it doesn't explain how a user is supposed to exercise those rights without circumventing DRM, which remains a felony regardless of whether infringement takes place or not.

This inherent contradiction in the law has led to some contradictory interpretations by the courts. In some cases, judges have ruled that the anti-circumvention rules apply only if the plaintiff can demonstrate that the defendant bypassed DRM in the course of actual copyright infringement. In other cases, judges have ruled that fair use isn't a viable defense against the DMCA's anti-circumvention clause, and that people who bypass DRM are liable even if they did so solely in the interest of exercising their rights. This uncertainty creates a classic "chilling effect," in which people and companies, uncertain of whether they're exposing themselves to liability or not, err on the side of caution and opt not to exercise their rights, thus rendering those rights effectively moot.

There is a small, wonky workaround to this dilemma in the DMCA, which requires the librarian of Congress to hold a "rule-making proceeding" every three years, granting limited exemptions to the anti-circumvention rule. At the time of writing, the most recent rulemaking in 2015 created exemptions for a variety of activities, including (1) using "short portions" of movies "for the purpose of criticism or comment"; (2) bypassing DRM on e-books to help sight-impaired or disabled readers get access to books they've purchased; (3) accessing a wireless communication network with permission from its operator; (4) "jailbreaking" smartphones, smart TVs, 3D printers, and vehicles to add, delete, or modify the software on them; (5) playing lawfully acquired video games "locally" without validation from an external server; and (6) accessing your own medical data from a networked personal monitoring device. Obviously, these rulemaking sessions are beneficial to free speech and user rights. Yet they fall significantly short of the bar set by the fair use provisions in copyright law. First of all, they are subject to the whims of the librarian of Congress and therefore to political tides; this is an appointed rather than an elected position, and even less beholden to the needs of the voters than a congressperson or senator would be. Second, unlike binding legislation, these rules last only three years; unless they are positively reaffirmed, they disappear in a puff of smoke, and with them go all the associated rights of filmmakers, gamers, medical patients, and other beneficiaries.

Finally, unlike fair use, these rulings cite specific exemptions rather than general principles. In doing so, they adopt the more restrictive methods that characterize "fair dealing" provisions in places like Europe rather than the more expansive ones, informed by the First Amendment, that characterize American fair use. In short, they're a welcome bandage to stanch the DMCA's bleeding, but not the reconstructive surgery required to make sure the law adequately protects fair use rights in perpetuity.

From Copyleft to Copyfight

Back when the battle over the digital commons was restricted to issues surrounding computer source code, the criticism and resistance to copyright was largely confined to the more radical wing of a fairly arcane technical field. Richard Stallman might have raised a big stink, but he did so in a very small space, and few outside of the software development community were aware of the disputes and legal innovations brewing within it.

As more of our cultural platforms have become digital and as the mainstream media industries have adopted the restrictive philosophies and tactics of the software titans, however, the battle has spilled out into the virtual streets (and, at times, into the actual streets). By the end of the 1990s, following the widespread adoption of the World Wide Web the enactment of the DMCA, and the high-profile disputes over P2P and other forms of "digital piracy," copyright became a (more) mainstream issue, and the "copyfight" became a popular cause among free speech and privacy advocates.

One of the early leaders of the copyfight was Harvard Law professor Lawrence Lessig, who had been involved in several high-profile legal matters surrounding law and digital technology, including the United States' antitrust suit against Microsoft (in which he served as a "special master") and *Eldred v. Ashcroft*, a case challenging the Copyright Term Extension Act of 1998, in which he served as lead counsel for the plaintiff (he ultimately lost, in a 7-2 Supreme Court decision).

Beginning in 2000, Lessig published a series of highly influential books critiquing intellectual property law in the digital age and elaborating a set of principles for protecting what he called the "creative commons." He also cofounded an organization with the same name, which took Stallman's innovations in open licensing and applied them broadly to cultural expression rather than just to software. Creative Commons licenses, currently in their fourth iteration, give authors, artists, musicians, filmmakers, photographers, game developers, and many other kinds of creators the ability to use their copyright powers to make sure their work remains accessible and adaptable by third parties, while still retaining some ownership and control. Creative Commons licenses are more flexible and adaptable than the GPL and many other free software licenses, allowing creators to decide whether they want to require attribution, prevent derivative works, and prevent commercial reuses of their works, as well as giving them the option to require that all licensees apply the same rules to their own derivative works.

Lessig cofounded the organization in 2001. At the time of writing, more than fifteen years later, over 1.2 billion works have been released under a Creative Commons license, including tens or hundreds of millions of songs, photographs, videos, games, and websites each, as well as thousands of full-length books.[8]

Just as the development of the GPL was a spark that helped to light the flame of the free software movement, Creative Commons has inspired millions of creators to share their work more freely and has also served as the platform for a great many libraries, universities, and other institutions interested in providing "access to knowledge" and "free culture" over the past decade and a half. Not only are countless posts and files on the world's top three websites (Google, YouTube, and Facebook, at the time of writing) licensed by Creative Commons, the fifth-largest site, Wikipedia, uses the license for every page and item it hosts.

Among the most enthusiastic adopters of these licenses are many of the creators whose work has presented such a challenge to our traditional understanding of art, media, and authorship: the mashers, modders, remixers, and other "configurable" culture makers who use digital cut-and-paste technologies to make something new from something old. According to my own survey research, the majority of people who create mash-ups and remixes have used a Creative Commons license to make their work more available to others, compared to only a small fraction of the general population.

While copyleft licenses such as the GPL and Creative Commons have helped to transform a range of creative fields over the past few decades, the copyfight also has a political dimension, rooted in various forms of resistance to IP laws and treaties, and marked by a growing awareness and concern about their broader social consequences. In the past decade, this resistance has taken the form of several large-scale popular protests—a new phenomenon in the centuries-old history of intellectual property.

In Europe, massive protests broke out a few years ago over a proposed treaty called the Anti-Counterfeiting Trade Agreement, or ACTA. This accord, which (like many of its kind) was negotiated between dozens of nations in secret, was leaked at various stages in its development, and its proposed provisions were widely criticized as a threat to free speech, privacy, market innovation, and civil rights. Advocacy organizations like the Electronic Frontier Foundation (EFF) have even argued that the agreement may not be constitutional within the United States (which was a signatory).

Tens of thousands of people took to the streets across Europe to demonstrate against ACTA, accompanied by various forms of online civil disobedience such as government website hacks and denial of service (DoS) attacks. Even some government members turned against the treaty, including dozens of Polish legislators who showed up to Parliament with Guy Fawkes masks reminiscent of the logo for the "hacktivist" collective Anonymous. Ultimately, following this widespread backlash, most of ACTA's signatories declined to ratify the accord, and at the time of writing, Japan remains the only official party to the agreement.

Around the same time that Europe was roiled by anti-ACTA protests, the United States was marked by demonstrations and civil disobedience related to a set of federal bills called the Stop Online Piracy Act and the Protect IP Act, criticized for many of the same threats to privacy and civil liberties as ACTA. While the crowds demonstrating in the streets were somewhat smaller than those in Europe, the online efforts were commensurately larger and better organized. Over 100,000 websites—including heavyweights like

Figure 18: Polish legislators wearing Guy Fawkes masks in Parliament.
(AP Photo/Alik Keplicz.)

Google, Wikipedia, and Twitter—participated in a coordinated blackout, hoping to communicate the potential censorship impact of these laws to their billions of collective users.

By some measures, these demonstrations were successful; more than 10 million voters contacted their elected representatives to protest the bills, and many more signed online petitions and took other online actions to register their displeasure. The bills were never passed, and the White House published a response to the petitions pledging not to "support legislation that reduces freedom of expression, increases cybersecurity risk, or undermines the dynamic, innovative global Internet."[9]

Yet four years later, President Obama signed a bill with some very similar provisions—and similar warnings from civil liberties advocates like the EFF and the American Civil Liberties Union (ACLU)—into law as an amendment to a consolidated spending bill. Unlike SOPA and PIPA, this bill (originally titled the Cybersecurity Information Sharing Act, or CISA) doesn't focus specifically on intellectual property; rather, it treats IP as one of many "national security" interests threatened by "cybersecurity risks." Ultimately, however, the outcome is the same: under this law, internet companies have immunity and incentive to spy on their users and share their information with government agencies, without a warrant—if those users are suspected of violating IP laws or otherwise compromising the law's broad definition of cybersecurity interests.

While most of the protest against IP laws and policies has been undertaken by citizens, advocacy organizations, and (at times) their allies in the commercial sector, there is also significant concern about and resistance to these policies within government agencies and political parties. I have already mentioned the symbolic protest staged within the Polish Parliament over ACTA. In the United States, Alejandro Mayorkas, deputy secretary of the Department of Homeland Security (DHS), authored a letter to Senator Al Franken sharing his concerns about the civil liberties implications of CISA, acknowledging that the law could "sweep away important privacy protections" while deluging the DHS with "large amounts of information with dubious value" in the fight against genuine cybersecurity threats.[10]

Even within the U.S. legislature, civil liberties advocates on both sides of the spectrum, from left-wingers like Senators Ron Wyden and Bernie Sanders to right-wingers like Senator Rand Paul and Congressman Darrell Issa, have opposed laws like SOPA, PIPA, and CISA, and have even pushed for alternate legislation that would guarantee online privacy and freedom of expression, regardless of countervailing concerns about IP infringement or cybersecurity. Yet, as we discussed in chapter 5, these efforts amount to little more than symbolic acts of protest without either consistently heavy lobbying expenditure or sustained voter support behind them—and, despite the growing visibility and volatility of the copyfight, neither is likely in the foreseeable future.

Thus the copyfight has made some strange bedfellows, bringing together traditional political rivals to form new coalitions both supporting and opposing intellectual property laws and treaties. Yet it has also opened the door to new political movements and organizations. Most prominent among these is the Pirate Party, a political movement founded in Sweden in 2006 and organized around a platform that explicitly privileges access to knowledge, privacy, and free speech over the privatization of cultural information (the details of the platform differ from chapter to chapter and region to region). At the time of writing, Pirate Party members hold hundreds of elected positions in dozens of countries, mostly at municipal and state levels of government, though there are also several members of national parliaments and even one member of the European Parliament. And in Iceland, following a very successful 2016 election campaign that more than tripled its representation in Parliament, the Pirate Party ran the national government.

Despite the party's ironic, self-deprecating name and its specialized focus on intellectual property laws, its purview and appeal have both broadened as it has grown. Today, the Pirate Party is beginning to develop into a more mature, populist movement—especially in Europe, where the parliamentary political system offers more of a platform for emerging political perspectives than the two-party system that characterizes countries like the United States.

Its appeal seems to be growing faster in the wake of revelations about the broad extent of state surveillance and the increasing role of dark money in national (and international) politics. These issues play directly into the Pirate Party's technologically savvy brand of populism. As one German Pirate Party operative explained to the BBC after some electoral successes in 2012, "We offer what people want. People are really angry at all the other parties because they don't do what politicians should do. We offer transparency, we offer participation. We offer basic democracy."[11]

Indeed, for many copyfighters on both sides of the divide, the increasingly acrimonious battles over intellectual property laws seem to have less and less to do with the details governing limited monopolies for incentivizing creators and inventors and more and more to do with the broader issues surrounding "basic democracy." For those in favor of treaties like ACTA and laws like CISA, such policies are absolutely necessary to further the growth of a vibrant international media and communications industry, and to provide financial security to pharmaceutical and technology researchers attempting to improve the quality of life for billions of people around the globe. For those opposed to them, these policies pose a dire threat to fundamental human rights and human dignity, while stacking the economic deck in favor of a handful of multinational corporations. There is precious little middle ground left between these ideological extremes.

Unfortunately, the copyfight is probably only getting started. As digital networks continue to increase in speed, complexity, and adoption, as markets and systems of governance become increasingly globalized, and as emerging technologies push the definitions of authorship and invention ever further from those understood by the original shapers of copyright, patent, and trademark laws, our societies will need to make some very difficult decisions about how to adapt IP laws and policies to suit these new realities. We will address some of these changes, and their implications in both the near term and the long term, in the conclusion.

Conclusion

The Future of Intellectual Property

Over the course of this book, we have covered a broad array of subjects, ranging from the prehistory of intellectual property to the backroom politics behind our laws and treaties to the front lines of the "copyfight" on streets and servers around the globe. For some readers, it may seem that we've gotten so deep into the proverbial weeds we can never find our way out. To others—those who have caught the IP bug—it may seem like we've only skated on the surface, and that each chapter and section of this book warrants a much deeper dive into the brackish waters beneath. My aim throughout has been to leave both groups dissatisfied—by telling the first more than they ever wanted to know, and by inspiring the second to find out more.

Another shortcoming of this book is that, like most publications, it is frozen in time while its subject continues to evolve. Already, in the course of writing it, I've had to go back to earlier chapters several times to revise passages that have been rendered obsolete by new legislation, judicial decisions, or political, economic, cultural, and technological developments. By the time you're holding this book in your hands or otherwise accessing its contents, I'm confident that many additional facts and analyses I've laid out here will have evolved as well. Yet I am also confident that the spirit of the book—a critical perspective that seeks to understand the needs and interests of all the stakeholders involved in IP, the historical contingencies of its development, and the consequences of these laws beyond their immediate application to information-based industries—will remain relevant even as the specificities continue to change.

Notwithstanding the necessarily dated scope of this book, it would be useful to conclude by considering the future of IP and the implications of this future for society. Without a crystal ball, the best I can offer is a guess based on current trends and developments. First, we'll review some of the agenda items on the lists of both lobbyists and reformists at the time of writing, and discuss briefly their potential outcomes and effects. Then, we'll peer a little deeper into the mist and discuss some of the longer-term questions hanging over the field. For any future readers, I'm sure this part will be especially entertaining in its omissions and oversights, though I hope you will also be pleasantly surprised by at least a few direct hits. Either way, this chapter should offer some illumination regarding the vector and tenor of developments in intellectual property during the second decade of the twenty-first century.

The Near Term: Customs, Trolls, Reforms, and Shakeups

During each congressional session in the U.S., hundreds of bills related to intellectual property are drafted and introduced into the legislative process. Only a handful eventually makes it into law. Yet for those of us who keep track of such matters, it's not a pure guessing game to anticipate which will succeed and which will fail. History shows that there are some useful indicators that help to predict whether a given bill (or at least its underlying agenda) will one day be enacted.

One factor that we've discussed extensively in this book is the amount of lobbying and campaign finance supporting the bill or agenda item in question. Obviously, the higher this figure is, the better the bill's chances. Another indicator is the number of times identical or substantially similar bills are introduced to Congress; it often takes several attempts before one finally becomes the basis for binding law. Yet another indicator is the amount of "buzz" surrounding an issue; the more op-eds, social media activity, and mainstream news coverage you see of a given issue, the more likely it is that someone is stoking public interest to add pressure to legislators to support a certain bill. Finally, if you put stock in such things, websites like PredictGov.com use statistically based algorithms to predict the percentage chance that any given bill will eventually become law.

Based on these and other factors, there are a number of changes in intellectual property law and policy that are likely to emerge in the near future. The first among these is one that was signed into law by President Obama (after twenty-eight separate bills attempting the same changes failed in both houses of Congress!), and has gradually been trickling down into actual policy. Officially titled the Trade Facilitation and Trade Enforcement Act, this law adds new funding to Customs and Border Protection (CBP) and Immigration and Customs Enforcement (ICE), with some strings attached. Specifically, it requires that these federal agencies drastically increase their efforts policing national borders for items that may infringe upon IP owned by American interests.

In the interest of accomplishing these ends, representatives of the private sector (for instance, entertainment and pharmaceutical companies) are being added to an "Advisory Committee" and asked to "educate" CPB and ICE employees about intellectual property and how to "enhance enforcement" of infringement. These enhanced efforts are overseen by a new taxpayer-funded unit within ICE, the National Intellectual Property Rights Coordination Center, run by an assistant director appointed by the secretary of Homeland Security. In addition to running the center, the assistant director is expected to coordinate with other federal agencies and with representatives of the private sector in order to conduct ongoing initiatives aimed at "combating the infringement of intellectual property rights."

In other words, this new law marks the continuation and escalation of a trend we discussed earlier: IP infringement is now being recast as a crucial element of national security, much as online "piracy" has been recast as an issue of cybersecurity. This is a brilliant legislative strategy because identifying an issue as crucial to the safety and well-being of the populace (as opposed to, say, crucial to corporate profitability or to the development and maintenance of a healthy public sphere) is the best possible way to garner widespread support within Congress and to assure support from the president.

It is unclear at this point whether shifting the focus of Homeland Security, CPB, and ICE *toward* policing IP infringement will necessarily require a shift *away* from policing things like drugs, weapons, and terrorism. If that is indeed the case, it seems like a policy whose utility and longevity might be limited; if these departments were to drop the ball on something genuinely threatening because they were otherwise occupied making sure that counterfeit handbags don't cross the border, and their balance of priorities came to light, it's easy to imagine a wave of justifiable anger and backlash within the government and among the American people at large.

Another important change that may be coming to U.S. IP law in the near future is patent reform, which has been the subject of over a dozen bills in both houses of Congress between 2010 and 2016 and was even mentioned by President Obama in his 2014 State of the

Union Address—the first such mention since 1946, when Harry S. Truman briefly listed "improving Patent Office procedures" as an agenda item in his annual address.

Why has patent reform risen to such an important agenda item over the past decade? The answer is simple: in the span of a few brief years, a crisis has emerged that threatens to put the entire patent system—as well as American industries—in peril. The agents of this crisis are technically called nonpracticing entities (NPEs), but they are widely referred to by a more meaningful and memorable name: "patent trolls."

Historically, as we have discussed throughout this book, the function of patents has been to grant inventors and discoverers of useful things a brief window of exclusivity to bring those useful things to market, in exchange for which they share the bounty of their inventions and discoveries with society at large by filing details about them in publicly available databases maintained by the USPTO and other similar governmental organizations around the world. Unlike the copyright system, this system has remained relatively unchanged over the years; patents still must be filed and granted (rather than automatically popping into existence), and they last only for twenty years in most cases (rather than, say, an author's life plus seventy years). Because of this, they continue to be a fairly functional and useful legal tool, and the world has benefited both from the thousands of patented items filed every year and from the wealth of inventions and discoveries whose twenty-year patent term has elapsed and that are now part of the public domain.

In contrast to these inventors and discoverers (and the corporations that employ or subsidize them), patent trolls are called "nonpracticing entities" because they do not actively use the inventions and discoveries in question. In fact, the great bulk of them do not ever invent or discover *anything*. Instead, these companies simply acquire patents cheaply from bankrupt companies, unfunded inventors, and other sources, and then make money by using these patents to threaten actual working people and organizations with lawsuits. As a recent study in the prestigious journal *Science* argued, trolls use these typically "low-quality" patents to engage in "opportunism."[1]

Specifically, patent trolls target two different kinds of victims: small companies or individual proprietors without the legal wherewithal to stand up to a sustained legal assault (in which case the payday is a small, quick settlement), and large, well-funded companies whose patents, technologies, or business methods seem vulnerable to attack by the right patent (in which case the payday is a big settlement or a court win with the prospect of ongoing royalties). In fact, the *Science* article demonstrated that being "cash-rich" makes a company twice as likely to get sued by patent trolls and less likely to be sued by legitimate patent holders.

A great example of a patent troll with both kinds of victim is a company called Personal Audio, LLC, which more or less claimed it owned the rights to the technology underlying podcasting and MP3 players. Based on two loosely worded patents covering an "audio program player including a dynamic program selection controller" and an "audio program distribution and playback system," the company (which produces nothing itself) set out in 2009 on a six-year string of litigations, both actual and threatened, against virtually all of the major players in the podcasting market.

First, Personal Audio targeted the biggest fish in the pond: Apple. After suing the company for $84 million in 2009, it won an $8 million decision in 2011. Two weeks after its victory, it took Apple back to court *again*, this time to cover additional products that had been released by the company in the two years since the original complaint was filed.

Over the next few years, Personal Audio sent letters to many of the most successful podcasters, demanding substantial licensing fees and threatening legal action if these fees were not paid. Unlike most forms of entertainment media, podcasting is dominated by independent practitioners, most of whom can't make a living at it until they have hundreds of thousands or millions of followers—enough to attract advertisers and create a stable base of revenue. Even those who are successful are hardly making the kind of money that's associated with a more corporate-dominated platform like television, radio, or cinema. So, for most of the targeted podcasters, these threatening letters gave them the unenviable choice between handing over some or all of their revenue to a third-party company that had done nothing whatsoever to deserve it, or facing the economically and emotionally crippling prospect of a sustained legal battle.

Ultimately, after ruining or imperiling several podcasters' lives and livelihoods, Personal Audio's litigation spree was stopped through legal efforts largely funded by the podcasting audience. First, popular comedian and podcast network owner Adam Carolla mounted a somewhat successful legal defense to the troll's infringement suit against him, using nearly half a million dollars in contributions crowdfunded via the platform FundAnything. Although Carolla didn't win the case, he did persuade Personal Audio to drop its lawsuit, and then he countersued, ending with a confidential settlement. Then the next year, the Electronic Frontier Foundation, using more than $76,000 raised from supporters via its own website, successfully petitioned the USPTO to invalidate the troll's two patents on the grounds that they were already "obvious" by the time they were filed. At the time of writing, Personal Audio is in the process of appealing to the USPTO, but for the moment, the shakedown racket has stopped.

This particular case of patent trolling was challenged successfully through the concerted efforts of defendants who were willing to undergo the risk, expense, and effort of pursuing the case in court rather than simply handing over the money demanded by the troll,

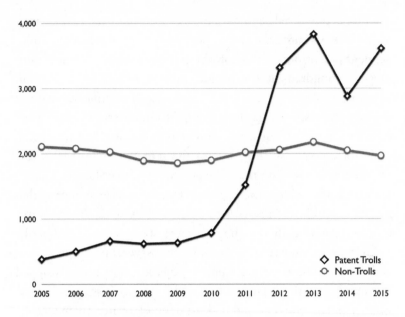

Figure 19: U.S. district court patent suits by trolls and non-trolls, 2005–15.

through the dedicated efforts of a policy nonprofit and via funds donated altruistically by thousands of supporters. Unfortunately, this was an exceptional case, impacting a visible and voluble industry with the power to raise awareness and support among millions of listeners.

The broader problem of patent trolling continues unabated, and it affects every industry in which patents hold sway, threatening to cripple startups and burden established market leaders while lining the pockets of unproductive, opportunistic phantom companies. Patent trolling also burdens the taxpayers by clogging the court system with thousands of spurious cases each year. In fact, the number of patent suits in U.S. district courts initiated by trolls ballooned tenfold between 2005 and 2015, from 381 to 3,613, while the number of suits by legitimate plaintiffs held steady at around 2,000 per year.[2]

Thus far, despite the well-intentioned efforts of American legislators, Congress has not yet managed to pass a bill putting a stop to the scourge of patent trolling. Part of the problem is lobbying by the trolls themselves. Part of the problem is uncertainty as to which measures will most effectively put an end to the practice without unduly hobbling legitimate patent holders. And a large part of the problem is plain old congressional gridlock; without significant funding from some interested party or sector, it's actually very difficult to pass legislation with any meaningful impact on business or policy. Furthermore, while the Obama administration identified patent trolling as a priority, the Trump administration at the time of writing has yet to evince any interest in the issue, nor has it expressed willingness to support such a bill even if it passes both houses of Congress. In fact, the president's son Donald Jr. has worked in recent years as a public relations consultant for "notorious" patent troll Macrosolve.[3] Yet, given the very real stakes for American industry and jurisprudence, there's still a real chance that patent reform will materialize in some form in the not so distant future.

In addition to patent reform, there are also a number of changes, large and small, currently in the works for copyright law. These include focused, industry-specific legislative efforts, sweeping changes to the contours of the law in general, and even drastic revisions to the regulatory apparatus behind the law's interpretation and enforcement. A good example of the first category can be found in the music industry. As we discussed in chapters 3 and 7, digital media platforms have contributed to some profound transformations in the way people make, distribute, discover, listen to, and share recorded music. New paradigms like streaming, remixing, and social media have become dominant over the past decade, while traditional ones like broadcasting and retail have struggled to reinvent themselves in contrast to, and conjunction with, these digital innovations.

The most visible legal consequences of these changes have come in the form of the copyfight and acrimonious public battles over "piracy" and sampling. Yet, behind the scenes, different factions within the music industry are also waging turf wars over borders and customs within this newly drawn terrain. To the casual observer, these many disparate bills and initiatives may seem unrelated and disconnected, but in reality, they are all part of a larger process. As the industry transforms itself structurally and economically, each stakeholder, from record labels to publishers to broadcasters to online services to the creators themselves, is jockeying to command a larger percentage of the revenue generated by recorded music, and to exert more control (and therefore to wield more power) over the actions of its partners and competitors.

One example of a "turf war" bill in the music industry is the Songwriter Equity Act, introduced to both the House and the Senate in 2015. This bill's explicit aim is very wonky: it changes the standards by which copyright royalty judges (CRJs) set royalty rates for the public performance of musical compositions, lifting a ban that previously prevented them from taking comparable rates for phonorecordings into account. Yet despite its highly technical methods and ostensible focus on one small legal mechanism, the actual purpose of this bill is straightforward and transparent: it would give composers and publishers a larger percentage of each dollar made from radio, streaming, and other "public performances" of music.

Another bill, the Fair Play Fair Pay Act, aims to do the opposite. This bill would require CRJs to establish a royalty rate for phonorecordings when they are played on the radio (currently, no such right or royalty exists, except in the cases of webcasting and satellite radio). The legislation would provide record labels and recording artists with a new, important revenue stream from broadcasting, and therefore would necessarily lower the percentage of revenue collected by composers and broadcasters (the revenue pie isn't going to grow, so the slices have to get smaller).

Other recently introduced legislation aims to change broadcast "retransmission" rules, to change webcasting costs, and to give rights holders more power to negotiate rates for the use of their work by broadcasters, webcasters, and/or digital music services. Like the two bills reviewed above, each of these initiatives positions itself in terms of making the economics of the music industry more "fair" for a given stakeholder but ignores the consequences for all the other stakeholders and overlooks the broader economic implications for the industry as a whole. Similar dynamics are unfolding in analogous copyright industries, from television to film to fine art: as digital media continue to transform the structures and economies of these sectors, everyone is lobbying for bigger slices, but few are thinking about how to grow the pie.

Of course, there are some people who have given a great deal of thought to the broader consequences of copyright legislation: lobbyists, legal scholars, and federal regulators. The lobbyist copyright agenda is laid out very clearly in a 2015 document published by the International Chamber of Commerce (ICC) that describes twenty-five "best practices" for IP rights enforcement. This agenda includes empowering customs officials to police and destroy infringing goods at the border (five months later, this policy was signed into law); updating the laws to make accused infringers pay the legal fees and "injuries" associated with their prosecution and infringement; ramping up criminal (as opposed to civil) penalties for infringement, including incarceration; placing the "burden of proof" on suspected infringers rather than on rights holders; requiring law enforcement to investigate infringement "without the need for a complaint" by a rights holder; undermining the safe harbors from secondary liability that protect digital service operators and ISPs; and amplifying the role of the federal government (and other national governments) in policing IP infringement. All in all, the vision is one in which IP enforcement is elevated to the status of an international priority, supported by a coordinated system of ubiquitous surveillance, proactive policing, and expedited judicial review.

By contrast, there are several legal scholars who have called for copyright reforms aimed at limiting or scaling back the power and scope of the law. Perhaps the most prominent among these is Lawrence Lessig (the cofounder of Creative Commons), who spent the first decade of the twenty-first century volubly and vociferously arguing for a variety of changes to copyright law, focused primarily on legitimizing new digital cultural practices and strengthening the commons. For instance, Lessig has advocated for a "right to remix," putting amateur sampling and cutting and pasting beyond the scope of copyright protection, and creating a compulsory license for professional remixing akin to the one that allows performers to "cover" popular songs without permission from composers, as long as they pay a statutory fee. Lessig has also argued for shortening copyright terms, returning the law to its initial fourteen-year span, and requiring registration and "maintenance" for creators who wish to extend that term (which would leave the vast majority of copyrighted works in the public domain after the initial fourteen-year period).

Another influential legal scholar who has laid out recommendations for reforming copyright is William Patry, whose 2011 book *How to Fix Copyright* argues that laws crafted in a bygone age of "artificial scarcity" serve no function in the age of digital abundance, other than to protect the dominance of legacy industries.[4] Like Lessig, Patry argues for much shorter copyright terms and wants to return copyright to a registration-based system, rather than automatically privatizing every expression as soon as it's been fixed in a tangible medium. He also advocates for greater clarity and efficiency, based on comprehensive global registries to keep track of who owns what, and streamlined licensing laws enabling more people to use more copyrighted work more easily. Finally, Patry takes issue with the widespread use of DRM and the "anti-circumvention" clauses of laws like the DMCA, arguing that they are threats to innovation, creativity, and fair use.

Yet another important voice in the copyright reform movement is law professor Jessica Litman, who has published prodigiously on the subject of copyright and digital media for nearly three decades. In a 2010 article entitled "Real Copyright Reform," Litman laments that the law is "old, outmoded, inflexible and beginning to display the symptoms of multiple systems failure."[5] Her prescription for realistic, achievable reform includes some fairly arcane but potentially transformative agenda items:

- "Radical simplification" of the law, which would make copyright understandable for laypeople, lower risk for startups and innovators, and divert a larger percentage of revenue into creators' pockets. In practice, one way of achieving this aim would be to create a "unitary commercial exploitation right" to replace the morass of overlapping and conflicting rights that currently constitute the law.
- Empowering creators by making it easier to reclaim the rights they've previously assigned to intermediaries such as publishers, labels, and distributors. Specifically, Litman recommends giving creators the ability to terminate any copyright grant, with five years' notice, after an initial fifteen-year period of use.
- Empowering audiences by expanding and elaborating user rights, making it clear that there are broad categories of noncommercial uses of copyrighted content that don't require permission from rights holders. Litman envisions achieving this end by explicitly acknowledging these rights in statute

and by appointing an "ombudsman" to the Copyright Office tasked with keeping the "public interest" paramount when considering new legislation and regulation.

- Streamlining the licensing process by getting rid of intermediaries wherever possible. For Litman, the best way to achieve this would be to "junk" all existing statutory licenses and start over from scratch, allowing individual creators to enter into new direct and collective licensing agreements. Any new intermediaries managing these collective agreements would be required by law to pay creators directly rather than funneling their revenue through third-party rights holders like publishers and labels.

As this brief review demonstrates, both industry representatives and legal scholars have weighed in on changes they'd like to see in copyright law in the near future—and these wish lists would be difficult to reconcile. Yet there is another voice calling for copyright reform, and this one is probably the most likely to have a direct role in shaping future legislation: the Copyright Office itself.

In 2013, Maria Pallante, then the register of copyrights for the United States, published an article in the *Columbia Journal of Law and the Arts* entitled "The Next Great Copyright Act" in which she called upon Congress to draft a "major copyright revision," addressing the substantial "frustrations" faced by those trying to interpret the outdated law in the context of a twenty-first-century media environment.[6]

Her proposal includes some elements that would strengthen rights holders' control over copyrighted works, such as giving content owners more discretion over licensing and elevating penalties for unlicensed streaming. It also includes some elements that would strengthen third-party access to protected works, such as exempting the "incidental copies" made in the course of legitimate digital services from copyright control and slightly paring back copyright's term to an author's life plus fifty years, allowing rights holders to renew for an additional twenty years if they continue to have an economic interest in the work.

Most of Pallante's recommendations, however, don't aim to benefit one party over another but seek merely to streamline the use and administration of copyrights overall and to clarify issues that have stymied courts in the digital era. These include the establishment of a small-claims court for smaller infringements (which would lower litigation costs and level the playing field); giving judges more discretion to match damages to the particulars of an infringement case; taking a holistic approach to music licensing reform in order to eliminate "gridlock"; and clarifying user rights such as first sale, fair use, and exceptions for people with disabilities (such as the right to have a book read aloud by a computer for sight-impaired users). Thus, while the article hardly answers all of the pressing questions about what the "next great copyright act" should look like, it does a good job of letting Congress know about many of the key issues that must be addressed.

At the time of writing, however, Congress has yet to begin the process of drafting a Next Great Copyright Act. If anything, we are further from this goal than we were when Pallante published the article. The increasing politicization of copyright law, which we have addressed throughout this book, has not only made it more difficult for Congress to enact visionary new legislation, it has also contributed to dysfunction within regulatory agencies themselves.

The Copyright Office is currently embroiled in a battle over the circumstances of its very existence. Historically, it has been housed within the Library of Congress, yet Pallante has actively argued that it should be a separate independent agency, and a bill introduced by Congressman Tom Marino in 2015 aims to mandate this move. Pallante and other supporters of an independent Copyright Office argue that this reorganization would make the agency more politically independent, institutionally streamlined and, in a word, be good for business.

However, opponents of this move—including consumer advocacy organizations like Public Knowledge and the librarian of Congress Carla Hayden—argue that it would make copyright policy more beholden to lobbyists and less invested in the public interest. There is ample evidence to support this view; for instance, the entertainment and communications industries are major donors to Marino's campaigns, and the list of lobbying clients associated with his bill includes nearly every major media conglomerate and copyright industry trade association.

In October 2016, Hayden, an outspoken champion of "equity of access" to information and consumer privacy, unceremoniously removed Pallante from her post as register. This move was widely interpreted (by both supporters and detractors) as a reprisal for Pallante's attempts to move the Copyright Office out of the Library of Congress. At the time of writing, it is unclear how these tectonic shifts in the policy landscape will ultimately play out, but it is safe to say that, given the increasingly political nature of copyright law, we are unlikely to reach a new consensus anytime soon.

The Longer Term: Thorny Questions from the Bleeding Edge

While there is a seemingly limitless number of pressing questions about the future of intellectual property, there are also some interesting longer-term questions resulting from the continuing (and, by some measures, accelerating) pace of technological change as well as the social and cultural shifts that accompany these changes. We will conclude with a brief review of some notable examples.

One of the foundational principles of intellectual property—especially copyright—is the concept of authorship. From the U.S.

Constitution to copyright statute to judicial interpretation and beyond, the law is rooted explicitly in the tripartite premise that (1) ideas are formed in the minds of individuals, (2) those ideas may be expressed in a tangible medium, and (3) copyright incentivizes individuals to share the expressions of their ideas by offering them a limited monopoly over their uses in the market. As we discussed early in the book, even the nation's founders were aware that this premise is partly fictitious (remember Jefferson's simile comparing the flame of a candle to an idea spreading from mind to mind?). Yet it has always been a convenient enough fiction to sustain the evolving body of IP law.

The problem is, this fiction has become less convenient in recent years, and is likely to become increasingly inconvenient in the future. As we discussed in chapter 4, the Romantic notion of authorship was under full assault within the visual, textual, and musical arts by the middle of the twentieth century, with styles and techniques from Dadaism to collage to cut-ups challenging its conceptual foundations. In 1967, the French literary theorist Roland Barthes even proclaimed the "death of the author," ushering in an age of postmodernist experimentation and a fair share of hand-wringing and soul-searching along with it. With the advent of digital media and the internet in the 1990s, these avant-garde techniques and styles became integrated into popular culture, and today mash-ups, memes, mixtapes, and other authorless or ambiguously authored works make up a significant portion of mainstream culture.

There is already a great deal of argument about how copyright should treat the digital products of "configurable culture." Is it fair use to turn an image from a popular film or a news agency into the subject of a meme? Can the copyright for "selection and arrangement" that applies to edited books and musical revues also be applied to sample-based music, mixtapes, and play lists? What is the copyright status of an authorless meme or, indeed, any piece of digital content with an untraceable source? While some of these issues have been litigated, such lawsuits usually end in nonprecedential settlements, so not only is there a total absence of statute to guide us in these matters, there is precious little case law as well.

While a Facebook meme may not have a single author, or an identifiable one, at least we can be reasonably confident that the person or people responsible for its existence were human. But there are at least two looming challenges to the concept of authorship in copyright in which this assumption does not apply. One is the question of animal authorship. As I alluded to briefly in the introduction, a recent copyright case in the U.S. centered on questions about the authorship and ownership of a selfie taken by a crested macaque with a camera belonging to a photographer named David J. Slater. Initially, Slater claimed copyright in the photo because he owned the camera and created the conditions under which the "monkey selfie" could be taken. This argument is not as unreasonable as it may seem, given the surprisingly vague legal history of photography, dating back to a nineteenth-century Supreme Court case about a photo of Oscar Wilde, in which the photographer prevailed because he had "superintended the arrangement" of the picture.

After a district court decision rejecting Slater's claims to the macaque's photo, the animal rights organization PETA appealed to the Ninth Circuit court on the photographer's behalf, arguing that copyright "does not depend on the humanity of the author, but on the originality of the work itself." Clearly, recognizing this particular animal's right in its own "creative expression" would be a major step toward recognizing animal rights in general, hence PETA's involvement in the case.

But what would it mean from a copyright perspective? Already, every *human* expression fixed in a tangible medium is automatically privatized for a functional eternity. If we assert author's rights for

Figure 20: The contested "monkey selfie."

this particular macaque, would the same apply for recorded bird songs, for the "choreography" of an antelope's mating dance, or for the patterns in a spider's web? Or even for the shapes produced by microbes in a petri dish? It's a slippery slope, and there's no clear cutoff point. Given that the monkey selfie case was ultimately settled out of court, it may be a while before we have any case law, let alone legislation, to guide us in answering these questions.

Another challenge to the concept of human authorship comes not from the natural world but from the artificial one. Increasingly, machines themselves play a crucial role in the generation of cultural information, and it's not at all clear who should own it. In some cases, such as Pandora's automatically generated music play lists or Snapchat's animated video filters, a computer algorithm is merely adding a secondary level of creativity to human expression, and doing so in a way that is fairly constrained in its own "creative" contribution to the process. Few would argue that these types of interventions deserve recognition as a form of authorship (although a case could certainly be made).

However, there are increasingly powerful forms of artificial intelligence (AI) taking on tasks that are traditionally understood as authorial in nature. Google's Magenta project has already produced several musical compositions and works of visual art that are not only unique but are indistinguishable from the work of a human being. A company called Narrative Science has developed an algorithm that writes news stories from scratch, and these stories have been published in the *L.A. Times* and elsewhere. The 2016 video game *No Man's Sky* allows players to fly around a procedurally generated universe containing 18 quintillion planets, each with its own unique life forms and ecology, none of which were designed directly by a human being.

It's no longer difficult to imagine a future in which most of the media we consume—from news to films to music to games—are produced algorithmically by AI to suit our unique circumstances and tastes. In fact, when I raised this possibility during a recent meeting with the head of artists and repertoire (A&R) at a major record label in New York, he responded enthusiastically and optimistically about the possibility. From the recording industry's perspective, algorithms represent a potentially cheaper and far less troublesome workforce than human beings.

Are computers authors in these cases? As in the case of animal selfies, attributing copyright to an artificial intelligence would open a Pandora's box of legal and ethical questions that reach far beyond the bounds of IP, challenging our foundational understanding of the human condition and forcing us to reconsider the definitions of selfhood and sovereignty in human society.

Furthermore, even if we were to accept the validity of AI authorship, that wouldn't necessarily require the extension of copyright to machines. Can computers be incentivized to create and share their work like a human can? If so, would the promise of wealth generated by a limited monopoly on the use of creative expression be an adequate incentive for a machine without a bank account or material needs beyond a few volts of electricity? If not, then there is no legal justification for extending copyright to AI authors—at least, not in America, where IP is rooted in the constitutional mandate to enrich the public sphere through incentivizing authors rather than in an abstract moral notion of an author's rights.

These questions have been asked in legal circles for decades—at least since 1969, when attorney and engineer Karl F. Milde Jr. published an article in the *Journal of the Patent Office Society* asking, "Can a computer be an 'author' or an 'inventor'?"[7] Yet at the time of writing, we are no closer to answering these questions than we were half a century ago, years before Apple or Microsoft had even been founded, when movie audiences were still boggling at the fictional, calculated evil of the artificially intelligent Hal 9000 computer in Stanley Kubrick's *2001: A Space Odyssey*.

The question of post-human authorship is only the tip of the iceberg when it comes to emerging technologies and intellectual property. Virtually every new platform that promises to reorganize our cultures and industries also entails significant challenges to our understanding of IP, and these challenges seem to be arising far faster than they can be resolved.

One transformative new technology is 3D printing. Today, this technology is still in the "early adopter" phase, but prices have dropped precipitously and consumer awareness is growing. Just as P2P file-sharing platforms gave users the power to copy and redistribute their entire digital media collections, 3D printing poses the possibility that material objects—from Lego blocks to Ikea cabinets to larger objects like cars and buildings—may be copied widely and reproduced cheaply within the relatively near future.

While many functional objects do not currently warrant IP protection in the U.S., the European Union has recently taken steps to strengthen and extend "design copyright" on functional objects such as furniture and appliances. Even within the U.S., there are a great number of patented objects that may be reproduced by 3D printers. There are even scenarios in which American copyrights are challenged by the technology—for instance, when it is used to copy sculptures and other works of visual art.

While legal scholars have begun to publish articles exploring the legal consequences of this technology (as well as the potential impacts, both helpful and harmful, of extending IP to cover 3D printing), there is not yet either statute or case law laying down any clear guidelines indicating what might constitute infringement, and what forms of copying may qualify as fair use or may otherwise be exempted from liability. In the meantime, the technology continues to advance; a new technique called "continuous liquid interface production" has recently increased the speed of production by 10,000 percent.

Another set of challenges to IP stems from the rapid advancement of biotechnology. Among many exciting capacities engendered by new technologies in this field, we are developing the ability to read, edit, and copy DNA sequences—the fundamental building blocks of life on Earth. In 2013, the U.S. Supreme Court ruled on its first case involving this technology, *Association for Molecular Pathology v. Myriad Genetics.*[8] In its decision, the court drew a distinction between naturally occurring DNA, which may not be patented, and synthetic DNA (sometimes called cDNA), which is protectable.

While this is a useful foundation for future legal analysis, it is only the beginning of what is bound to be a long and convoluted coevolution between law and biotech. For instance, a new tool called CRISPR (itself the subject of a bitter and protracted patent dispute) allows scientists to edit DNA directly at a molecular level, replacing any one of its four nucleotides (abbreviated as G, A, T, and C) with any other at any point in a genetic sequence. In other words, humans now have the ability to rewrite their own genetic code—a power that may be used altruistically, for instance, to engineer diseases out of existence, or selfishly, for instance, to "upgrade" a person's attractiveness, intelligence, or other desirable hereditary traits.

Another way to put this is that DNA has now become an expressive medium, and just as the binary code of computer software qualifies for copyright protection, one could make similar claims for the quaternary code of an edited or constructed DNA sequence (as in the case of software, the fact that it's patentable doesn't mean it's not also copyrightable). While some legal scholars have claimed that copyright could—and should—apply to "authored" DNA sequences, others disagree, and there is not yet any legislation or case law providing any guidance whatsoever in this matter.[9] Given the rapid pace of technological and cultural development, however, it seems it will be only a matter of time before judges begin grappling with the issue.

Other emerging technologies—from the "internet of things" to space travel to virtual reality—offer similar challenges to our understanding of culture, ethics, and industry, and pose similarly daunting questions for the future of intellectual property, both in the U.S. and on a global scale. While there is no room to explore their implications in the final pages of this book, it is a tantalizing subject for scholars of intellectual property, and there are no doubt many great books yet to be written on these and related issues.

In closing, I will simply observe that, although intellectual property has evolved significantly over the years, from an obscure and narrow corner of property law to a far-reaching and hotly contested complex of legislation, case law, regulation, and international entanglements, its story is only beginning.

In recent years, we have witnessed the rise of the "information society," in which creative expression and technological innovation are not merely boons to industry but the foundations of all social and economic development. We also have witnessed the digitization and networking of information of every kind, and data as diverse as our health records, family photos, and investment portfolios now live side by side on servers in the "cloud." In the near future, we will see even more intimate dimensions of our lives, from our genetic profiles to our cognitive processes, translated into 1s and 0s and then collected, stored, and analyzed by increasingly powerful computers (and by the powerful state and corporate institutions that control them). In short, there is little about the human experience that will not soon be reducible to digital information and distributed via communication networks, and therefore potentially subject to IP laws of one kind or another.

Already, we are beginning to adjust culturally to the more central role that IP is bound to play in human affairs. New political institutions like the Pirate Party have recently emerged, which treat information and intellectual property as integral to the political process rather than as a peripheral issue best left to lobbyists and policy wonks. "Hacktivist" organizations from Anonymous to Wikileaks have begun to play transformative roles in public affairs, based on radical approaches to information transparency and a rejection of traditional notions of property and control. We are even witnessing the birth of new spiritual belief systems that fundamentally challenge the ethics and morality of IP; for instance, Kopimism, a religion founded in Sweden and officially recognized by the state in 2012, holds that "the internet is holy" and maintains that it is the sacred duty of humanity to copy, mix, and share information, unfettered by the constraints of IP or any other law.

These developments probably don't presage the end of intellectual property (to the chagrin of many hacktivists and Kopimists), but they certainly do suggest that, to stay useful to industry, relevant to society, and acceptable to the public at large, these laws will have to transform radically in the years to come. As the old lines between public and private, business and culture, and local and global continue to blur, the legal justifications for intellectual property, rooted in distinctions like idea versus expression, original versus derivative, and commercial versus noncommercial, will have to evolve as well.

As they do, legislators and enforcers will need to make sure that the balance of power doesn't tip too far in either direction, maintaining that sweet spot between privatization and freeloading in which the public sphere is both enriched by new ideas and creations and strengthened by the freedom to reuse and reimagine older ones. Our future as a society will depend upon it.

Notes

Introduction

1. Kevin A. Hassett and Robert J. Shapiro, "What Ideas Are Worth: The Value of Intellectual Capital and Intangible Assets in the American Economy," Sonecon, accessed October 5, 2016, http://www.sonecon.com/docs/studies /Value_of_Intellectual_Capital_in_American_Economy.pdf. As I will discuss elsewhere in this book, such sweeping economic generalizations should be taken with a heavy dose of salt. The study cited, for instance, was funded in part by the pharmaceutical industry, which has a vested interest in strong, well-policed IP laws.
2. John Tehranian, *Infringement Nation: Copyright 2.0 and You* (New York: Oxford University Press, 2011).
3. Feist Publications v. Rural Telephone Serv. Co., 499 U.S. 340 (1991).
4. Matthew Haag, "Who Owns a Monkey Selfie? Settlement Should Leave Him Smiling," *New York Times*, September 11, 2017, https://www.nytimes .com/2017/09/11/us/selfie-monkey-lawsuit-settlement.html.
5. These patent materials were a gift from the New York State Bar Association after I spoke at one of its events. The illustration hangs proudly in my office.
6. Diamond v. Chakrabarty, 447 U.S. 303 (1980).
7. David Bollier, *Brand Name Bullies: The Quest to Own and Control Culture* (Hoboken: John Wiley and Sons, 2005), 195.
8. White v. Samsung, 989 F. 2d 1512 (U.S. App. 1993).

9. Technically, trademark and trade secret laws are rooted in article 1, section 8's commerce clause, which empowers Congress to "regulate Commerce with foreign Nations, and among the several States." Rights of publicity, which are state rather than federal laws, are generally based in state constitutions' privacy or commerce clauses.

10. U.S. Copyright Office, *Circular 92: Copyright Law of the United States: and Related Laws Contained in Title 17 of the United States Code*, December 2011, http://copyright.gov/title17/circ92.pdf.

11. U.S. Patent and Trademark Office, *Consolidated Patent Laws—March 2017 Update*, https://www.uspto.gov/web/offices/pac/mpep/consolidated_laws.pdf; U. S. Patent & Trademark Office, *U.S. Trademark Law: Rules of Practice & Federal Statutes*, July 11, 2015, http://www.uspto.gov/sites/default/files/tm law.pdf.

12. Jonathan Weisman, "After an Online Firestorm, Congress Shelves Anti-piracy Bills," *New York Times*, January 20, 2012, www.nytimes.com/2012/01 /21/technology/senate-postpones-piracy-vote.html.

13. "World Intellectual Property Organization," accessed October 5, 2016, http://www.wipo.int/wipolex/en/profile.jsp?code=US.

14. Michael Geist, "The ACTA Copyright Treaty and Why You Should Care," *GigaOm*, May 3, 2010, https://gigaom.com/2010/05/02/the-acta-copyright -treaty-and-why-you-should-care/.

15. Metro-Goldwyn-Mayer Studios Inc. v. Grokster, Ltd., 545 U.S. 913 (2005).

16. "Instagram Terms of Use," accessed October 5, 2016, https://help.instagram .com/478745558852511/.

ONE

The Origins of Intellectual Property

1. Michael Baxandall, *Painting and Experience in Fifteenth-Century Italy*, 2nd ed. (Oxford: Oxford University Press, 1988).

2. Movable type, the technology underlying the printing press, had actually existed in Asia for about five hundred years prior to this invention, but for a variety of fascinating reasons that are unfortunately beyond the scope of this book it did not have an equivalent speed of adoption or contribute to the same types of cultural and social changes in that region.

3. Adrian Johns, *Piracy: The Intellectual Property Wars from Gutenberg to Gates* (Chicago: University of Chicago Press, 2010), 24.

4. Lyman Ray Patterson, *Copyright in Historical Perspective* (Nashville: Vanderbilt University Press, 1968), 6.

5. Patterson, *Copyright*, 139.

6. Patterson, *Copyright*, 179.

7. Patterson, *Copyright*, 78.

8. Chris Dent, "'Generally Inconvenient': The 1624 *Statute of Monopolies* as Political Compromise." *Melbourne University Law Review* 33, no. 2 (2009): 415, http://law.unimelb.edu.au/__data/assets/pdf_file/0003/1705278/33_2_4.pdf.

9. Christine MacLeod, *Inventing the Industrial Revolution: The English Patent System, 1600–1800* (Cambridge: Cambridge University Press, 2002), 7.

10. Dominic Basulto, "Patents Are a Terrible Way to Measure Innovation," *Washington Post*, July 14, 2015, https://www.washingtonpost.com/news/innovations/wp/2015/07/14/patents-are-a-terrible-way-to-measure-innovation/.

11. This is a necessarily condensed version of a much more complex set of arguments. Not only were there far more factors at work in these debates (the balance between federal and state power, interstate and international trade relations, etc.), but Madison and Jefferson themselves were far from consistent on these issues, changing and evolving somewhat over the course of their lives and from one context to another.

12. William Patry, *How to Fix Copyright* (New York: Oxford University Press, 2011), 131.

13. Lawrence Lessig, *Free Culture: How Big Media Uses Technology and the Law to Lock Down Culture and Control Creativity* (New York: Penguin, 2004).

14. U.S. Copyright Office, *Copyright Law of the U.S.*, 17 U.S.C., § 102.

15. U.S. Copyright Office, *Copyright Law of the U.S.*, 17 U.S.C., § 101.

16. U.S. Patent and Trademark Office, *Consolidated Patent Laws*, 35 U.S.C., § 101.

17. U.S. Patent and Trademark Office, *U.S. Patent Activity: Calendar Years 1790 to Present*, accessed June 24, 2017, http://www.uspto.gov/web/offices/ac/ido/oeip/taf/h_counts.htm.

18. "2014 Patent Litigation Study," *PwC*, July 2014, http://www.pwc.com/us/en/forensic-services/publications/2014-patent-litigation-study.html; Gene Quinn, "The Rise of Patent Litigation in America," *IPWatchdog* (blog), April 9, 2013, http://www.ipwatchdog.com/2013/04/09/the-rise-of-patent-litigation-in-america-1980–2012/.

19. Executive Office of the President, "Patent Assertion and U.S. Innovation," *The White House*, June 2013, https://obamawhitehouse.archives.gov/sites/default/files/docs/patent_report.pdf.

20. The term *common law* refers to rules that are derived not from legislation but from customary practices, widely held principles, and judicial rulings.

21. Mathew Sag, "IP Litigation in United States District Courts: 1994 to 2014," *Iowa Law Review* 1065 (2016), https://papers.ssrn.com/sol3/papers.cfm?abstract_id=2570803.

TWO

The Limits of Intellectual Property

1. Brent Lang, "Charged Again with Fakery, *Catfish* Filmmakers Sued over Song," *The Wrap* (blog), December 3, 2010, http://www.thewrap.com/charging -fake-threshold-media-sues-catfish-filmmakers-23007/; David Clinch, "The 'Ten Commandments' of Using Eyewitness Video," *First Draft News Medium* (blog), August 28, 2015, http://medium.com/1st-draft/the-ten-commandments -of-using-eyewitness-video-c3bd560f8061; Eric Bangeman, "New NLPC 'Top 50' List Spotlights Pirated Movies on Google Video," *ArsTechnica* (blog), July 18, 2007, http://arstechnica.com/tech-policy/2007/07/new-nlpc-top-50 -list-spotlights-pirated-movies-on-google-video/; Ashkan Karbasfrooshan, "Why Big Media Is Going Nuclear against the DMCA," *Tech Crunch*, November 6, 2011, http://techcrunch.com/2011/11/06/big-media-nuclear-dmca/; "Why Spotify Is Not the Enemy of Artists and Who Is," *The Trichordist* (blog), July 29, 2013, http://thetrichordist.com/2013/07/29/why-spotify-is -not-the-enemy-of-artists-and-who-is/.

2. Although this process unfolded throughout Europe in the late Middle Ages and early modernity, the British began the process earlier, and pursued it more aggressively, than did their neighbors on the mainland.

3. This formulation is cited in Gilbert Keith Chesterton, *What's Wrong with the World* (New York: Dodd, Mead, 1912), 89. More recently, David Bollier has cited a slightly different version in several publications, dating the poem to the mid-eighteenth century. The earliest printed citation I have seen is in William Cobbett, *Cobbett's Weekly Political Register* 15 (1809).

4. Garrett Hardin, "The Tragedy of the Commons," *Science* 162, no. 3859 (1968): 1244, doi: 10.1126/science.162.3859.1243.

5. Susan Jane Buck Cox, "No Tragedy of the Commons," *Environmental Ethics* 7, no. 1 (1985): 49–61, doi: 10.5840/enviroethics1985716.

6. Matt Ridley, *The Origins of Virtue: Human Instincts and the Evolution of Cooperation* (New York: Penguin Books, 1997), 288.

7. James Boyle, "The Second Enclosure Movement and the Construction of the Public Domain," *Law and Contemporary Problems* 6, no. 1 (2003): 37.

8. Michael Heller, The *Gridlock Economy: How Too Much Ownership Wrecks Markets, Stops Innovation, and Costs Lives* (New York: Basic Books, 2010).

9. The term *public domain* doesn't appear in patent or trademark statutes.

10. James Boyle, *The Public Domain: Enclosing the Commons of the Mind* (New Haven: Yale University Press, 2009), 38.

11. Boyle, *The Public Domain*, xv.

12. Genetical Pharmaceutical Association, "Generic Drug Savings in the U.S.," in *Genetical Pharmaceutical Association*, 5th ed., 2013, http://www.gphaonline .org/media/cms/2013_Savings_Study_12.19.2013_FINAL.pdf.

13. "William Shakespeare," IMDb, accessed June 5, 2018, http://www.imdb.com /name/nm0000636.

14. Paul Heald, Kristofer Erickson, and Martin Kretschmer, "The Valuation of Unprotected Works: A Case Study of Public Domain Photographs on Wikipedia," *Harvard Journal of Law and Technology* 29, no. 1 (Fall 2015): 1–31, http://jolt.law.harvard.edu/articles/pdf/v29/29HarvJLTech1.pdf.

15. Pierre N. Leval, "Toward a Fair Use Standard," *Harvard Law Review* 103, no. 5 (1990): 1105, 1107.

16. Folsom v. Marsh, 9 F. Cas. 342 (C.C.D. Mass. 1841).

17. Bobbie Johnson, "Murdoch Could Block Google Searches Entirely," *Guardian*, November 9, 2009, http://www.theguardian.com/media/2009/nov/09 /murdoch-google.

18. See, for instance, North Jersey Media Group Inc., Plaintiff v. Jeanine Pirro and Fox News Network, LLC, Defendants, 13 Civ. 7153; North Jersey Media Group Inc. v. Fox News Network, LLC, 14 Civ. 7630; Yunghi Kim and Contact Press Images, Inc., Plaintiffs v. Fox News Network, LLC, 13 Civ. 4589. Full disclosure: I served as an expert witness for the defense in each of these suits.

19. American Intellectual Property Law Association, "AIPLA 2015 Report of the Economic Survey Shows Trends in IP Litigation Costs," *American Intellectual Property Law Association*, July 28, 2015, http://www.aipla.org/about/news room/PR/Pages/150728PressRelease.aspx.

20. Patricia Aufderheide and Peter Jaszi, *Reclaiming Fair Use: How to Put Balance Back in Copyright* (Chicago: University of Chicago Press, 2011).

21. Patricia Aufderheide and Aram Sinnreich, "Documentarians, Fair Use, and Free Expression: Changes in Copyright Attitudes and Actions with Access to Best Practices," *Information, Communication & Society* 19, no. 2 (2016): 178– 87, http://dx.doi.org/10.1080/1369118X.2015.1050050; Aram Sinnreich and Patricia Aufderheide, "Communication Scholars and Fair Use: The Case for Discipline-Wide Education and Institutional Reform," *International Journal of Communication* 9 (2015): 2456–66, http://ijoc.org/index.php/ijoc/article /view/3657.

22. The U.S. Department of Commerce's Internet Policy Taskforce, *White Paper on Remixes, First Sale, and Statutory Damages*, January 2016, 1–107, http:// www.uspto.gov/sites/default/files/documents/copyrightwhitepaper.pdf (hereafter cited as White Paper on Remixes).

23. Katherine J. Strandburg, "Patent Fair Use 2.0," *UC Irvine Law Review*, no. 2 (2011): 305.

24. TufAmerica, Inc. v. WB Music Corp. et al., 13 Civ. 7874 (2014). The following year, the Ninth Circuit Court of Appeals came to a similar and more precedential decision in a case regarding a sample used in Madonna's 1990 hit "Vogue." This case established definitively that the de minimis rule applies to

all copyrighted works, without exception. See VMG Salsoul v. Madonna Louise Ciccone, nos. 13-57104 and 14-55837 (9th Cir. June 2, 2016).

25. Bridgeport Music v. Dimension Films, et al. 410 F. 3d 792 (6th Cir. 2005)
26. The U.S. Department of Commerce's Internet Policy Taskforce, *White Paper on Remixes, 58.*
27. Kirtsaeng v. John Wiley & Sons, Inc., 133 S.Ct. 1351 (2013).
28. Kal Raustiala and Christopher Sprigman, *The Knockoff Economy: How Imitation Sparks Innovation* (Oxford: Oxford University Press, 2012), 172.

THREE
Intellectual Property and Industry

1. U.S. Copyright Office, *Copyright Law of the U.S.*, 17 U.S.C., § 101.
2. The fascinating data behind these geographical trends are available at popvs soda.com, a website maintained by geographer Alan McConchie.
3. Technically, the petition goes to the Trademark Trial and Appeal Board (TTAB), which is located organizationally within the USPTO.
4. World Intellectual Property Organization (WIPO), "Committee of Experts on the Legal Protection of Computer Software, Second Section (Geneva, June 13 to 17, 1983): Report (Adopted by the Committee of Experts)," *Copyright: Monthly Review of the World Intellectual Property Organization (WIPO)*, September 1983, 272, http://www.wipo.int/edocs/pubdocs/en/copyright/120/wipo_pub_120_1983_09.pdf.
5. Alice Corp. Pty. Ltd. v. CLS Bank Int'l, 134 S. Ct. 2347 (2014);Steven Callahan, "Alice: The Death of Software-Related Patents?" *Northern District of Texas* (blog), May 1, 2015, http://www.ndtexblog.com/?p=3550.
6. Aleecia M. McDonald and Lorrie Faith Cranor, "The Cost of Reading Privacy Policies," *I/S: A Journal of Law and Policy for the Information Society* 4, no. 3 (2008–09): 543–68.
7. For instance, at the time of writing, the Apple website TOS, the software license agreement for Apple's OS X operating system, and the Apple privacy policy are all between three thousand and thirty-five hundred words.
8. Yannis Bakos, Florencia Marotta-Wurgler, and David R. Trossen, "Does Anyone Read the Fine Print? Consumer Attention to Standard Form Contracts," *Journal of Legal Studies* 43, no. 1 (2014): 35.
9. Mike Masnick, "Proof That (Almost) No One Reads End User License Agreements," *Techdirt* (blog), February 23, 2005, https://www.techdirt.com/articles/20050223/1745244.shtml.
10. "Oculus Terms Of Service," last modified September 26, 2017, https://www.oculus.com/en-us/legal/terms-of-service/.

11. Richard Anderson, "Pharmaceutical Industry Gets High on Fat Profits," *BBC*, November 6, 2014, http://www.bbc.com/news/business-28212223.

12. Jack DeRuiter and Pamela L. Holston, "Drug Patent Expirations and the 'Patent Cliff.'" *US Pharm* 37, no. 6 (2012): 12–20.

13. Aaron E. Carroll, "$2.6 Billion to Develop a Drug? New Estimate Makes Questionable Assumptions," *New York Times*, November 18, 2014, http://www.nytimes.com/2014/11/19/upshot/calculating-the-real-costs-of-developing-a-new-drug.html.

14. Charles Ornstein, Ryann Grochowski Jones, and Mike Tigas, "Now There's Proof: Docs Who Take Company Cash Tend to Prescribe More Brand-Name Drugs," *ProPublica* (blog), March 17, 2016, https://www.propublica.org/article/doctors-who-take-company-cash-tend-to-prescribe-more-brand-name-drugs; Joseph Engelberg, Christopher A. Parsons, and Nathan Tefft, "Financial Conflicts of Interest in Medicine," *SSRN* (2014): 1–60.

15. Joseph Walker and Austen Hufford, "FTC Sues Endo, Alleges Company Paid off Generic Drugmakers," *Wall Street Journal*, March 31, 2016, http://www.wsj.com/articles/ftc-accuses-endo-of-paying-off-generic-drugmakers-1459437000.

16. U.S. PIRG, "Top Twenty Pay-for-Delay Drugs: How Drug Industry Payoffs Delay Generics, Inflate Prices and Hurt Consumers," July 11, 2013, http://www.uspirg.org/reports/usp/top-twenty-pay-delay-drugs.

17. Justin Antonipillai and Michelle K. Lee, "Intellectual Property and the U.S. Economy: 2016 Update," prepared by the Economics and Statistics Administration and the United States Patent and Trademark Office, September 2016, https://www.uspto.gov/sites/default/files/documents/IPandtheUSEconomySept2016.pdf.

FOUR

Intellectual Property and Cultural Expression

1. These data are available at http://www.bls.gov/data/.

2. Nielsen, "2015 Nielsen U.S. Report," 2016, http://www.nielsen.com/content/dam/corporate/us/en/reports-downloads/2016-reports/2015-year-end-music-report.pdf.pdf.

3. Jesse Holcomb and Amy Mitchell, "The Revenue Picture for American Journalism and How It Is Changing," *Pew Research Journalism Project* (blog), March 26, 2014, http://www.journalism.org/2014/03/26/the-revenue-picture-for-american-journalism-and-how-it-is-changing/.

4. These data are available at https://www.bea.gov/.

5. These data are available at https://www.census.gov/construction/c30/historical_data.html.

6. The dynamics I describe here are applicable to a range of other cultural histories and trajectories outside Europe as well. Yet, as in chapter 1, I choose to focus on Europe because that is where modern notions of intellectual property originated. Thus, the comparison between pre- and post-IP aesthetics is most acute in these instances. In the coming chapters, especially chapter 6, I will discuss the relationship between Westernized IP regimes and non-Western cultural traditions and political systems in greater detail.

7. Mark Rothko and Christopher Rothko, ed., *The Artist's Reality: Philosophies of Art* (New Haven: Yale University Press, 2006), 106.

8. Carmen C. Bambach, *Drawing and Painting in the Italian Renaissance Workshop: Theory and Practice, 1300–1600*, (Cambridge: Cambridge University Press, 1999).

9. Lisa Pon, *Raphael, Dürer, and Marcantonio Raimondi: Copying and the Italian Renaissance Print.* (New Haven: Yale University Press, 2004).

10. Mark Rose, "Technology and Copyright in 1735: The Engraver's Act." *Information Society* 21, no. 1 (2005): 63–66.

11. Quoted in James E. B. Breslin, *Mark Rothko: A Biography* (Chicago: University of Chicago Press, 1993), 305.

12. Rothko and Rothko, *Artist's Reality*, 123.

13. We'll be discussing the relationship between IP and cultural imperialism in greater depth in chapter 6.

14. "Sherrie Levine," *Contemporary Photography Index* (blog), April 27, 2010, https://contemporaryphotographyindex.wordpress.com/2010/04/27/sherrie-levine/.

15. Jonathan Francis, "On Appropriation: *Cariou v. Prince* and Measuring Contextual Transformation in Fair Use," *Berkeley Technology Law Journal* 29, no. 4 (2014): 10, doi: 10.15779/Z383M6C; Anthony R. Enriquez, "The Destructive Impulse of Fair Use After *Cariou v. Prince*," *DePaul Journal of Art, Technology & Intellectual Property* Law 24, no. 1 (2013): 1–48.

16. Arifa Akbar, "Hirst Demands Share of Artist's £65 Copies." *Independent*, December 6, 2008, https://web.archive.org/web/20081217021308/http://www.independent.co.uk/arts-entertainment/art/news/hirst-demands-share-of-artists-16365-copies-1054424.html.

17. Michael Lobel, *Image Duplicator: Roy Lichtenstein and the Emergence of Pop Art* (New Haven: Yale University Press, 2002), 59.

18. Louis Armand, "Jean-Michel Basquiat©: Identity and the Art of (Dis)empowerment," *Litteraria Pragensia* 11, no. 21 (2001): 94–106, http://web.ff.cuni.cz/~lazarus/basquiat.html.

19. Gerald Abraham, *The Concise Oxford History of Music* (Oxford: Oxford University Press, 1979), 72.

20. Richard Taruskin, *The Oxford History of Western Music*, vol. 2 (New York: Oxford University Press, 2009).

21. Adam Baer, "Wolfgang Amadeus Copycat: Did Mozart Plagiarize?" *Slate*, February 13, 2002, http://www.slate.com/articles/arts/culturebox/2002/02/wolfgang_amadeus_copycat.html.

22. Reuven Tsur, "Metaphor and Figure-Ground Relationship: Comparisons from Poetry, Music, and the Visual Arts," *PsyArt: An Online Journal for the Psychological Study of the Arts*, January 11, 2000, http://psyartjournal.com/article/show/tsur-metaphor_and_figure_ground_relationship_; Stephen Hinton, "Not 'Which' Tones? The Crux of Beethoven's Ninth," *19th-Century Music* 22, no. 1 (1998): 61–77, doi: 10.2307/746792.

23. Aram Sinnreich, *Mashed Up: Music, Technology and the Rise of Configurable Culture* (Amherst: University of Massachusetts Press, 2010).

24. John H. Roberts, "Handel and Vinci's 'Didone Abbandonata': Revisions and Borrowings," *Music & Letters 68*, no. 2 (1987): 141–50.

25. Hannu Annala and Heiki Matlik, *Handbook of Guitar and Lute Composers* (Pacific, MO: Mel Bay, 2007). The British coverage was based on the landmark court case *Bach v. Longman*. Statutory coverage for music didn't exist in Britain until 1842.

26. Taruskin, *History of Western Music*, 15.

27. Robert Schumann, *On Music and Musicians*, trans. Konrad Wolff (Berkeley: University of California Press, 1946), 35.

28. Susan McClary, *Georges Bizet: Carmen* (Cambridge: Cambridge University Press, 1992).

29. Blume v. Spear 30 F. 629 (C.C. S.D.N.Y. 1887).

30. Bright Tunes Music v. Harrisongs Music 420 F. Supp. 177 (S.D.N.Y. 1976).

31. Quoted in Kembreu McLeod, "How Copyright Law Changed Hip Hop," *Alternet*, May 31, 2004, http://www.alternet.org/story/18830/how_copyright_law_changed_hip_hop/.

32. Quoted in McLeod, "How Copyright Law Changed Hip Hop."

33. McLeod, "How Copyright Law Changed Hip Hop."

34. Grand Upright v. Warner 780 F. Supp. 182 (S.D.N.Y. 1991).

35. Bridgeport Music v. Dimension Films, et al. 410 F. 3d 792 (6th Cir. 2005).

36. "Underground" and noncommercial sample-based music, such as mixtapes and mash-ups, have very different standards and aesthetics for a variety of reasons that are fascinating but beyond the scope of this chapter. For more information, see Sinnreich, *Mashed Up*.

37. TufAmerica, Inc. v. Warner Bros. Music Corp., et al. 67 F. Supp. 3d 590 (S.D.N.Y. 2014).

38. Estate of James Oscar Smith v. Cash Money Records 253 F. Supp. 3d 737 (S.D.N.Y. 2017).

FIVE

The Politics Behind Intellectual Property

1. See Frank R. Baumgartner, Jeffrey M. Berry, Marie Hojnacki, Beth L. Leech, and David C. Kimball, *Lobbying and Policy Change: Who Wins, Who Loses, and Why* (Chicago: University of Chicago Press, 2009); Martin Gilens, *Affluence and Influence: Economic Inequality and Political Power in America* (Princeton: Princeton University Press, 2012).

2. Center for Responsible Politics, "Revolving Door," accessed June 26, 2017, http://www.opensecrets.org/revolving/.

3. Jessica Litman, "The Politics of Intellectual Property," *Cardozo Arts & Entertainment Law Journal* 27, no. 2 (2009): 314.

4. Litman, "The Politics of Intellectual Property," 315.

5. Litman, "The Politics of Intellectual Property," 315.

6. Raquel Alexander, Stephen W. Mazza, and Susan Scholz, "Measuring Rates of Return on Lobbying Expenditures: An Empirical Case Study of Tax Breaks for Multinational Corporations," *Journal of Law & Politics* 25, no. 4 (Fall 2009): 451–53.

7. Matt Nesto, "Lobbying Works! Big Spenders Reap Big Stock Gains, Says Trennert," *Yahoo! Finance*, July 23, 2012, http://finance.yahoo.com/blogs /breakout/lobbying-works-big-spenders-reap-big-stock-gains-143308537 .html; "Money and Politics," *Economist*, October 1, 2011, http://www.econo mist.com/node/21531014.

8. Data available at followthemoney.org.

9. The comparison of forty campaign donors to forty-eight lobbying clients is based on the nature of available public data. In the first case, these are the only publicly available figures, and in the second, the data are grouped by number of reports filed, and the forty-eight companies in question were those that had filed twelve or more lobbying reports for the year.

10. Michael J. Cooper, Huseyin Gulen, and Alexei V. Ovtchinnikov "Corporate Political Contributions and Stock Returns," *Journal of Finance* 65, no. 2 (2010): 719, doi: 10.1111/j.1540–6261.2009.01548.x.

11. https://www.opensecrets.org/news/2016/02/outside-spending-for-2016 -hits-200m/.

12. U.S. Chamber of Commerce, "About the U.S. Chamber," accessed June 7, 2018, https://www.uschamber.com/about-us/about-the-us-chamber.

13. "Exclusive Investigation: Donald Trump Faces Foreign Donor Fundraising Scandal," *Telegraph*, October 24, 2016, http://www.telegraph.co.uk/news/2016 /10/24/exclusive-investigation-donald-trump-faces-foreign-donor-fundrai/.

14. David Krevets, "U.S. Copyright Czar Cozied Up to Content Industry, E-mails Show," *Wired*, October 14, 2011, https://www.wired.com/2011/10/copyright -czar-cozies-up/.

SIX
Intellectual Property in the Global Arena

1. Johns, *Piracy*, 13.
2. United Nations Statistics Division, "GNI in US Dollars—All Countries for All Years—Sorted Alphabetically," accessed June 7, 2018, https://unstats.un.org/unsd/snaama/dnlList.asp.
3. Susan K. Sell, *Private Power, Public Law: The Globalization of Intellectual Property Rights*, Cambridge Studies in International Relations (Cambridge: Cambridge University Press, 2003), 7.
4. Sell, *Private Power, Public Law*, 8.
5. Madeleine Berg, "The Most Expensive Movies Ever Made," *Forbes*, April 27, 2016, http://www.forbes.com/sites/maddieberg/2016/04/27/the-most-expensive-movies-ever-made/.
6. Peter Drahos, "Thinking Strategically about Intellectual Property Rights," *Telecommunications Policy* 21, no. 3(1997): 201–11.
7. World Trade Organization, "WTO-WIPO Agreement," December 22, 1995, https://www.wto.org/english/tratop_e/trips_e/wtowip_e.htm.
8. Peter K. Yu, "TRIPS Wars: Developing Countries Strike Back," in *Flashpoints*, ed. Alexandra George (New Orleans: Quid Pro Press, forthcoming), http://ssrn.com/abstract=2671664.
9. Sell, *Private Power, Public Law*, front matter.
10. Sell, *Private Power, Public Law*, 47.
11. Center for Responsible Politics, "Intellectual Property Committee," accessed November 7, 2017, https://www.opensecrets.org/lobby/clientsum.php?id=F107735.
12. Sell, *Private Power, Public Law*, 46.
13. Sell, *Private Power, Public Law*, 55.
14. Sell, *Private Power, Public Law*, 96.
15. https://www.vox.com/2016/7/21/12253426/donald-trump-acceptance-speech-transcript-republican-nomination-transcript.
16. ChinaFile, "Document 9: A ChinaFile Translation," November 8, 2013, http://www.chinafile.com/document-9-chinafile-translation.
17. Tim Winton, "Tim Winton Condemns Government Plans for 'a New Colonial Era of Publishing,'" *Sydney Morning Herald*, May 20, 2016, http://www.smh.com.au/entertainment/books/tim-winton-condemns-government-plans-for-a-new-colonial-era-of-publishing-20160519-goze20.
18. Starbucks Coffee Company, "Ethiopia Yirgacheffe™ Chelba," accessed June 26, 2017, http://www.starbucks.com/coffee/reserve/organic-ethiopia-yirgacheffe.
19. World Intellectual Property Organization (WIPO), "The Coffee War: Ethiopia and the Starbucks Story," accessed June 26, 2017, http://www.wipo.int/ipadvantage/en/details.jsp?id=2621.

20. Gregory Younging, "Traditional Knowledge Exists; Intellectual Property Is Invented or Created," *University of Pennsylvania Journal of International Law* 36, no. 2 (2015): 1082, http://scholarship.law.upenn.edu/jil/vol36/iss4/5.

21. Quoted in Thiru, "Human Rights Council Adopts Watershed Resolution on Access to Medicines," *Knowledge Ecology International* (blog), July 1, 2016, http://keionline.org/node/2605.

22. Thiru, "Human Rights Council."

23. Joe Karaganis, ed., *Media Piracy in Emerging Economies* (n.p.: Social Science Research Council, 2011).

24. Figures cited in Thomas S. O'Connor, "Development of Intellectual Property Laws for the Russian Federation," *Journal of Business Research* 64, no. 9 (2011): 1011–16. As with all estimates of market harm by interested parties, these figures should be taken with a grain of salt.

25. Karaganis, *Piracy in Emerging Economies*, 211.

26. Fan Yang, *Faked in China: Nation Branding, Counterfeit Culture, and Globalization* (Bloomington: Indiana University Press, 2015).

27. U.S.-China Economic and Security Review Commission (USCC), *2015 USCC Annual Report*, November 2015, U.S. Government Publishing Office, 217. https://www.uscc.gov/sites/default/files/annual_reports/2015%20Annual%20Report%20to%20Congress.PDF.

28. Jeremy Malcolm, "Captured U.S. Trade Agency Resorts to Bullying Again in 2016 *Special 301 Report*," *Electronic Frontier Foundation*, April 28, 2016, https://www.eff.org/deeplinks/2016/04/captured-us-trade-agency-resorts-bullying-again-2016-special-301-report.

29. Aram Sinnreich, *The Piracy Crusade: How the Music Industry's War on Sharing Destroys Markets and Erodes Civil Liberties* (Amherst: University of Massachusetts Press, 2013), 173.

SEVEN
Copyright Piracy

1. For an in-depth discussion of this concept, see Daniel Heller-Roazen, *The Enemy of All: Piracy and the Law of Nations* (New York: Zone Books, 2009).

2. Johns, *Piracy*.

3. Johns, *Piracy*, 38.

4. International Copyright Association, *International Copyright: Meeting of Authors and Publishers at the Rooms of the New York Historical Society* (New York: International Copyright Association, 1868).

5. "Wireless and Lawless," *Electrical World*, May 20, 1907, 1023.

6. Sydney S. Biro, "International Aspects of Radio Control," *Journal Radio Law*

2 (1932): 45; Louis G. Caldwell, "Piracy of Broadcast Programs," *Columbia Law Review* 30, no. 8 (1930): 1087–1114.

7. Alva Johnston, "Profiles: Czar of Song," *New Yorker*, December 17, 1932, 22.7

8. Mike Hennessey, "U.K. Piracy Rate World's Lowest," *Billboard*, June 19, 1982, 9.

9. Stephen Traiman, "Pro & Semi-Pro: All Systems Go," *Billboard*, May 12, 1979, TAV-3.

10. Sony Corp. of America v. Universal City Studios, Inc., 464 U.S. 417 (1984).

11. For a more in-depth discussion of these findings and conclusions, see Sinnreich, *Piracy Crusade*, chapter 4.

12. Full disclosure: I served as an expert witness on behalf of both *Grokster* and *LimeWire*.

13. Krysten Crawford, "Hollywood Wins Internet Piracy Battle," *CNN/Money*, June 27, 2005, http://money.cnn.com/2005/06/27/technology/grokster/.

14. International Federation of the Phonographic Industries, *IFPI Online Music Report 2004*, accessed June 26, 2017, www.ifpi.org/content/library/digital-music-report-2004.pdf.

15. Sinnreich, *Piracy Crusade*, 126–27.

16. Ernesto, "100,000 P2P Users Sued in US Mass Lawsuits," *Torrentfreak* (blog), January 30, 2011, https://torrentfreak.com/100000-p2p-users-sued-in-us-mass-lawsuits-110130/.

EIGHT
Copyleft and Copyfight

1. Moore's law, a principle coined by Intel founder Gordon Moore, holds that the amount of computer processing power available at a given price will double every eighteen months.

2. While "open-source" is a technically accurate way to describe GNU, Stallman himself objects to the use of this term, preferring to call it "free software" in order to emphasize the political implications of this philosophy.

3. Richard Stallman, "The GNU Manifesto," *Dr. Dobb's Journal* 10, no. 3 (March 1985): 30.

4. Stallman, "The GNU Manifesto," 30.

5. As we discussed in chapter 2, a cultural commons is not necessarily the same thing as a public domain. In fact, many of the disputes surrounding copyright in a digital context stem from the tension between our cultural experience of digital culture as a commons and our legal requirement that we understand it as a form of property.

6. This is not a hypothetical scenario but a tragedy taken directly from my own life experience.

7. Charlie Sorrell, "So Long, and Thanks for All the Cash: Yahoo Shuts Down Music Store and DRM Servers," *Wired*, July 25, 2008, www.wired.com /gadgetlab/2008/07/so-long-and-tha/.

8. Including my own book *Piracy Crusade*.

9. Macon Phillips, Victoria Espinel, Aneesh Chopra, and Howard A. Schmidt, "Obama Administration Responds to We the People Petitions on SOPA and Online Piracy," *The White House: President Barack Obama* (blog), January 14, 2012, https://obamawhitehouse.archives.gov/blog/2012/01/14/obama-admin istration-responds-we-people-petitions-sopa-and-online-piracy.

10. Alejandro Mayorkas to Al Franken, July 31, 2015, http://www.franken.senate .gov/files/documents/150731DHSresponse.pdf.

11. Stephen Evans, "Germany's Pirate Party Riding High," *BBC News*, May 12, 2012, www.bbc.co.uk/news/world-europe-18017064.

Conclusion

1. Lauren Cohen, Umit G. Gurun, and Scott Duke Kominers, "The Growing Problem of Patent Trolling," *Science* 352, no. 6285 (2016): 521–22.

2. Cohen, Gurun, and Kominers, "The Growing Problem of Patent Trolling."

3. Cory Doctorow, "Donald Trump, Jr Is a Patent-Troll and His Biggest Client Now Does Business with the US Government," *BoingBoing* (blog), March 13, 2017, https://boingboing.net/2017/03/13/christ-what-an-asshole-3.html.

4. Patry, *How to Fix Copyright*.

5. Jessica D. Litman, "Real Copyright Reform," *Iowa Law Review* 96, no.1 (2010): 3.

6. Maria A. Pallante, "Next Great Copyright Act," *Columbia Journal of Law and the Arts* 36, no. 3 (2012–13): 315.

7. Karl F. Milde Jr., "Can a Computer Be an 'Author' or an 'Inventor?'" *Journal of the Patent Office Society* 51, no. 6 (June 1969): 378.

8. Association for Molecular Pathology v. Myriad Genetics, 689 F. 3d 1303.

9. For more on this debate, see Susan Neilson, "Copyrighting DNA Is a Bad Idea," *Nautilus*, June 15, 2016, http://nautil.us/blog/copyrighting-dna-is-a -bad-idea.

Further Reading

ONE
The Origins of Intellectual Property

Kaplan, Benjamin. *An Unhurried View of Copyright*. New York: Columbia University Press, 1967.

May, Christopher, and Susan K. Sell. *Intellectual Property Rights: A Critical History*. (Boulder: Lynne Rienner, 2005.

Patterson, Lyman Ray. *Copyright in Historical Perspective*. Nashville: Vanderbilt University Press, 1968.

Silbey, Jessica. The Eureka Myth: Creators, Innovators, and Everyday Intellectual Property. Stanford: Stanford Law Books, 2014.

Vaidhyanathan, Siva. *Intellectual Property: A Very Short Introduction*. New York: Oxford University Press, 2017.

TWO
The Limits of Intellectual Property

Aufderheide, Patricia, and Peter Jaszi. *Reclaiming Fair Use: How to Put Balance Back in Copyright*. Chicago: University of Chicago Press, 2011.

Bollier, David. *Think Like a Commoner: A Short Introduction to the Life of the Commons.* Gabriola, British Columbia: New Society, 2014.

Boyle, James. *The Public Domain: Enclosing the Commons of the Mind.* New Haven: Yale University Press, 2009.

Heller, Michael. *The Gridlock Economy: How Too Much Ownership Wrecks Markets, Stops Innovation, and Costs Lives.* New York: Basic Books, 2010.

Hyde, Lewis. *Common as Air: Revolution, Art, and Ownership.* London: Farrar, Straus and Giroux, 2011.

Okediji, Ruth L., ed. *Copyright Law in an Age of Limitations and Exceptions.* Cambridge: Cambridge University Press, 2017.

Raustiala, Kal, and Christopher Sprigman. *The Knockoff Economy: How Imitation Sparks Innovation.* Oxford: Oxford University Press, 2012.

THREE
Intellectual Property and Industry

Donaldson, Michael C., and Lisa A. Callif. *Clearance & Copyright: Everything You Need to Know for Film and Television.* 4th ed. Los Angeles: Silman-James, 2014.

Fishman, Stephen. *Trademark: Legal Care for Your Business & Product Name.* 11th ed. Berkeley: NOLO, 2016.

Gabriel, Joseph M. *Medical Monopoly: Intellectual Property Rights and the Origins of the Modern Pharmaceutical Industry.* Chicago: University Of Chicago Press, 2014.

Gordon, Steve. *The Future of the Music Business: How to Succeed with the New Digital Technologies.* 4th ed. New York: Hal Leonard Books, 2015.

Gortych, Joseph E. *Consider a Spherical Patent: IP and Patenting in Technology Business.* Boca Raton: CRC, 2014.

Ryder, Rodney D., and Ashwin Madhavan. *Intellectual Property and Business: The Power of Intangible Assets.* Thousand Oaks, CA: SAGE, 2014.

FOUR
Intellectual Property and Cultural Expression

Boyle, James, and Jennifer Jenkins. *Theft: A History of Music.* Durham, NC: CreateSpace Independent Publishing Platform, 2017.

Demers, Joanna. *Steal This Music: How Intellectual Property Law Affects Musical Creativity.* Athens: University of Georgia Press, 2006.

Further Reading

Hick, Darren Hudson. *Artistic License: The Philosophical Problems of Copyright and Appropriation.* Chicago: University of Chicago Press, 2017.

Pon, Lisa. *Raphael, Dürer, and Marcantonio Raimondi: Copying and the Italian Renaissance Print.* New Haven: Yale University Press, 2004.

Sinnreich, Aram. *Mashed Up: Music, Technology and the Rise of Configurable Culture.* Amherst: University of Massachusetts Press, 2010.

Woodmansee, Martha. *The Author, Art, and the Market: Rereading the History of Aesthetics.* New York: Columbia University Press, 1996.

FIVE
The Politics Behind Intellectual Property

Baumgartner, Frank R., Jeffrey M. Berry, Marie Hojnacki, Beth L. Leech, and David C. Kimball. *Lobbying and Policy Change: Who Wins, Who Loses, and Why.* Chicago: University of Chicago Press, 2009.

Drutman, Lee. *The Business of America Is Lobbying: How Corporations Became Politicized and Politics Became More Corporate.* New York: Oxford University Press, 2017.

Lessig, Lawrence. *Republic, Lost: Version 2.0.* New York: Twelve, 2015.

Litman, Jessica. "The Politics of Intellectual Property." *Cardozo Arts & Entertainment Law Journal* 27, no. 2 (2009): 313–20.

Reich, Robert B. *Saving Capitalism: For the Many, Not the Few.* New York: Vintage, 2016.

SIX
Intellectual Property in the Global Arena

Calboli, Irene, and Srividhya Ragavan, eds. *Diversity in Intellectual Property: Identities, Interests, and Intersections.* New York: Cambridge University Press, 2015.

Drahos, Peter, and John Braithwaite. *Information Feudalism: Who Owns the Knowledge Economy?* New York: New Press, 2007.

Karaganis, Joe, ed. *Media Piracy in Emerging Economies.* N.p.: Social Science Research Council, 2011.

Sell, Susan K. *Private Power, Public Law: The Globalization of Intellectual Property Rights.* Cambridge Studies in International Relations. Cambridge: Cambridge University Press, 2003.

Yang, Fan. *Faked in China: Nation Branding, Counterfeit Culture, and Globalization.* Bloomington: Indiana University Press, 2015.

Further Reading

SEVEN
Copyright Piracy

Cummings, Alex Sayf. *Democracy of Sound: Music Piracy and the Remaking of American Copyright in the Twentieth Century.* New York: Oxford University Press, 2013.

Dunbar-Hester, Christina. *Low Power to the People: Pirates, Protest, and Politics in FM Radio Activism.* Cambridge, MA: MIT Press, 2014.

Heller-Roazen, Daniel. *The Enemy of All: Piracy and the Law of Nations.* New York: Zone Books, 2009.

John, Nicholas A. *The Age of Sharing.* Malden, MA: Polity, 2016.

Johns, Adrian. *Piracy: The Intellectual Property Wars from Gutenberg to Gates.* Chicago: University of Chicago Press, 2010.

Sinnreich, Aram, *The Piracy Crusade: How the Music Industry's War on Sharing Destroys Markets and Erodes Civil Liberties.* Amherst: University of Massachusetts Press, 2013.

EIGHT
Copyleft and Copyfight

Coleman, E. Gabriella. *Coding Freedom: The Ethics and Aesthetics of Hacking.* Princeton: Princeton University Press, 2012.

Doctorow, Cory. *Content: Selected Essays on Technology, Creativity, Copyright, and the Future of the Future.* San Francisco: Tachyon, 2008.

Herman, Bill D. *The Fight over Digital Rights: The Politics of Copyright and Technology.* New York: Cambridge University Press, 2013.

Jenkins, Henry. *Convergence Culture: Where Old and New Media Collide.* Rev. ed. New York: NYU Press, 2008.

Lessig, Lawrence. *Free Culture: How Big Media Uses Technology and the Law to Lock Down Culture and Control Creativity.* New York: Penguin, 2004. Independently published, 2017.

Raymond, Eric S. *The Cathedral & the Bazaar: Musings on Linux and Open Source by an Accidental Revolutionary.* Cambridge, MA: O'Reilly Media, 2001.

Index

Note: An italicized page number indicates a figure.

Index

artificial scarcity, 236

artistry, 114

ASCAP. *See* American Society of Composers, Authors and Publishers

Association for Molecular Pathology v. Myriad Genetics, 246

AstraZeneca, 131

AT&T, 139

Aufderheide, Patricia, 64–65

Auros, 196

auteur theory, 82

authorship, 6, 74; AI, 244; animal, 242; in film industry, 82–83; romantic, 241

awareness campaigns, *195*

Babylon, 29

Bach, Johann Sebastian, 115

Band-Aids, 87

Basquiat, Jean-Michel, 111, *113*

Basulto, Dominic, 36

Bathes, Roland, 241

Baxandall, Michael, 29

the Beatles, 120

Beethoven, Ludwig van, 115, 117

Bell, Robert, 180

Berkeley Software Distribution (BSD), 210

Berne Convention, 44, 105, 118–119; treaty terms, 153

Bertelsmann, 193

best practices, ICC, 235

Betamax, VHS and, 188, 192, 205

Beyoncé, 80

Bible, 102

biopiracy, 165, 177

Biopiracy: The Plunder of Nature and Knowledge (Shiva), 165

Biotechnology Industry Organization, 131

BitTorrent, 193, 196

Bizet, Georges, 118

Biz Markie, 122

BLS. *See* Bureau of Labor and Statistics

BMG, 193

BMI, 131

Bo, Eddie, 66, 123–124

Boehner, John, 133

Bollier, David, 16, 42

borrowing, plagiarism compared with, 124

Boyle, James, 56–57, 58

BPI. *See* British Phonographic Industry

Brand Name Bullies (Bollier), 16

brands, 87

brick-and-mortar retailers, 81

Bridgeport v. Dimension, 67

Bright Tunes Music v. Harrisongs Music, 120

Bristol-Myers Squibb, 131

British Phonographic Industry (BPI), 186–187

Bryant, William Cullen, 181

BSD. *See* Berkeley Software Distribution

Buck, Gene, 184

burden of proof, 235

Bureau of Labor and Statistics (BLS), 100

Cage, John, 121

campaign donors, *141*

Canon, 12

Capitol Legislative Strategies, 132

Carey, Matthew, 180

Index

Samsung, 12, 17, 91
Sanders, Bernie, 127, 222
Schaeffer, Pierre, 121
Schering-Plough, 131
Schumann, Robert, 118
Schumer, Amy, 75
Schumer, Charles, 72
Schwitters, Kurt, 107
Science (journal), 230
secondary liability, 69–76
second enclosure movement, 56–57
secret negotiations, 142–148
selfies, monkey, 242, *243*
Sell, Susan K., 155, 161
semiconductor chip rights, 155–156
Shakespeare, William, 7; public
    domain and, 61
shell corporations, 142
shipping, 200
Shiva, Vandana, 165–166
Shkreli, Martin, 96
Shocklee, Hank, 122
Sibelius, 80
sildenafil, 95
Sinnreich, Matt, 24
Skype, 85
slash fiction, 200
Slater, David J., 242
smartphones, jailbreaking, 217
Smith, Jimmy, 124
Smith, Lamar, 20
Snapchat, 93, 243
Snatched (film), 75
social media, fair use and, 64
Soderbergh, Steven, 19
soft money, 139
Software Alliance, 131
Soghoian, Christopher, 147, 148

Songwriter Equity Act, 234
Sony Pictures, 78
Sony v. Universal, 188
SOPA. *See* Stop Online Piracy Act
source code: battles over, 204–210;
    IBM and, 206; privatization and,
    207; programmers on, 207–208
South Korea, 67
space-shifting, 186, 199–200
Special 301 Report, 174
special master, 218
Spotify, 68, 80, 196
Sprigman, Christopher, 74
stakeholders, 137; in IP, 226
Stallman, Richard M., 208–209,
    217–218
standard form contracts, 91–92
Starbucks, 166–167, *168*
Star Chamber, 33
Star Trek, 200
Star Wars (film), 61
State of Union Address, 228–229
stationer's copyright, 32
Statute of Anne, 34, 104, 180
Steamboat Willie, 43
Stella Artois, 15
Stop Online Piracy Act (SOPA), 3, 20;
    opposition to, 222–223
Story, Joseph, 63
Strandburg, Katherine J., 66
Strategas, 138
Sunlight Foundation, 128
Super PACs, 142
Supreme Court (U.S.), 10, 63, 68, 90,
    91, 188, 242, 246
Sweden, 223, 248
Sydney Morning Herald (newspaper),
    165

Index

USPTO. *See* U.S. Patent and Trademark Office
USTR. *See* United States Trade Representative
utility patents, 9–10

Valenti, Jack, 186
van Dyke, Henry, 181
VCRs, 185, 196
Venice, 35
Verizon Wireless, 85
VHS, Betamax and, 188, 205
Viagra, 95
vicarious liability, 70
visual art, IP and, 102–113
von Bingen, Hildegard, 114

War of 1812, 178
Warhol, Andy, 108
Washington, George, 22
Washington Post, 36
Watch List (WL), 174
wave-length piracy, 183
Western art, 106
Westlaw, 194
White, Vanna, 17
Wikileaks, 175, 248

Wikipedia, 61, 71; GPL on, 219
Wilde, Oscar, 242
Winton, Tim, 165
WIPO. *See* World Intellectual Property Organization
Wired (magazine), 215
WL. *See* Watch List
World Intellectual Property Organization (WIPO), 21, 28–29, 159; on trademark registrations, 50
World Trade Organization (WTO): China and, 172–173; establishment of, 154; membership of, 154
World War II, 50, 185
WTO. *See* World Trade Organization
Wyden, Ron, 222

Xerox corporation, 87

Yahoo!, 214–215
Yang, Fan, 172–173
Younging, Greg, 168
YouTube, 25, 203
Yradier, Sebastián, 118

zines, 200